# A
# Mountain
# Stands

## Confessions of a Suppressed Genius

*Scott Sonnon*

For information on Scott Sonnon and RMAX.tv Productions, please contact:

RMAX.tv Productions P.O. Box 501388
Atlanta, GA 31150
USA
Website: www.rmaxinternational.com

Comments and questions should be sent to: info@rmaxinternational.com

Printed and bound in the United States of America

ISBN: 0692205098
ISBN-13: 978-0692205099

Credits
Editing: Bruce McLaughlan
Design and Layout: Wade Munson · www.wadeincreativity.com

# DEDICATION

To my fellow dyslexics — the 1 in 5 of the world's population, who, despite being ignored, neglected, and in many cases, abused and shamed for our unique neurological wiring, are among the greatest contributors to our world. Remember you stand among giants: from both Edison and Tesla in electricity, from both Wright brothers to Richard Branson in the power of flight, from Alexander Graham Bell to Steve Jobs in telecommunications, from Sir Isaac Newton to Stephen Hawking in physics, from Da Vinci to Disney in art, and Washington to Kennedy in politics.

Your dyslexia is your genetic advantage. Own your genius proudly, and regardless of the hardships you face, do not allow your light to be suppressed.

Fight the darkness of prejudice against you, not by greater darkness within you, but with unabashedly beaming the light of your creative brilliance upon the world.

Shine on.

# EDITOR'S NOTE:

Each day, Scott Sonnon uses his personal Facebook page and other social media postings to share significant and often painful stories from his life with his tens of thousands of followers. This book is a collection of those life events, the lessons he learned from them and the broader application for his readers. It was written one chapter per day, and is now interwoven for the first time into an autobiography.

# CONTENTS

# ACKNOWLEDGMENTS

My mother, for being my first hero and teaching me anything I dream is possible, though it'll take more work than I could dream possible, so work hard, be smart and never give up.

To Doctor Jonathan Ellsworth Winter for teaching me that to love wisdom, first you live and then later you can philosophize; so travel, experience life, and thrust yourself into your greatest fears.

General Alexander Ivanovich Retuinskih for teaching me that flow is an integration of breathing, structure and movement, and when you integrate those three, flow cannot be compartmentalized, it floods throughout your life.

Sri Mata Amritanandamayi Devi for teaching me that my greatest courage comes from compassion, that it is not a weakness or liability, but my most profound strength and an unlimited source of energy.

To my business partner and best man, Nikolay Travkin, for teaching me that if you work together, you can transform even the craziest idea into a reality IF you're tough enough to question every little step along the way to ensure that you're taking care of every detail.

To my teammate and right hand, Alberto Gallazzi, for teaching me that if you want to get big work done, you're going to have to be straight with people, and that sometimes, compassion is the hardest slap on the face.

To my wife, for teaching me that you can't strive for "more" as the goal or you lose everything; that real life happens between and within goals, not after them; and that love is something worth working for every day, without quitting because it gets hard.

To my children, for teaching me that if you truly love one another, you can start so much farther ahead in life, that you do not have to go through suffering even if you experience pain, that you do not have to doubt your possibility even if you believe that others believe in you, and that we can change as a species if we are willing to live by example for the next generation, and not try to trick ourselves into believing that we must compromise our integrity so that they don't have to.

To my Legion, for believing in me, for teaching me that we may be alone but we are alone together, that we may be different but we are common in our diversity, and that we may be deemed individually incompetent by others but together through our mutual support we are stronger than anyone or anything.

Scott Sonnon
www.facebook.com/sonnon

# INTRODUCTION

One the first day of classes, a meditation teacher brought a large Plexiglas tube into his classroom. He filled it with rocks. "How many of you think the tube is full?" He asks. Every student raised his hand.

He smiled, and poured in a bag of smaller rocks, which fitted nicely into the gaps between the large ones. "NOW how many of you think the tube is full?" About half the class raised their hands.

He smiled, and poured in a bag of gravel ... which fitted into the gaps between the small stones. He repeated the question, and this time about a third raised their hands.

And he poured in a bag of sand. Repeated his question. This time, the students were starting to "get it," and only a handful raised their hands.

And this time, of course, he poured in a bucket of water.

He looked at them. "Imagine that your life is like this beaker. The obstacles you will face are like the rocks, the gravel, the sand. Your life will seem 'full' of insurmountable troubles as long as you are bound by your egos. But your true being is like clear water. When you step away from your ordinary mind, no matter how crowded your life is with obstacles, you will find the clear space to navigate, to grow, to find joy. That is what we will explore: the flowing, fluid state of No-Self."

Flow. Everyone who has ever achieved at a high level has experienced that time of grace, of presence without tension, action without attachment. And Scott Sonnon, Master of Sport, inventor, author, international champion, teacher, coach, businessman, husband, and blissful father – has been teaching us how to access it, under killing pressure, for twenty years now. With a hunger and facility to seek and find Truth I've never seen in another athlete, Scott has sacrificed flesh and blood and treasure and comfort to travel the world, learning from and fighting the best, and then relating what he has learned to life off the mat.

# A Mountain Stands: Confessions of a Suppressed Genius

I've said this many times, and will again, right now: Scott Sonnon is the smartest human being I've ever met who applies that intelligence to the realm of physical performance. While that's impressive, the truth is that it isn't enough to earn my respect: I've encountered very smart, very focused people before, and some of them are nightmares in private life, so focused they are like the houses at Universal City: look great from one angle, and absolutely nothing at all from the side or back.

Not Scott. He is a good and decent family man with a lovely, powerful wife and amazing children. A successful businessman who has been voted one of the top ten coaches in the world ... creator of "the world's most intelligent workout" ... "top ten most influential martial artists in the world"... and so many other awards that at this point I've lost count.

All I can say is that he is, while the same flawed clay as the rest of us, one of a tiny handful of people whose capacity and integrity I trust most. I have coached him, and he has coached me. We've been business partners and friends. I've been frustrated with him, and at other times so proud of him I could hardly contain my joy.

He is my brother.

I cannot pretend to be objective about Scott, and as you read this biography you'll notice that certain themes, and references to certain events in his life are repeated multiple times. His autobiography is not "elegant," as one might expect from a work compiled from a series of articles published individually and written over more a period of many months. But it is astoundingly heartfelt, and honest, and powerful. When a person writes as he speaks, and speaks his heart, just reading his words takes you behind his eyes, into his essence, and has the potential to transform you.

There is a saying:
*He who knows not and knows not that he knows not: He is a fool, ignore him.*
*He who knows not and knows that he knows not: He is a child, teach him.*
*He who knows and knows not that he knows: He is asleep, wake him.*
*He who knows and knows that he knows: He is wise, follow him.*

Scott Sonnon has followed the warrior path deeply enough to find genuine wisdom in that arena. And REAL wisdom can be moved from one arena to another, is "generative." Whenever you find such a person ... drink deeply of what they have to say.

Scott is the real thing, warts and all. And if you open your mind and heart, and read of his struggles and triumphs and how he found his Flow in the midst of travail, there is much to learn.

There will always be the big rocks, the small rocks, the gravel, the sand.

Be the water.

Steven Barnes
NY Times bestselling author, former Kung Fu columnist for Black Belt Magazine
www.diamondhour.com

# FOREWORD

Not often does a teacher re-encounter a former student who has earned her or his spurs as a truly educated human being. Then, to re-encounter one who has excelled at human living is a rarity that can only be called a blessing.

Scott Sonnon fits that rarity admirably – with 15 other former students I know about – as realized after 39 years of teaching students during 87 years of living, learning, loving.

There is little I could add to his story, principally two viewpoints. One: it is circumstances that make us, such as being born with certain genes that determine much of what we are; in due time we make our own circumstances, such as educational choices, that then re-make us. Two: some first circumstances can never be un-created; they are with us always, we cannot oust them. Nevertheless, we can use those circumstances as foundations to become greater than they: a new creation!

John Rushkin, eminent Victorian writer and artist, attended an English country garden tea party when a lady bumped an ink well on her lace handkerchief. The inkblot ruined her cherished family treasure. Rushkin asked for the kerchief. Weeks later the lady received a package, heirloom within. The artist had transformed the inkblot rudiment into a beautiful painting of a garden, which handkerchief became the rave of London.

Mr. Sonnon vividly details how personal rudiments can be regenerated into new creations of the human experience for the benefit of oneself – and for the world.

John Ellsworth Winter, Ph.D.
Professor of Philosophy Emeritus, Millersville University of Pennsylvania
Guest Professor of Philosophy, University of Vienna, Austria

Scott Sonnon

# PART 1

---

# A THOUSAND WHIRLING QUESTIONS

# WHEN TEACHING AND LEARNING COLLIDE

Crying silently at the end of that terrible day, I rode the school bus to the stop at our trailer court. The kids scowled at me and shoved me down the aisle toward the exit, crumpled paper catapulting off my body like esteem-battering siege engines.

The bus driver shook her head and grabbed my arm as I passed. "If you're going to cause this much trouble, get your parents to drive you home from school." She shoved me down the steps.

Believe me, I thought to myself, I wish that my mom could.

The substitute teacher that day had screamed in frustration at my test answer, "Are you kidding? If you're going to deliberately make a mockery of my class, go to the office," his finger pointing to the exit, waving my paper for all of the kids to see.

I was a mirror-writer, so my work was only readable by its reflection. At 6, I couldn't understand why my hand couldn't make the words look like everyone else's. But my mother, despite being a single mom of four kids working two full-time labor jobs, found alternative educational support: Total Physical Response for my language skills, Chisanbop for my mathematics, and Phonics for my spelling.

But it wasn't any one of these specific alternatives that changed my life. It was simply THAT she COULD.

If an alternative educational approach worked, that meant to my young mind that it wasn't me who was broken; rather, the class wasn't being taught in a way that allowed me to learn. Now, I could have gone down the road of blaming the teachers (I did for a time), but my family helped me to realize a different route: self-education through alternative learning styles validates and empowers like no conventional education could.

My grandmother looked at my red-inked schoolwork and said, "WOW! Isn't this great, Hon?" I was still crying, and her reaction confused me. She asked, "Do you know how many people can write upside down and backwards? I sure can't. That is some superpower you have! I wonder what else you can do that we don't know about!"

Superpower! Somehow, I was exceptional, but no one could understand it.

That support from my mother and that belief from my grandmother sufficed. I could endure the ridicule (eventually) if I was secretly a superhero, like a childhood version of Clark Kent. Instead of being ashamed of my superpowers, I'd practice them, grow them, hone them.

The tears stopped, and I went back to my room to read my comics and think. "What if I AM Superboy growing up?"

The next year at school, the most wonderful teacher of my scholastic life came over to my desk the first week of class.

Overlooking my mirrored writing, she said, "Scott, I love how clean and crisp you make your letters with your right hand. Can we play a game for a second, please?" At my nod, she took the pencil from my right hand and placed it in my left. Smiling, she continued, "I bet you can do it with both." (Before her arrival, the entire class had been forced to write right-hand, so she was a bit of a heretic in the school, I came to learn, for her so-called "alternative witchcraft," as another teacher scoffed in whispers.)

Cautiously touching lead to paper, I felt the letters and words travel down my arm... Without mirror-writing. What!? I wrote more and compared it to my right-handed work. Another Superpower! My left hand could do what my right hand could not, and my right hand could do what NO ONE else could!

The teacher beamed, tossed my hair, and said, as she walked away, "See! You CAN write with both hands!"

I played with it, writing with both hands at the same time. "WHOA! That's so neato," yelled the kid next to me, "I'm going to try that!" She couldn't, but in seconds, everyone had two pencils, one in each hand, trying to repeat my trick. No one could. A few kids ran over to my desk and asked me to show them how to write "backwards and upside down." Looking up I saw my teacher sitting there, smiling. She said, "Go ahead, Scott! Show 'em whatcha got!!" A crowd formed, and everyone tried it out.

It was the best day ever.

Superpowers.

I dedicated the rest of my life to unearthing hidden abilities. It wasn't an easy, confident or direct route. That great day was only one. Many dark years of turmoil lay ahead, eventually leading to institutionalization in a childhood psychiatric hospital. But even there, the seed had already germinated... Superpowers. Nothing would stop me from transforming from my Clark Kent childhood into the future cape wearing Kal-El. That one great day was enough to cement in place the idea that within me lies greatness, and those who can't see it, don't yet realize their own.

When someone says that a person cannot do something, is incapable, incompetent, inept ... I feel very sad, because they can't see the hidden superpowers of the person they're judging; worse still is when the judged individual believes them, too. But we are all part of a league of super— heroes and super-heroines. Some just can't see it yet. A sad few suffer their entire lives not realizing this potential.

Be your own superhero ... so that you can crusade for others to become theirs.

Thank you to all of the teachers who have helped me along my growth.

You're doing incredible, life-altering work with just the simplest gesture, smile and supportive belief in our potential. Thank you to all the parents who love their children so unconditionally that they realize their children have untapped potential beyond what they can comprehend. Your love will unearth their superpowers, and they will grow into those abilities, despite all the hardships they face now.

# HEAD-STRONG FROM THE FIRST

The first words the doctor said when I was born, in uncontrolled exclamation, "Oh my God, look at its head."

They thought from my head size that I was hydrocephalic, but fortunately, it was a harmless condition into which I eventually grew.

When you're a mother, the last words you want uttered should be surprise at a deformity. My mother snatched me away from the doctor who couldn't control his unprofessional tongue, and said, "Give me my boy! He's beautiful and perfect!"

Eleanor Roosevelt said that "beautiful children are accidents of nature, but beautiful old people are works of art."

I had thought to myself when I was told my birth story that I could at least become my own sculptor, and shape a life to fit the size of my imagination. The disadvantages of my body could be overcome by the advantages of my vast dreams and aspirations.

An extraordinarily large head on a long neck makes for mechanical disadvantage, so my "accident of nature" contributed to my neck breaking the day I was landed on my head at the 1995 Grand National Championship by a suplex. It crackled like fireworks in my spine when we hit. Although I managed to win the gold by a mere point, I spent the 12 years following the victory recovering from the pulverized vertebrae and resulting fissures. The nerve pain became motivation for seeking solutions to my anguish.

Were it not for my large skull and long neck, and their eventually parting of ways, I would not have sought alternative health methods around the world. Who would go to all that effort in a "normal" situation? But now these skills have become highly useful to other people. And now I no longer travel the world looking for help, but supply it. That is the true miracle.

Were it not for that early childhood experience, maybe I would not have felt so alien to my environment; perhaps I would have had a more cheerful youth. But it did compel me to look to my own solutions. When I encountered a wall resisting my seeking mind, I'd imagine a way under, over, around or through it. Most people would advise me to give up and just be complacently happy with what I had been "lucky" enough to achieve. But though I can be content, I can never be complacent.

I don't believe in luck; or rather, if I did, it seems the harder, longer and smarter I endure on a puzzle, the luckier I seem to get at solving it.

We imagine life will be a straight line of success, but we don't realize that when we encounter a wall, we will often need to circle back, widely around major hurdles, not necessarily because our path had steered us wrong, but because the process of the journey holds greater importance than the outcome of the destination. How we handle the hardships we face becomes our work of art, and our gift from God.

*"You gain strength, courage and confidence by every experience in which you really stop to look fear in the face. You are able to say to yourself, I have lived through this horror. I can take the next thing that comes along. You must do the thing you think you cannot do,"* said Eleanor Roosevelt.

As the Dalai Lama said, *"This is my simple religion. There is no need for temples for it. No need for complicated philosophies to explain it. Our own brain, or own heart is our temple, and our philosophy is kindness."* I can be safe, sure and fulfilled, right now, inside this temple.

Though drama still reaches out its tendrils, I wear this cipher on my finger — in my mind and in my heart — my super-secret ring allows me to decode these daily mysteries, and allows me to not participate in and enable them; it allows me to rise above my lower, base reactions and risk a higher response, an inner calling to true resolution.

You are not alone. Together, though separate, we can as a community don our super-secret decoder rings, and select higher responses to the dramas in which we once participated. It may be that simple, but it certainly is not easy. The more we share our stories, the more strength others can gain through our daily heroism in the most insignificant of higher choices.

# NOURISH THE ACTIVE MIND

In kindergarten, my mind would swirl with such violent chaos from the inability to form a cogent thought. I'd hold my head as if to steady the vortex. My grandmother would comfort me by singing to me a tune which ironically became a seed upon which my adult mental life has elegantly germinated.

"The mind is a garden, with your thoughts as the seeds. You can grow flowers, or you can grow weeds."

So, I'd sit down, tears streaming, and she would let me talk through my chaos. Because of my dyslexia, it was nearly impossible in my childhood to take the mental fragments and form them into an idea on my own, as my mind felt like a collection of cacophonous instruments playing random clatter. But my grandmother's tune would slowly soothe the noise, as the disorder would take root, and begin growing into one clear stem of thought at a time.

I had no idea at the time that my grandparents' farm would become a metaphor for my mental life. But reflecting upon it, these simple wisdoms she imparted became the garden of who I am. Those mental skills grew into conscious strategies for even my teaching career and project development, as well as my personal growth: Collect the seeds, plant them deep, take care of the soil, shine down, feed the flowers and pull the weeds.

Simple discipline for daily living.

If you want a rich garden for your mental life, prepare to get dirty. When you find a negative thought, be detached from it. Don't associate it with your identity, as it is merely a weed, a natural consequence of the fertile mental soil that you've established. Then, pluck not just the stem, but every bit of its root.

Be vigilant of these unintended, but naturally occurring weeds. However, remember that your garden cannot flourish by becoming consumed with patrolling for the negativity of these invaders. You also must nourish your positive crop of ideas. Be fastidious about supporting the light of your Higher Source with daily meditation and prayer, and water it with constant care, for the seeds of your thoughts remain thirsty for attention, discipline and love.

# DEFINE THE MORAL OF YOUR STORY

When I was 7, my mother read me a short poem:

*Only as high as I reach can I grow*
*Only as far as I seek can I go*
*Only as deep as I look can I see*
*Only as much as I dream can I be*

She'd quote that final line throughout my childhood whenever I'd talk of the bold things I wanted to do with my life, saying: "Only as much as you dream, can you be." Whenever I pursued something, she would tell me that however strongly I believed in my dream determined if I would achieve it. And she stood behind those words with her parenting.

I remember I was 7 because it was that Summer that I asked my mom if my friend and I could pull my mattresses into the back yard to use as mats. She nodded with a puzzled expression, and we began a ritual for afternoons that Summer, and even into the Fall: Backyard Kung Fu Theater.

We'd create massive battles choreographed with martial arts techniques we "learned" from watching television. Once practiced, we would act them out with great flourish and panache for my mother, who always applauded at the end.

She would ask, "What is the moral of this story?" So, I would elaborate on the reason and the reluctances, the righteousness or the regrets. She would clap her hands again, and tell me how fascinating she found my imagination. She catalyzed my future career as a fighter and a writer, as a teacher and a speaker, with her simple questions, and constant reminders to reach high, go far, look deep, and dream big.

David Schwartz stated, *"Attitudes mirror our mind. How we think shows through in how we act."* My mother never encouraged me to fight for a living; neither did she ever try to stop me. However, her practice of asking me the moral within each battle I faced formed the foundation to all my actions in later life. Her repeated question became the filter with which I formed my own attitudes toward challenges.

Today, I cannot help but view each challenge with the same attitude: What is the moral of the story? You can define the value of each, as much as you dare dream. Whatever you're facing right now, emotionally, nutritionally, physically, relationally, vocationally, financially, even spiritually, you can ask yourself, and define the moral of the story that you want to learn.

Dream it large, hold that attitude through all of your choices, and you WILL find your way through to brighter, better days.

# HUNGER FOR A BETTER WORLD

With my mother laid off, we subsisted on Welfare and food stamps and were about to lose our home. One night we only had gravy and bread for dinner, and at 7 years old, I cried that I was still very hungry. My mother gave me the final piece of bread.

When I realized later that she had not had any food for herself, I cried the entire night at my selfishness and my mother's sacrifice. Though I was trying to be quiet, and she was bone-weary from walking a snow-frozen picket line from dawn to dusk, she overheard. Coming in to our room, she comforted me, saying that everything would be fine; that I should not worry because things feel much harder as a child than as an adult.

She explained that a grown up can easily sacrifice everything for her children. But when you're a child, that responsibility feels impossible. And she kissed me for being brave.

She tiptoed out of the room and quietly downstairs. I sneaked out of my room after her, and as I looked down the staircase, saw her quietly crying, face in her hands, at our barren Christmas tree. The tree seemed like the most beautiful thing I had ever seen, even with only the few presents under it.

That night, I wished that Christmas Eve, with a tree scant of wrapped presents, Santa would bring my Mom some food so she was no longer hungry, instead of bringing me gifts. When I fell asleep, I dreamed that I could grow up into a man who could take care of my family and others so that other people would never be so sad or feel so alone.

Witnessing my mother's internal strength impacted me forever … and became a lifelong passion to do my best to help others whenever and wherever possible. I cannot afford to think I can help; I must keep faith and KNOW that I can.

On this holiday, wishes can transform into dreams, and dreams into passions. The key ingredient in the recipe causing this transformation, in my experience, is faith in a higher/deeper/other Source, and the responsibility to sacrifice your own comfort so that others who are not yet capable of your awareness, due to their suffrage, can feel a moment's reprieve.

I have one wish this holiday season. Let us dream of a day when those we see and reach can be comforted ... and like my mother's sacrifice, we find the strength of responsibility to make this dream become a reality, if only for one day.

You can't merely hope it's possible. You can't think it's possible. You must KNOW that you can make a dramatic, life altering difference in the lives of others, even if only through a word of comfort. Find the strength within you, like a parent sacrificing for a child, and KNOW that every action you take makes a world of difference.

# THE TRUEST GIFTS COME WRAPPED IN LOVE

My favorite Christmas gift came when my mother had been laid off from her job as a steelworker in the 1970s, the first female to do the job in Pennsylvania.

We had shopped for gifts at the thrift store, and wrapped hand-me-downs from the older siblings to the younger. We made Christmas dinner with food from welfare stamps; and wrapped our tree with wreathes of strung popcorn and paper cut snowflakes. That simple beauty lingers with me.

Christmas morning, I unwrapped the best gift I have ever received. My mom had taken clothespins from the back yard line, and hand painted each one as the pieces of a chess board, and then drew the board by hand. We played on that board until the paint chipped away. (Learning the intricacies, my brother went on to compete at state championships at chess.)

The Dalai Lama said that, *"If you think you're too small to make a difference, try sleeping with a mosquito."* Similarly, Rickson Gracie proved with exhaustive example that, "If size mattered, elephants would be kings of the jungle."

Although a humble, heartfelt gift can seem insignificant, especially when others appear glutted with opulence, the humblest present can hold the greatest meaning, and its lesson last the longest.

I hope you have a wonderful Christmas and that the real gift of family and fellowship will remain with you. Let us strive to make every day Merry, even if in the smallest, most seemingly insignificant act.

# DEDICATION BRINGS DREAMS TO LIFE

May 31st, 1993, my mom whispered, "The dedicated are the luckiest." She kissed me and continued, "You're so lucky, and I'm so proud of you."

After 4.5 hours of fighting, I walked straight to her to thank her. I had just earned my black belt in Russian Sambo, one of the most physically demanding martial arts ever created.

Against advice to set "realistic expectations," I chose to pursue the impossible. Despite all odds, I became a five-time world champion, earned my master of sport, and was inducted into the Hall of Fame, because of my mother's definition of luck. When I was 8 years old, she hung a sign above the door of my bedroom. It now hangs next to my NEAR-SHORT-LONG TERM whiteboard in my office. It reads:

*If while pursuing distant dreams*
*Your bright hopes turn to gray,*
*Don't wait for reassuring words*
*Or hands to lead the way.*
*For seldom will you find a soul*
*With dreams the same as yours.*
*Not often will another help you*
*Pass through untried doors.*
*If inner forces urge you*
*To take a course unknown,*
*Be ready to go all the way,*
*Yes, all the way alone.*
*That's not to say you shouldn't*
*Draw lessons from the best;*
*Just don't depend on lauding words*
*To spur you on your quest.*
*Find courage within your heart*
*And let it be your guide.*
*Strive ever harder toward your dreams*
*And they won't be denied.*                    *Love you, Mom.*

# TEN STEPS TO FINDING THE STRENGTH

I had cried to my mom about how overweight I was. She said that all I had to do was eat less junk.

I whined to her that it was too hard.

My mother was a simple woman who had parented demonstratively, so she put me in the car and took me to a shelter where people had been lined around the street for a bowl of hot soup. She said, "When you feel you're not strong enough, remember how strong these people are for rebuilding their lives with whatever small amount they are given by people who care enough to help. If it gets too hard for you, go help people who have it harder."

Recently, a friend argued that I should concentrate only on sharing the sciences and technologies that I've been taught and have developed in nutrition, exercise and recovery. I will continue to share those techniques and create and refine more of them, but these are just things. Research shows the number one determinant of whether an approach works is compliance. What REALLY matters to us involves more than what we use, but rather what is our motivation to work hard enough to not give up. Placed in context on how much harder it could be, our current challenge shrinks.

My top ten techniques for improving my life don't involve a collection of tools, but an array of attitudes:

1.  Remain aware that you are in control of change. You WILL change even if you're out of control, but you CAN change consciously, if you don't sacrifice awareness for distraction.

2.  Let go of mistakes when they happen! But hold your attention longer next time so you do not make those specific mistakes again. You've learned from them and are stronger from making them.

3. No idea alone will get you there; so even if you don't believe you can, just start. What separates us from our former selves is not intelligence, or even confidence, but the will to act.

4. As you change, take care of yourself in the moment. Push hard but be compassionate of your recovery and strengthening process. If you ignore caring for yourself, you will only push backward.

5. Everyone you meet is fighting a hard battle. Don't judge others, or compare yourself to them. If you want help on your own path, then start helping others on theirs. Your path will grow easier as a result.

6. If you can't see your strengths, and don't know where to find willpower, visit others who are going through their hardships. Help them, and you may find yourself working harder than ever.

7. If you truly believe in something, make it congruent throughout your life. Consistency in compliance is the number one denominator of success in anything.

8. Authenticity means being true to yourself no matter how the current situation appears to want you to be different. Be authentic and you will find that you grow more completely.

9. Don't hide your growth. Be transparent, even when no one is looking. Hold yourself accountable to never having a choice hidden from yourself, and you will keep your awareness.

10. Don't just grow. Evolve. Life isn't a collection of experiences, but a deepening appreciation of them. Realize the omnipotence of your courage to become a purer version of yourself ... for others will be encouraged by your ongoing evolution ... even if others don't like it at the time.

# FORTUNE FAVORS THE BOLD

Walking down the bridge, I dodged kids who were attempting to kick out my shoes for being the "fat dork." I stumbled, tripping down the stairs and turned, enraged, punching the culprit as hard as I could. All I heard in his puffed exhale was, "kill him!"

And the chase was on.

With my third grade girth, I didn't get far. Kids dragged me to the ground and jumped into the boot party like a looting mob.

I scrambled from beneath the pile of 10 or more, who were thrashing and kicking like some cartoon donnybrook. They all looked up to see me running, and restarted pursuit.

I felt myself slowing, unable to outrun them. I stopped and turned, digging my toes into the ground with my back against a tree. The fastest kid arrived and I felt as if I were about to vomit as I lunged forward to grab him. I missed, but so did my would-be tackler, who ran right into the tree. He fell down unconscious, entirely of his own doing, though to the onlookers I must have appeared to be a Judo champion.

The other kids stopped cold and paused, looking at the prone, still body, then back at me. They suddenly en masse scattered, running away and thinking that someone would be going to prison.

At the nearest house, I yelled for help. As the ambulance arrived, the boy stirred, delirious and concussed. The EMT told the boy he was very lucky to have a friend to take care of him the way I did. He looked at me and we both acknowledged the moment with conscious sobriety.

I was never bothered again for the year we remained at that school.

Gandhi said, *"Strength does not come from physical capacity but from an indomitable will."*

Everything you deserve to become, all of your fathomless potential, each dream burning in your heart for realization, lay on the other side of your fears.

These personal demons we flee, the emotional dragons we pretend do not exist, the problems we ignore out of fright … they signal to us; they guard the door; the very fear they induce shows the direction we ought turn to realize the strength of our true character.

Fears cast an illusion of doubt that pursues you with snapping teeth as you flee but evaporates when you turn and step directly into its illusory jaws.

Feel the fears on the hackles of your neck. Turn. Run right toward them. You need not fight them for they are not real. You fight only the temptation to avoid their confrontation.

The stronger you've let them grow, the more real pain they may seduce you into believing, but keep going and you will discover that the wounds are nowhere to be found. And you are free.

# BECOME WHO YOU TRULY ARE

I waddled down the hall under the dangerous sway of my hyperlordosis, loaded by my obesity and made fragile by my joint disease. Book after folder was knocked from my hands; the back of my head shoved to the floor; my torso kicked to the wall; the snickers of the onlookers at my helplessness cutting like tiny scalpels. I thought to myself, "If I'm going to escape this persecution, I must change the way I walk and the way I talk."

Even at that early age, I realized that it wasn't my obesity that was the problem, but how I carried it which caused me to appear the victim. I recognized it wasn't my thoughts, ideas and dreams that must alter, but how I expressed them to the world — the mirror writing and dyslexic speech — needed to be refocused, so that I would not create such negative attention to myself.

I didn't change who I was. I merely awoke to who I truly am. With my improved quality of movement and food skills, my obesity slowly faded away; and with my improved writing and speaking skills, my dyslexia gently disappeared from outside notice. But these two conditions, the way I walked and the way I talked, amounted to aversion from pain.

As I grew older, I aspired to become a champion for others, a great writer and speaker defending those who wished to pursue their dreams. With each chance I took to sacrifice how others defined me in order to become more truly myself, the criticisms of those early years returned. Though I disagree with much of Aristotle's work, one insight of his I have conceded, "If you want to avoid criticism: say nothing, do nothing, be nothing."

The greatest gift you can give those dear to you, those you reach with your work, and those they reach, is your personal growth. Internal development remains our greatest investment in the future of everyone we touch, and everyone they do.

As Jim Rohn wrote, *"You take care of you for me, and I will take care of me for you."*

Don't buckle under the negativity. When you're attacked for awakening to more of who you truly are, exhale and celebrate how much work you've done to become a purer version of yourself. Perhaps one day, others will, too. But by then, you won't care about those criticisms, for your dreams will have been realized, and everyone, all of us, will be better for your courage to endure that growth.

# BELIEFS CAN BLOT OUT POSSIBILITIES

"If you didn't act like such an imbecile, maybe other kids wouldn't hate you so much," my fourth grade teacher said after I returned with recess' scrapes and bruises.

I retorted, "Maybe I'd do better in class, if you stopped the other kids from beating me up."

His face turned red, and he pulled out a waffled paddle. Bending me over his desk, in front of the class, he began to hit me with it, yelling, "No child is going to tell ME how to run me classroom, especially the class idiot!"

"Grades don't measure intelligence and age doesn't determine maturity," my grandfather told me. He continued, in a way that provided comfort, "Keep learning things your way, even if no one gives you credit. But to survive, learn why they do things their way. So, maybe when you're bigger, you can figure out what belief caused them to do things so wrong. A belief can sometimes be worse than ignorance, because we're convinced we're right, and blind that we're not."

His words validated my own unique, but untapped, learning styles; acknowledged the possibility that even authorities could be wrong; and encouraged me to start down a path of illuminating beliefs which were limiting the growth of others, in addition to myself. That one key event catalyzed the course of my career and empowered me to challenge any injustice I observed or experienced.

Without that event:

I would not have pursued alternative educational methods through movement, as a dyslexic, kinesthetic learner, and challenged the domination of verbal/linguistic methods in the school systems.

I would not have developed my own approach to reading, my own writing style, my own form of public speaking.

I would not have begun research on strengthening my connective tissue against joint disease, explored the "myofascial matrix" as a movement model for functional fitness, and traveled the world seeking modalities to make me truly healthy and strong.

I would not have revisited beliefs about nutrition and hydration over and over, to challenge the heavily marketed processed synthetics that led to my childhood obesity, nor returned to the simple eating approach of my grandparents, and therein found an abundance of vitality never known throughout my life.

I would not have invested decades in training in efficient forms of martial art, and debunked the attrition mentality of force against force; for I found in the abuse of my youth, a flaw, and only in absorbing and retranslating the aggression expressed toward me was I able to create a true solution to it, and be free from fear.

I would not have poured myself into the science underpinning stress, to decipher the riddle of my father's tortured rage after returning from war, how our family disintegrated, and how the disorder not only could have been prevented but could have been transitioned, supported ... even cured before it spalled out of control.

I never would have developed the systems, tools and technology to address this specter of distress; tools that now have become incumbent in government agencies across the globe.

And I never would have become the things that I feared most: a writer, speaker and teacher. I never would have written a single book, produced a single video nor taught a single course.

My grades didn't predetermine my direction in life. The immaturity of some of my adult authorities couldn't deter me from following it, no matter how many times I surrendered and submitted in hopeless desperation.

If you don't follow your own path no matter how frighteningly unexplored, others' beliefs will conscript you to follow theirs, even if in an unjust, wrong, but popular direction. Find teachers who will help you clear the underbrush on your own path, allies who will walk next to you, friends who will help you up when you pitfall, and the courage to do it alone when you must.

The bad news? There is no key to your success.

The good news? It isn't locked; though we're often distracted by convincing, inaccurate beliefs to look in the wrong direction.

Look within. And keep going.

# PAIN BECOMES THE CATALYST

Grabbing me by the hair, the teacher pulled me to the front of the class. Removing a waffled paddle from his drawer, he told me to bend over the desk, announcing, "You've always been difficult. All of the teachers think so. Now we know it's because YOU are the troublemaker. Since you aren't learning what we're teaching, the lessons are now going to be much more painful."

They were.

They didn't understand my learning disabilities, so they assumed that I was being deliberately difficult. I remember thinking that if I could CHOOSE to understand what they were teaching, I'd trade anything in the world to do so.

I'm so glad now that I could not give them the obedience they expected. Because of my learning challenges I was blessed to discover an inherent flaw in how they'd been taught to teach:

Not learning in the conventional way is not a learning disability; it's a learning style with a different lens. Not everyone learns in the same way; there is a multitude of learning styles. Learning is a gift, even when pain is the teacher. It may not be seen as a gift by the sadist delivering it, but it is a blessing for the one brave enough to embrace its illumination.

The gift I received that day was the conviction to get myself out of my situation no matter what it required. The first step toward getting somewhere is deciding not to stay where you are. I decided to find my unique styles of learning.

Thirty years later, my lower back blew out while I was fighting in Russia. That initial crack on my back from the teacher's paddle eventually splintered and broke under the pressure of martial arts.

After I was unable to move for three days, Russian doctors told me that I needed surgery or I wouldn't be able to walk. I refused. Every day, I worked on minute mobility drills that remained under the radar of the agonizing spasms in my back.

Without pain killers, each movement felt like it was sending hot pokers into my spine; even when I was only shifting my weight.

Babe Ruth once suggested, "It's hard to beat up a person who never gives up." There was no way that I was going to go to surgery in a different country, especially when I had no money or health insurance and hardly spoke the language. So I moved a little every day, staying just under the spasms. Movement heals. It delivers all of our nutrition, recovery and natural medicine.

One of my greatest discoveries in life, from which I gained great confidence each time it happened, was doing that which others said I could not do. I eventually got out of bed and walked and to this day have not had surgery on my spine.

My body learns, and heals, through movement.

I'm flawed. I've been broken many times. I've caved in to others' expectations and definitions. I've surrendered and submitted more times than I can count.

But I've gotten back up one more time than that countless number. I've triumphed not despite my flaws, but BECAUSE of them.

Better to become a diamond with many flaws than to remain a perfect lump of coal. You may be smacked down. You may have your back broken. You may be full of flaws and imperfections. But your uniqueness is what makes you unassailably beautiful.

Confucius reminded us that, *"Everything is beautiful, even if no one sees it."*

Don't give up. Get up.

Don't give in. Get going.

You're more beautiful than you realize, more powerful than you believe, and more intelligent than you imagine BECAUSE of your uniqueness. Do not regret what has been done; relish what you now have been confidently committed to unearth.

# ACCEPT THE GIFT OF UNIQUENESS

"You're useless! Can't you get ANYTHING right?" The math teacher berated me in front of the class. I had struggled with math but due to a special kinesthetic mathematics method my mother had found for me, called *Chisanbop*, I had managed to compensate for my dyscalculia: one of the types of dyslexia which impacts math.

The teacher was frustrated that I couldn't answer his problem in the way he wanted. Though I could get the correct answer almost every time, I wriggled around my desk without pencil and paper to solve it.

Slapping me on the back of my head, he bounced my face off the desk. My nose exploded with blood. The teacher exasperatedly yelled at me, "Jesus, just go to the nurse! You're getting blood everywhere! It's not like you're going to do anything worthwhile in class. Just go!!"

My mom picked me up from the nurse, nose pinched shut with tissue. I told her the story and furious, she nearly returned to confront the teacher. I pleaded with her to take me home because it would make it worse for me at school.

She calmed and said, "Your worth doesn't decrease because someone else can't see it! Who do you know who can count six different numbers at the same time?"

My mom referred to a trick *Chisanbop* combined with my dyslexia had let me perform. It allowed me to follow multiple arithmetic sequences simultaneously. I could count up to six different numbers and remember them because the score was held on my body, not in short term memory.

My math teachers at school didn't understand all my "fidgeting" was actually how I performed solutions. No matter the attempts at explanation, they laughed and called it "voodoo" and threatened to return me to the "retarded class" if I didn't apply their rote method of answering the questions.

My kinesthetic approach to mathematics integrated as the foundation of my fitness system called TACFIT: tracking and measuring multiple streams of data points — time, technique, effort, discomfort and heart rate.

My data tracking methods are now used by universities, federal agencies and military and police units worldwide.

Recently, a naval academy asked me to conduct the commencement speech for their graduating class. They asked me to focus on the reality of the hardships they'll face. I told them with candor: You're going to face a disparity between what you feel is valuable and what the world has come to expect as status quo.

To be worthwhile means to be true to yourself. You don't need to be accepted by everyone. Accept yourself. Know your own worth. Value your contribution.

If you have the courage to face the enormous weight of others' expectations, disbelieving your unique ideas are valuable, and yet you persevere ... then, the entire world, all of us, can improve because of you.

Rumi wrote, *"Do not be satisfied with the stories that come before you. Unfold your own myth."* Be strong. Even those who resist you will benefit from your determination.

# HUMBLY ACKNOWLEDGE YOUR NOBILITY

In elementary school, I was humiliated by other kids for my "mirror writing" which only could be read by its reflection. "Backwards," they chided me as a nickname. And I began to feel "Backwards" in everything I did, often getting lost walking between classes, because of poor directional sense.

During a field trip to the planetarium, when we were told to find all of the constellations, I finished far faster than anyone else. The teacher pulled me aside and said to me, "You may have trouble making shapes as fast as everyone in the class, but you're the fastest at finding them. Maybe you only get this special ability by seeing things in a way that others have not. That may make it difficult for you in some things now, but may become your superpower as a grown-up."

She continued talking while pointing up at the planetarium's pinholes of light, "Did you know that everyone in here, everyone everywhere, once came from the stars? We must all be humble because we are all so small in this big universe. But we can each be noble because we are all made of star dust and each capable of changing the world. Compared with the stars in the sky, you are both tiny and huge; it all depends upon your perspective, and how you use your special abilities."

I will never forget that teacher. Though all of my other teachers dumped me into an intellectual garbage can, she viewed my unique perspective as a power I needed to refine and develop. She also taught me that I needed to address the drawbacks of my special abilities by working extra hard at the typical subjects in school.

Decades later studying biomechanics in Russia, my teachers were astounded that I could throw athletes who were obviously physically superior, and more experienced. Much like the constellations at my childhood planetarium, my "special ability" allowed me to read patterns of tension like code in computer programming; I could predict the potential movement before my opponents took action, feeling the tension of their intention … and exploit it before they could overpower me with their superior strength and speed.

My childhood teacher planted this lesson long before; to look for how my unique perspective gave me an advantage in a situation where I appeared severely disadvantaged. Now, when things become very difficult, I smile because I know that if I can invert my perspective, I can find my hidden advantage in the opportunity.

Remain humble but become your innate nobility. In every difficulty, flip your perspective and find your hidden powers. When you feel small, look at your true reflection, and you will see how massive you truly are.

# IMPRISONED BEHIND WALLS OF IGNORANCE

"Why are you doing this? I hate you!" The words vomited from my agonized throat as the heavily reinforced door shut.

The terrifying epiphany arrived that I had not been picked up early from school to visit a new dentist, as I had been told, but to be taken to a psychiatric hospital. My mother wept on the other side of the tiny reinforced window of the door. And my hateful words cut through them.

I was trapped, and it was her fault, I thought. Why would she lock me in a mental asylum? I just didn't learn things like everyone else.

My learning disabilities led to poor grades. Since the school punished anyone involved in a physical altercation, regardless of right or wrong, the ridicule of classmates over my abysmal class performance coupled with my obese appearance led to repeated disciplinary actions by the superintendent.

The teachers felt frustrated at not being able to teach me, the administrators for not being able to rehabilitate my delinquency. My mother felt desperate that I needed help. So one day, rather than the dentist, I was at the children's psychiatric hospital.

*"All blame is a waste of time. You may be successful in making another feel guilty about something by blaming him, but you won't succeed in changing whatever it is about your attitude which is making you unhappy,"* Wayne Dyer cautions.

For many years, I blamed my mother for her desperate decision; I blamed my teachers for their inability to teach me; I blamed the school administrators for unjust policies that punished those victimized by aggressors; I blamed the doctors for attempting to convince me that I was broken and flawed, needing to be "fixed."

Yet, the blame led me nowhere but circling down into hopelessness.

The hospital didn't work as the doctors, administrators and teachers had thought.

The eyes are useless when the mind is blind. They didn't see me because their definitions of my predicament categorized my nature as the problem, rather than part of an interactive circumstance which, if we had been able to zoom out and see, could have been understood very readily. But blaming any one of them would not alter my situation.

Thirty years ago, no one understood my learning disabilities, and our educational predation of teachers and administrators failed them. My doctors held only the perspectives they had been taught. My dear mother had only done what she could do to help her son, when she felt she had no alternatives remaining. Even the youths who attacked me are not to blame, because they only feared what they didn't understand, and that fear devolved into violence.

Marvin Ashton wrote, *"If we could look into each other's hearts and understand the unique challenges each of us faces, I think we would treat each other much more gently, with more love, patience, tolerance and care."* A situation of violence is never justifiable, but it is understandable. If you take the time to extract yourself from the victimization mentality of your own involvement, you can see the circumstance clearly. It's all just ignorance.

If we are to take effective action in our lives for change, we will be required to do what we feel no one else is doing: to compassionately understand the source of ignorance in all of the inextricably intertwined behaviors, actions and attitudes. It doesn't justify what was done. But it does give you the ability to become empowered to change your circumstances.

For many years, I feared that if others would learn of my institutionalization as a child, that it would injure my career. Now, I recognize that if I intend to make any change in the circumstances for others, I must embrace and share my story, and show how only my attitudinal changes allowed me to step free of my circumstance. No one could rescue me. No one could help me. I had to stop feeling paralyzed by my victimization, and even if no one could support me, I had to realize the source of ignorance for all of us. And by my empathy, become free.

When something happens in your life, you have three possible attitudes: you can allow it to define you and accept that definition, you can let it destroy you and remove hope from your spirit, or you can let your understanding of the God's eye view of the circumstance strengthen you. For as ignorance is the source of life's tragic maladies, only self-education can begin to restore our freedom.

When in a bad situation, remember someday all of this will make perfect sense. So for the time that things go badly, exhale, laugh at the confusion, empathize with the ignorance, smile through the tears, and remind yourself that everything happens for a higher purpose. You are being called to greater service through your courage to take personal action upon our own ignorance, so that others may be given the opportunity to take action upon it themselves.

# JUDGE A COVER BY ITS BOOK

Children resiliently make friends wherever they are, and when I was institutionalized in a children's psychiatric hospital for my learning disabilities, to the degree that the doctors permitted fraternization between us, I made friends with some of the other patients.

One of the patients called his father and mother during the permitted period, and asked: "I was told that I may be able to come home soon, and I have a favor to ask. I have made a friend here that I would like to bring home with me."

"Of course," his parents replied, "we would love to meet him."

"There's something you should know," their son continued. "He's gay."

"Oh. Well… you know how your father and I feel about that, but if he is your friend, I guess we can just avoid the topic when he visits."

"No, Mom and Dad, he doesn't have anywhere else to go. I want him to live with us."

"WHAT?" said the father. "Son, you don't know what you're asking. We have our own lives to live, and he has a very different lifestyle of his own. We can't just take somebody in off the street. I think you should just come home and forget about the friend you made at a hospital. You can come back and make new friends in our own town."

At that point, the son hung up the phone.

A few days later, the parents received a call from the hospital, telling them to come immediately. On their arrival, the doctor told the worried parents that their son attempted suicide, and he gave them the letter the boy had written. It said only the following, "I am sorry that I'm gay."

Crushed by the weight of their actions, they wept, and asked if they could see their son, and take him home.

The parents in this story are like many of us. We judge people who have different beliefs and lifestyles. We allow these filters to compartmentalize people into "us" and "them." But at our core, if we viewed "them" with the same clarity with which we view those we love, we would only see "us." And we would be so, so much better.

# TRUST IN YOUR OWN MADNESS

When you sit in a mental institution, and calmly explain to the physician that you're not broken, not flawed, not even damaged, and instead, "dare to think differently," do not expect the gatekeeper to throw open way for your release. In fact, the more calm that you become, the more convinced they must be that something is wrong with you.

"Really, Scott, what rational person would think that they've been put in here by mistake," the doctor asked me. "This one," I replied raising my hand with a chuckle. He didn't find me amusing.

I later learned the behavior that they wanted to witness: irrational fits, tear-filled pleas. Also, the didactic therapies they applied required a struggling submission: too quick to give in and you'd be suspected of trickery. I must admit that despite my misplacement in the child's psychiatric hospital for my learning disabilities, I did learn a great deal about human behavior, albeit not entirely as intended by the staff.

I had lost my mind; but I had no intention of going to find it. Years later, after entering University, and my first semester studying Zen and the Art of Motorcycle Maintenance, I had decided that the only way that I would be able to make any significant contribution to stopping this from happening to other children would be to erase the thin line distinguishing insanity and genius and be entirely comfortable defined as either.

It takes a degree of madness to refute an incumbent belief system, such as the belief that childhood learning disabilities are genetic flaws, when they're truly unique gifts hidden from view by the dominance of specific educational learning styles; such as the belief that obesity is a character defect of sloth and gluttony, rather than a biochemical and hormonal sensitivity reaction to toxic processed additives in aggressively marketed "ingestibles" that are mislabeled as food.

When confronted by a socially defined limitation, you must first disprove it by your own example. Transform yourself and you can stand firm on your own self-evident truth. But that is not the most difficult challenge you'll face; for once you do, you will be redefined as a "fluke" — an isolated case that does not disprove the belief. The challenge comes when helping others discard their limiting beliefs. And when you do ... then, the cascade of transformations will erode those socially imposed limitations like a glacier breaking free, rewriting the landscape with its rush.

In my inbox yesterday, I received a beautiful message from a mother whose child wrote her a Mother's Day note: "Mom, thank you so much for believing in me. I wanted to end it all, but because of you, I now trust in myself to BECOME it all." The mother thanked me for the messages I have written regarding the educational lie of learning disabilities and the great corporate deception of obesity.

She wrote, "Your belief in yourself and support in others believing in themselves, gave my husband and I the courage to stand strong when our daughter's situation threatened to write her off. She's now going to college for her first year. Happy, fulfilled and self-willed. God bless you."

Believe in yourself. Find something that you would die for and live for it. You will face resistance far greater than you can imagine, so steady yourself. You can and WILL do it, but it will require every ounce of your energy, commitment, and persistence. Now, go kick ass, my crazy brothers and sisters.

# OTHERS CANNOT DEFINE YOU

I was placed in a children's psychiatric hospital because they didn't know how to address my learning disabilities. Now, research has come to demonstrate that dyslexia is a form of neurological wiring predisposing us to accelerated development through alternate (to the convention) learning style education.

My learning disability allowed me to learn and understand movement in a manner most "normally wired" people cannot, and led me to world champion after championship, and the honor of coaching others to the same. It allowed me to develop a unique writing style for which I have become known, and a speaking style that carries me across the world, sharing the experiences of overcoming my challenges of being "defined" by others.

*"Care about what other people think and you will always be their prisoner,"* Lao Tzu wrote. Like the recent victory of Miss Montana, despite others claiming her autism defined her limitations.

People, conditions, circumstances, experts cannot define you. Only you define yourself. Believe. To be free from the prison of definitions, be outrageously, audaciously you.

# BETRAYED BY THOSE IN POSITIONS OF TRUST

A well-known publishing firm has begun interviewing me for a biography on how I came from physical disability to become a multi-sport champion martial artist and acclaimed yoga guru, from mental disability to Mensa International Member and best-selling author, and from an impoverished trailer park to become an internationally acclaimed speaker.

In discussing the early, violent years of my childhood, they keyed on one story which I thought would help others who feel trapped, persecuted and deprecated as I was. I haven't shared this story publicly before because of the pain it once caused me, and because of the long-festering shame that accompanied it.

I have been very reluctant to write about that part of my life for fear that disclosure would injure my company and my staff.

But thanks to the encouragement and support of key individuals over the recent years, I realize that this series of events served as a crucial catalyst for who I am today.

"And he shall be known by how he moves and how he speaks…"

I was only a young adolescent when I was re-immersed into mainstream population of the public school system. The school administration was under strict legal confidentiality to not disclose that I had spent the better part of a year in the psychiatric hospital.

I had been committed due to mental conditions that hadn't at the time been fully understood, and the emotional problems I experienced adjusting socially to my unique neural wiring. When news of my hospitalization spread to the teachers, within a week it had leaked to the student body.

Already socially ostracized, this only magnified the violence visited upon me. But it was the emotional ridicule that cut deeper than knives. One day, I was receiving my daily "flat-tire" treatment from two seniors: annoying but harmless as they stepped on the back of my shoes to pop off the heel. I stopped to fix my shoes, and then they kicked the books out of my hands.

They laughed at this and at my fumbling waddle because of being an "obese" kid further afflicted with osteochondrosis and dyslexia. I shrugged it off and returned to collecting my scattered papers. Then came a slap on the side of my head as he began boxing my ears. Back and forth pin-balling my skull.

With ears still ringing I heard, "Hey Freak, now that you're out of the rubber room, you gonna kill your mommy?"

And I lost it. I lunged at the senior, twice my height. I punched him as hard as I could.

As he went down gasping, I turned to grab my book bag and run; with his friend still laughing.

I remember looking over my shoulder to see him standing, veins bulging with embarrassment at my successful counterattack.

I remember being grabbed in a front headlock; pulled, running. I saw the concrete wall; then blackness.

When I awoke in the nurse's office, the vice-principal was talking to my mother at my bedside. In my delirium, I made out phrases like, "We don't know how the other students found out. Maybe someone from your family released the information."

My mother was never a woman to be trifled with. In the years of the steel foundry strikes during the 1980s when the steel industry was going belly-up, I watched her lay in front of a bus of "scabs" who tried to cross her picket line and watched as the tires touched her body while she cursed at the top of her lungs. She never moved as the rest of the picketers enraged flew against the bus and over-turned it.

I saw my mother's livid reaction to the vice-principal's scapegoating denial. He said she shouldn't consider me her "fault" because some kids are just "bad eggs." And she exploded with a seething chain of expletives.

She scooped me out of bed and helped me to my feet, the concussion still causing nauseating vertigo. Once again, it seemed, my mother escorted me out of the violence of an indifferent and ignorant educational system. Unfortunately, we were leaving during a break between classes, and I had the "long walk of shame" from the nurse's office to the front entrance of the school.

And then those eyes. … Each student and teacher, glaring, giggling, pointing, snarling on up-turned noses. It was one of the slowest marches of my life, because those students who hadn't already known about my year in the psychiatric ward now had each been apprised amid the gossip wildfires.

As I waddled out of that social prison, the thought appeared in my head as if implanted: to escape from this hell-hole, I need to change how I move and how I speak.

I thought this because they were the primary focal points of ridicule: my anomia and apraxia caused me great difficulty in speaking, not to mention the intense fear of public speaking for obvious reasons; and my osteochondrosis and dyslexia wrought havoc on my coordination, causing me to fail at following motor directions, incapable of "normal" exercise.

Other aspects of dyslexia made actual thinking a chore where most people take logical thought sequence for granted; this was the most difficult aspect, as I felt adrift on an ocean of random and disconnected ideas.

I remember thinking at that age, unduly matured by physical and emotional trauma, that changing how I moved would lift me out of "this place" and changing my words would give me access to more intelligent alternatives, options and ideas. I realized that these people weren't "bad" — just ignorant. The educational system basically only offered wastebasket for "abnormal" kids. But a few key individuals quietly sparked a pinhole of hope within me that I could delimit my potential; that I could rise above my circumstances and actually become grateful for them.

And they were absolutely right. As strange as it sounds, without that "pressure" my motivation would have remained a "lump of inert coal."

That was the pivotal point for me, the crystallization of my obsessive drive for the "diamonds" of grace and wisdom. And recounting it to the interviewers writing this biography led me to reflect on that turning point in my life.

For so many of my childhood years, I actually believed them — that I was "crazy." Think about it. How could one "defective" social outcast be "right" and an entire community be "wrong?"

Decades of over-achievement and over-compensation later, I realized that I had spent my years trying to prove to myself that they were wrong. I felt that I needed concrete validation that I wasn't physically invalid, so I turned myself into a martial arts champion, a published yogi, and record-holding strength athlete. I felt that I needed proof that I wasn't mentally incompetent, so I transformed myself into a best-selling author, globally acclaimed public speaker, Hall of Famer and patent-holding inventor.

But those things aren't the point. They were just examples of the real issue. And that point, the message I want to share with you, if you've continued to read through this story, is that you will change your life, if you change your movement and if you change your speech. Each motion, each word, is a choice and a chance!

# TRUST YOUR IDEAS, NOT REACTIONS TO THEM

Disabled, diseased, destitute — these make you invisible to most people. It takes a special person to truly "see" you, rather than driving by the cardboard-signed indigent and pretending not to notice. It wasn't until one person showed me that my invisibility cloaked my freedom that I reframed my learning disabilities, obesity and impoverishment.

One coach taught me that if ignored, I could take advantage of opportunities that others could not see. So, I set out like a wraith to learn alternative methods of growth and development.

Other students laughed when they saw me counting with my fingers in math classes. They chided me when they'd see me acting out physical skills as if I were on a grand stage. Humiliation felt worse than invisibility, and I so wanted to creep back into the comfort of being unseen, but a counselor suggested that others laugh uncomfortably at what they don't understand. "If you're being laughed at, you must be doing something different. Different is good — unless you want more of the same?" she asked. I feverishly shook my head, "No.'

Released from the psychiatric hospital, I clutched my backpack to my chest so that my notes and journals couldn't be stolen again. Helping me pick up my sprawled books after they were thrown to the ground by a group of students, a teacher whispered, "Keep going. Most people don't like change. If others have such strong negative feelings toward your ideas, and those ideas will help others rather than hurt them, you must be close to something big."

Decades later, I saw the work I had been doing reproduced by many others. These solutions to my early childhood suffering were very hard earned, so I fought to protect my intellectual property.

My teacher asked me, "If people so love what you've done that they feel compelled to adopt it as their own, have you not succeeded at the change you hoped to make? Let go. Heal. You've won."

Humbled, I turned away from protecting my ideas, and started to give them away. Success had given me the opportunity to truly be free to patron the change others wanted to see, and so I aspired to become for others those teachers along my path who whispered the perfect message I needed to hear to keep going.

I've seen many come and go over the years. Some with very good ideas and intentions. The universal trait of those who have succeeded has been the ability to endure. If you just persist, you can have poor material and even bad intentions and still succeed. No short-cuts, as everyone must pay their dues, but you can facilitate success by never quitting.

When launching a new career, as Gandhi advised: Firstly, you'll be ignored because you're new; don't think that abandoning your ideas will help you. Keep researching and working. It sounds like effort, because it is.

Do good by the ideas you've been blessed with and you will eventually get caught doing it.

Next, you'll be laughed at as people start to scrutinize your unique ideas as improbable. Stay true to your ideas, and the values which support them. Don't cave to peer pressure to conform. Don't fall into the trap of trying to be everything to everyone as you'll dilute your ideas.

Then, you'll be hated in a last ditch attempt to discredit you. Others may try to tear you down for every foible you've ever committed, actual or fabricated. Don't get pulled down by the desperation of perceived scarcity, and give up your passion for conformity. Keep focused on abundance.

Finally, you win because you've stood the test of time and you've weathered all of the attacks that the process ensues. Don't attach personal worth to the feedback you receive, good or bad. You're just the messenger of your ideas, attempting to do good by others with the gifts you've been given. Yes, you worked very hard, but you did so to make opportunities available to others. Let go of any attachment to the fruits of the labor, and express your gratitude at being given such incredible abundance to do so.

When you're initially ignored, you can mistake your ideas as lacking value. Shouldn't they pay attention if you have a good idea? No. Others don't know about you and even if they did, how can they trust that you're legitimate? That's not your fault, but it is your responsibility to continue growing. You have good ideas, but you have to pay your dues and develop a good reputation. It'll take time, but you can make the process a lot longer by doubting yourself.

When you are laughed at, you can make the error of trying to change who you are because maybe you're unique. You'll need a thick skin or you'll develop one, because you're going to be ridiculed. Keep true to yourself and be courageous. Don't compromise your values to fit into a preexisting definition. If you do, then you no longer are unique and you become redundant and unnecessary.

When you're eventually hated, you can lash back. You can fall prey to the aggressive feedback loop and become swept up in the drama that cannibalizes your energy and misdirects your path. You can police your intellectual property for theft and plagiarism. You can micromanage your liability, your administration of your company, and your customer service. Exhale. When things are toughest, and believe me they will get very tough, smile because you've almost won.

When finally you win, you can even become disillusioned into believing that it's because of "you" rather than because the universe needed you to share your potential with the world in order to make other things happen that it needed. I had always wondered why all successful people "Thank God" in one way or another. The process of successfully bringing an idea to reality provided them with the critical ingredient of humility. When you succeed, stay small, no matter how big your ego may feel… and keep doing the work you've been so blessed to do.

There are so many pitfalls… but persist sharing your good ideas and keep directed with your internal moral compass and do not become personally attached to your ego in the process. You may be ignored, ridiculed and even hated, but eventually, you will triumph.

*"If people keep throwing dirt at you and they are not true. Do not let them drag you down. Think of it like a mud spa, it will eventually fall off and your real skin will glow."* ~ Dodinsky

# BECOME SOMEONE'S GOOD SAMARITAN

I crumpled into a ball, blood pouring from my hand as the kid who pushed me arrived, laughing.

I pressed off the ground as hard as I could to shove him away, but he was too close and I was too low. The impact hit his groin, and he snapped to the ground in pain. I heard him gasp, "Get him," but I was already running.

Severely overweight, I didn't even make it across the park before his friends grabbed me from behind and pulled me to the ground.

My eyeglasses had broken so I could only see his vague shape approaching. Without a word from him, to the sound of cheers from his friends who held me, his shoe landed between my ribs. Like kicking a tire full of water, air vomited from my lungs. The next kick was to my head.

Dazed, my ears ringing, I saw only a shape move as, lifted by an unseen force, I was placed on my feet and the gang of kids dispersed in all directions. A big adult face appeared in front of my eyes asking, "Are. You. Okay?" Reflexively I nodded, and the woman said, "You had better get home and have your parents look at those cuts." She then walked away.

The mystery Samaritan left an indelible impact. When I see suffering now, despite others' insistence to "mind my own business," I recall the woman who saved me from a worse beating. Her simple intervention ended my pain. How could I now sit by and watch others suffer?

Reach down into someone's darkness and lift them up to the light. Strong people use their strength not only to stand up for themselves, but for others.

Run to help when you can. Object. Never forget that your simple hand-up could very well be the one that saves a life and changes it forever.

# PITY THE JUDGMENTAL

At my childhood church, we had an annual "slave auction" where kids were "sold" in exchange for donations to labor at the houses of those who "bought" them. When I stepped up, not one person met the opening "bid." Hearing the murmurs and giggling about my body and face, I looked around the stage for help. Finally, my cousin's family saved me from further embarrassment by offering to buy me. Still, I felt humiliated.

The pastor saw that I was having trouble, and pulling me aside, said something so powerful that I have never forgotten:

"Should you find yourself the target of other's prejudice, fears, insecurities or small mindedness, and feel the sting of their venom, remember it could be much worse. You could be one of them."

I never understood what "turn the other cheek" meant. Extending forgiveness doesn't mean to permit harm. The people who interpreted the parable that way obviously never had been the target of a gang attack.

But pastor helped me realize pity for the ignorance they suffer. Though it can feel very difficult when YOU are the target of venomous attacks, if you maintain this objective perspective, you realize that only ignorance would cause people to behave so debasingly toward one another.

That doesn't make it okay. But it should give us pause. Think how much worse it would be to suffer that ignorance than to be the target of it.

You wouldn't even know that you were the problem, as you would think it was everyone else.

That pastor shifted my goal from defending against the attacks of others, to pitying them for their myopia. This almost instantly raises the question, "Where am I still ignorant? Where am I doing this to others?"

Years later, studying philosophy and practicing martial art while attending University like my childhood hero Bruce Lee, I ran upon this advisement by Lao Tzu : *"If you want to awaken all of humanity, then awaken yourself. If you want to eliminate suffering in the world, then eliminate all that is dark and negative within yourself. Truly, the greatest gift you have to give is your own self-transformation."*

I held negativity and darkness within me for many years. How could I help others when I secretly held onto the umbrage of my early experiences? The wisdom of my pastor and Lao Tzu solved my dilemma. I didn't need to try to change the darkness and negativity in others, but to release that which I held inside myself. I could not fight off darkness with greater darkness, but my internally revealed light would ignite a spark within others.

Those who hurt innocent people, pity them. Stop them, but pity them. And know that you will ultimately defeat them not through defending against their attacks, but by living a life of such brilliant positivity that your self-transformation spreads like an inoculation to ignorance across everyone you touch, and everyone they touch, and so on…

Be bright.

# BEHIND VIOLENCE LIES IGNORANCE

They knocked me off my brand new bicycle, picked it overhead and threw it into the lake. Devastated, I fell to my knees in tears. It was the first bike my mom ever had enough money to buy me, and now because I'd foolishly ignored the danger of teenagers drinking beside the lake, I had lost the beautiful birthday present she had worked extra hours to buy for me.

One began to mock my crying, which helped turn my sorrow to anger. No matter what, I was getting my bike back, I thought. My mother had worked too hard for it. I dove into the water. Overweight, I wasn't a strong swimmer. I sank fast to the bottom.

In the murk, I couldn't see anything, but felt around until my hands found the knobby back tire. Grabbing hold of the frame, I tried to lift it, but it wouldn't budge, the bike entangled in debris. The desperate pressure in my chest began to build, but I couldn't let go.

I remember thinking, "It's my birthday, and I'm not going to tell my mom that I had lost the bike."

But eventually I could struggle no more. The worst feeling of my life bubbled up: I had to let go. I had to give up. I had to quit. I wasn't strong enough. I didn't have the energy to swim back up to the surface. I had waited too long, and was about to inhale water into my bursting lungs.

Suddenly, hands grabbed my jacket and pulled me up the embankment. Many voices barked, but only one traveled clearly to my consciousness. "Why do you think that was funny? Go back in there and get this kid's bike right NOW or you'll never see me again!"

Coughing the lake out of my lungs, my vision eventually cleared but the burden of submission weighed heavily on my heaving chest.

I had failed. My bike lay there on the bank. The gang had expected me to be elated that they retrieved it from the lake, but my focus had changed. I had lost something more significant than my mother's hard-earned birthday gift. I had lost my will.

Picking up the bike, I rode home, deflated in my humiliation.

*"The strength of your will cannot be imprisoned by other people's ignorance,"* suggests Dodinsky, author of "In the Garden of Thoughts."

But when you're working to emancipate yourself from circumstances, it can feel as if the cage remains impossibly locked, that your will cannot break the bondage within which it feels hopelessly trapped.

Today, I receive messages from others who feel locked in the prison of others' ignorance, desperate to find the will to escape. You don't realize how strong you are, but you will. Sometimes the strongest among us smile through pain, cry behind closed doors and fight battles that no one knows about.

Most obstacles melt away when you decide to walk boldly through them. That DOES indeed demand such heavy boldness that the line between boldness and foolishness blurs. But a few obstacles, no matter your daring, may still remain tall. We may not understand why we cannot scale them, and the impossibility humbles us to our knees.

Sometimes, we encounter obstacles, not so that we will overcome them, but so we can learn from them.

I remember the girl who pulled me out of the water, who threatened to leave her boyfriend if he didn't undo his ill-deed. Her courage inspired me to stand alone, if I had to, against even friends and family, to object to wrongdoing.

The true measure of a person's character is how you treat someone who can do you absolutely no good. Do something right, and no one may remember. Do something wrong, and no one may ever forget your name. I neither remember the teens who threw my bike into the water, nor will ever forget the face of the girl who saved me from drowning and rescued my bike.

When I speak to people now, I recall finding what felt like my maximum potential, the limits of my will, the bottom of my heart... and what it felt like to feel insufficient to the obstacles I faced. Only your foolish heart, only your daring courage to find that edge may inspire others, like the girl from my past, so that others may endure the injustices in their lives and learn from their own impassable obstacles.

There is always a way.

# FIND YOUR 'PERFECT FIGHT'

Awakening in an ambulance, I blearily looked upward at the seated paramedics. Lifting my pounding head, I saw blood covering my torso and legs, and another body stretched unconscious next to me. "Oh God, what happened," I tried to speak, but couldn't utter.

Then I recalled the attack, three seniors shoving me into a wall, my head bouncing like a racquetball.

Then... nothing. Just fleeting images of my face meeting fists and ephemeral ghost memories of unhinging and lunging toward them.

Later, I learned that in the delirium of concussion from the first impact, I had exploded upon them with the rage of a cornered animal. I jumped on the closest, who stumbled backward into a light switch, whose sharp edge opened his skull and sprayed his blood upon us both. I turned on the next two assailants, crazed and frothing. As they ran, teachers dragged me to the ground, and I passed out. This was the story I was later told. In an age before high school video cameras, we will never know if this was an accurate account.

In the hospital, as they checked my concussion, I thought to myself, "Maybe now, I'd finally be left alone." But I was very wrong. Returning to school, the stalking terror doubled in ferocity. The attacks resumed, but this time, with lookouts, with my arms pinned, with concealed shots to only my belly or back where bruises could not tell a story.

It did not end. It was not over.

Many years of martial arts practice passed. After half a lifetime spent training and competing, I stood in the middle of the mat, at the world championships, feeling the intense pressure of the live video streaming to the Internet, my reputation on the line, my livelihood as a teacher based upon my performance. My students — near and far — DESERVED a chance for something better than my continuation of this senseless, ceaseless cycle of fighting.

I had only come out of retirement to hold myself accountable for remaining absolutely centered, for finding my "perfect fight" and holding heaven inside the hell of controlled violence. If I could do this, if I could finally remain in the eye of the storm, the cycle of violence that I carried upon my shoulders could lift. The baggage could be dropped; I would be free.

How many others who would see this, or hear the story, could then hope for such a possibility in their own lives? How many young kids, terrorized as I once was, could dream of a life free of fear?

Winning was insufficient. Becoming the best was just ego. I didn't need to better my opponents, but with the pressure of thousands of young athletes watching, I needed to better myself. If a lifetime of pressure was to produce a diamond from the lumps I had taken all my life, I knew that I must hold my peace, remain centered, and perform with grace.

It all ended like a dream, and I've walked unfettered since then. The baggage did not fall off, but as I have realize over time that I no longer need carry it, I am setting pieces down one-by-one through my writing.

Several years have passed since receiving that divine gift of a minute's sangfroid clarity in the most dire challenge. Its value still unfolds; a climactic frame in the mental movie of my life, an elegant crystallization point for decades of strife.

I stumble and overstep still, but without no doubt that I can reclaim my center. My peace has been proven to me even in the most terrifying of challenges. We must only prove it to ourselves once.

We can beacon peacefulness with readiness. We can remain gentle without being weak, be humble and pious without being harmed or persecuted, be calm and clear without being crushed or coerced. Yes, our daily practice extending this lesson of peace throughout every crisis and choice CAN and DOES make it so. It is possible. We can set down our rusty, ill-fitted armor, and move unburdened.

When encountering your fear, when destabilization threatens your emotional center, don't allow others to push you into their hurricane; pull them into your tranquility. Your center will gently ripple outward and calm your world.

# YOU CAN CHANGE YOUR SELF-DEFINITION

I had dreamed of a super-secret decoder ring appearing in my cereal box, like becoming a member of the Captain Jet Jackson Flying Commandos that my grandfather would let me watch on the black and white. To hold the decryption key to secret messages, what excitement it held for my boyish mind! That excitement has never faded, and I never truly "grew up" or perhaps "out" of searching to decode mysteries. My enamored boyhood still adventures today with the same excitement whether scouring ancient disciplines or studying today's most cutting edge discoveries.

From a violent, broken home, to the abuse and ridicule I faced in the outside world, I turned inward to books for the safety of their solitude, and the escape their stories brought. Ironically, I did very poorly in school because my imagination became perpetually preoccupied with the next adventure. Pillaging bookshelves, I'd find myself under a tower of encyclopedia before the librarian gave me a fifteen-minute warning for closing time.

From non-fiction to fantasy, my mind shifted to other odysseys as I began role playing games: departing upon grand campaigns into the mythologies of foreign lands became a welcome escape from a world where I was labeled as obese and learning disabled. It didn't help my social estrangement, the beatings I faced, nor failing grades at school, and I continued to feel the distance from traditional teaching methods where learning remained inaccessible.

During one such campaign, I noticed that curiously, my game character's personality held undesirable traits exactly like those of the prior characters I had created. How could a cleric, a paladin, a magician and a barbarian all have the same personality flaws? All four continually whined about the injustice of their predicaments, became trapped in unsolvable dilemmas, alone without any support from their parties, and died tragically because of their insufferable drama.

Walking home that night, I rounded the corner with my books, dice and maps in hand to discover a group of older kids. This was not good, so I quickly spun and reversed direction. Running after me, the gang yelled for me to come back, amidst a slew of deprecating expletives. Reaching the front of the building where we had been gaming, they caught up with me, rotund and panting, and kicked out my feet. My gaming gear tattered across the sidewalk and into the road in every direction. Rolling onto my back, I raised my hands to protect my face as their shoes started to rain down.

That night, bruised and ashamed, I sneaked through my bedroom window clutching my puddle-soaked books and torn maps.

Lying in bed, the connection between my earlier discovery regarding my characters' flaws and the event that had just ended deciphered itself. "The commonality between all of my characters is ME. Those are my characters' traits. They are the traits that I have with people."

Digging deeper, I wondered: "What would happen if I decided to use different traits in my characters? Courage, confidence, conviction, leadership? What would happen then? What would happen to me? Would these circumstances change?"

Recalling that crystallization point in my childhood, I now see how it decoded a transformation that forever altered my perception and interaction with my world.

The negative drama in my life could not continue if I chose to stop playing my part in it. When I started to select bravery over fear, certainty over doubts, commitment over evasiveness, and supporting others rather than complaining of lacking support, drama began disappearing in direct proportion to my own level of faith that I could hold these new traits.

Drama could not exist without my active participation. Like turning on a light, this realization dispelled the dark illusion of previously inescapable walls. Like a super-secret decoder ring, I had unearthed a cipher: a key to decrypt a continual mystery in my life. "Why am I continually placed in these unfair circumstances?" I couldn't change other people, and some of the events I could not alter, but I could change my attitude about being a victim of them. I could choose to stop participating in the drama by playing a different part.

I know full well that it can be hard to accept the truth when lies are much more comforting. Yes, it's unjust; others should support, save and protect you. But often, you must begin alone. No, it's not right. No, you shouldn't have to. No, it's NOT your fault that it is the way it is. But you CAN do something. You don't have to change for anyone else, but you can indeed change for YOU. You have a super-secret decoder ring which can decipher traits that aren't serving you.

My life turned a corner with that discovery. There are still "gangs" of would be threats, but my attitude toward them has changed. In recent years, through my teachers' guidance, I've decided to encode even more daring traits than those original modifications. Patience, empathy, compassion, even (*gasp*) love… I'm still in the process of accepting these new traits at full strength, but the results remain undeniable: These higher level traits decipher drama-free events that let me actually be of help to others.

# LET YOUR INNER SELF BURST FREE

"What are you doing, Scott?" my grandfather said as he appeared behind me at the chicken incubator. I said I was trying to help one of the chicks that was having trouble getting out; trying to crack open its shell.

"Scott, helping isn't always helpful. If you crack that egg from the outside, the chick's life will end. If she cracks it from the inside, her life will begin. Cracking it open from the inside makes her strong enough that she will live, but if you do it for her, she probably won't survive, and if even if she does, she may remain weak all her life."

At barely six years old, I couldn't realize the lesson that my grandparent's farm had given, but now, looking back on those many simple wisdoms, I see how they've shaped me into the father and husband I have, and continue to, become.

Struggling to overcome my obesity and joint disease, I gained an internal value for healthy nutrition and fitness, giving us a vibrant, pain free life, versus the external appearance of physique, which can slowly cannibalize our quality of movement and health.

Struggling to overcome my learning disabilities, I grew aware of the inner perception of HOW we think – of learning how our thoughts shape our reality — rather than merely consuming bits of information like a passive memory stick.

Struggling to overcome the abuse, violence and terror of lacking personal safety, I became sensitive to the validation of boundaries and protection of liberties, and how honoring that self-space allows us, like the trapped chick struggling for freedom, to live a strong life for others. Our perception of our life tells us everything we need to know about how we see it. Life isn't so much what is brought to us, but the attitude we bring to life; not so much what things in life happen to us, but how we perceive we are happening to our lives, and others.

As Benjamin Franklin once wrote, *"The only thing more expensive than education is ignorance."* If you think that the ignorance others point toward you feels challenging, imagine living with the cost of that ignorance every day. What is the cost we pay for the ignorance with which we perceive the world? How can we struggle to overcome that challenge? What opportunity will that long, hard struggle make us strong enough to grasp?

Like the chick facing the eggshell, the only seemingly impossible wall we need to strive against is the one we create for ourselves. Create a life that feels strong on the inside, not just one that looks strong on the outside, and that internal strength will give re-birth to a new perception of our world forever.

# EVEN SCARS CAN CONTAIN MAGIC

The group of local kids chasing me for my "weirdness" (learning disabilities) caught and threw my rotund body to the ground, not seeing the jagged pipe protruding there. Bouncing off the lacerating end, my now bloodied face turned toward them and the kids scattered.

"Oh my God we killed him. Run before someone sees him!"

My grandmother found me stumbling down the road, hands covering my blood-spewing face. Assessing my condition, her face transformed from grief to gaiety as she exclaimed, "Did you know that only a magic silver dollar can heal a wound like that and I just happen to own one?!"

Taking me inside, she placed the silver dollar in the freezer. After laying me down and cleaning my wound, she retrieved the coin and dipped it in rubbing alcohol. Placed on my cleaned wound, it initially shocked me like fire. She gasped, "See? The coin's magic works and has already begun healing you! Even though it was in the freezer it feels hot, right?"

I nodded.

She advised me to hold it there for an hour. And to the background sounds of Looney Tunes, that cold coin, rubbing alcohol and pressure stopped the bleeding, reduced the swelling and began to mend the wound.

As my mother returned from work my grandmother said to me, "You earned a magic silver dollar today. Years from now when you're an old man, if you look closely you'll see our President Eisenhower."

Looking at my facial scars, I sometimes see the man my grandmother spoke of, remember her magic, and smile to myself. We all have fantastical imaginations, and if you've ever survived incredible pain and trauma, you know that belief in a little magic never hurts, and sometimes heals.

# FIRST, DEVELOP PERSEVERANCE

Incessant worry was a searing hot white noise in my mind. I worried I'd get into another fight, get another beating by the teachers, be humiliated in class, be shamed by doctors, be abandoned again by my family, become broke without food or medical attention, be ill-prepared, incompetent, unworthy ... I worried death would come too early before I had the chance to understand the purpose behind my despair and suffering.

My grandmother had seen it on my face. She cupped my face, and looking down at me, said, "Worry is a total waste of time. It can't change anything. It robs you of your joy by keeping you very busy doing absolutely nothing. You want to stop worrying so much? Start laughing and DO something about your situation. You may look crazy but you'll feel great. ... You may not make the right choice to change the situation, but you won't be worrying anymore, and eventually you'll figure out the right choices."

Only later in life, when I started to make nutrition and exercise changes to resolve my health issues, did I come to understand what she meant. When you first start exercising, you heart pounds, your head hammers, your lungs burn, your muscles strain, your joints ache, your stomach turns, your mind races with every imaginable excuse to stop, why you're going to get hurt, why you're not capable, competent, prepared, why you can't possibly continue. This is called: "first wind."

You suffer because the mind doesn't know that this is not the end of your fitness, only the end of its initial gear ... until you laugh it off and keep going. Then, something amazing happens in your brain: it rewires to a new gear of efficiency; it floods your receptors with feel-good chemistry, your heart synchronizes, your head clears, your breathing normalizes, your muscles groove the movement, your joints smooth out the motion, and your mind focuses on your tempo and technique. This is called "second wind" — a cerebral adaptation that scientists call neuroplasticity.

But we have to survive our first wind. Most of us, most of the time, stop before we get to our second wind. And don't you think for a second this only applies to exercise! Everything we do is a physical activity for our nervous and endocrine (hormonal) systems; even sitting or laying down. When you worry, your brain lights up EXACTLY as if you were in a crisis!

We stop before the shift happens. We surrender before giving the miraculous design of the human body a chance to adapt and provide us with the clarity, energy and effortlessness that WILL come.

The cells in your body react to everything your mind thinks. When you stop in first gear, perseverating with worry, despair and suffering, you make yourself literally ill.

Most of the groups that I train — soldiers, police and firefighters — have an average mortality of age 54, specifically because of the horrific stress they must endure, and how it slowly erodes their immune systems; the number one killer for them being stress-related diseases.

Negativity suppresses your immune system. Positivity, on the other hand, bolsters it. So, the best choice to make when you feel stuck at first wind is to insert a positive attitude. Unfortunately, we usually only try wishful thinking. Wishful thinking tries to convince us that this is good for us, that something better will come, that it'll soon be over, that it isn't real.

But wishful thinking rarely can survive against the potency of worry, despair and suffering in life's true battles.

Positive thinking is a decision; a choice to fight against the vacuum pulling us down into negativity. When you worry, laugh out; when you despair, take action; when you suffer, hang on. Laughter, action and perseverance are the antidotes to worry, despair and suffering.

Practice these in every small thing you do, like your choice in meal preparation, like your commitment to today's exercise, like your discipline to set aside your prayer and meditation time, when you face a child's tantrum, a coworker's ire, a spouse's argument. If you practice it daily in these small things, you will accumulate your power to apply them in the big things in life.

Second wind comes, if you laugh, act and endure. You can, you must, you will succeed. Stay strong.

# HOPE CONTAINS INCREDIBLE POWER

I had fallen backward down the stairs of my father's house, and was trapped. My family was across the street at the neighbor's and I had sneaked back to get a toy. Running inside, I slipped, and instead of turning the corner, I tumbled down into the basement.

The doorknob slipped from my hands and shut me into darkness as my feet pitched back over my head, something sharp piercing my skin like a hot poker. I yelled for anyone to help get me out, but no one could hear.

I tried to brace myself to stand but each time the fire shot up my leg and I fell onto my back clutching my knees to my chest. The wound, wet and warm, spread like electric shock up my spine with each failure.

My grandfather's voice began in my head, "You can't beat the Devil by hiding in the shadows, Boy. Fight the darkness by letting out your light." Taking it literally, I let my eyes adjust, and then crawled on my belly up the stairs toward the horizontal thread of light winking under the door.

Propping myself to my knees, the knob smeared under my bloody hands, refusing to turn. My grandfather's voice continued, "You won't know your limits until you push them, Scott. Push." So I pushed with my shoulder ... and fell forward fast as the door hadn't fully latched shut.

My mother found me lying there, passed out from fatigue and blood loss. How long would I have lain undiscovered had my grandfather's guidance not encouraged me?

Carl Jung suggested that, *"Facing your own darkness is the best method for empathizing with the darkness others encounter."* When you find yourself standing next to or within the troubles others are experiencing, take a moment to reflect upon your own challenges.

Like my grandfather did for me, if you want to help someone push their edge, you have to give them hope to find it in the dark. Even a little illumination during our darkness travels a long, long way.

Perhaps instead of repulsion from and resistance to other's troubles, through empathy, we can offer an ember of support instead; as a candle cannot be dimmed by sharing its flame.

# THE BOTTOM OFFERS FIRM FOOTING

Within the prison of my mind, I had gone mad. It felt for me, as it does for many, that I was trapped within the walls of my skull, unable to communicate with the soap opera outside, or alter the predictable, declining trajectory of my life.

The learning disabled labels were self-fulfilling: because of the low and immutable expectations to which I was held, none of my behaviors could be seen in light of my actual intent. As a result, I seemed to worsen my situation each time I struggled against it, like an emotional quicksand it sucked me further down the more I fought.

Grabbing the grille of my football helmet, my coach pulled me to the sidelines. "Sonnon, are you stupid, or is that head of yours filled with fat? They're running over you. You're the biggest kid on the field, so plug that hole and don't let any of their defensive line come through it!"

When you're the round kid, stuck in the trenches because your team hopes you're too heavy to be moved, you tend not to view yourself as powerful; you're just a cork. So I imagined I was coach: big, confident, like a tank. Tucking my elbows, touching fingers down, I poised for the snap. "You're a tank; you're immovable," I repeated in my mind. The ball was snapped. The line crashed over me and sacked our quarterback again.

I stood up, humiliated and crushed by the look from my teammates, my coach, the spectators. "I'm worthless," I thought, chin dropping. The laughs, cheers and snipes echoed from the other team, as their coach yelled, "Keep hammering that fat kid!" I felt the prison door of my mind soldered tight. No escape, no appeal, no end to my sentence.

I couldn't pretend to be different than my definitions. "Fake it till you make it" works only for the courage to try; confidence only comes from evidence. I was bullheaded enough to try anything, but had zero belief it would work.

Years passed, I had been given my diploma even though I had mostly failing grades, as they didn't want me to return, or else pitied me. Adrift, I continued a destructive spiral downward into juvenile delinquency, until one day I awoke surrounded by unconscious drunk and drugged strangers, unaware even of my whereabouts. I looked for an exit. No car, money, not even a home, I couldn't wake these strangers and ask for help; help to do what — help to go where?

That was my bottom. I couldn't fall farther. But at that bottom, I stood up, and walked out. Cold air burned my lungs, my sweatshirt offering little protection against the snow. But I was walking.

The homes became more familiar, and I stopped. "Where now?" So, I kept walking. ... Many hours later, I found myself in front of my mother's house. Without a key, I just stood there, afraid to knock. "I'm worthless. Why would she let me in?"

But my mother had always been an early riser, always excited to get up and get some work done, and she passed the door, glanced through the window and saw me shivering there. Opening the door, she pulled me in, "Sit down. I'll make you breakfast."

Dropping down into a seat, I cried soul-deep at her table. She sat, arm draped over my shoulder, and comforted. ...

"Sweetheart, crying isn't a sign of weakness. It's a sign that you've been trying too hard for too long, running into or running away from your problems. Stop underestimating yourself. Stop holding onto what hurts, and make room for what heals."

The quaking of my body under her arm began to release the pressure of an entire childhood of perceived worthlessness.

My worst was the best thing that could have happened to me. Hitting bottom became firm under my feet. I could not fall anymore, so I could stand. Leaving the carnage of that debauched environment and walking "home" became my action to change.

I couldn't pretend to change. I couldn't act as if things were better. They weren't. I had to take action. So I stood, walked, found refuge, released and began to heal.

Climbing would take more time, but I knew at that point, that it WAS time. Moving back into my mom's house, I started a third-shift fulltime position at a convenience store, and began the paperwork on my own to acquire student loans, to pass my SATs, and request admission to college. Humble beginnings, but it WAS a beginning! Though the journey had only started, for the first time in my life, I felt confident. I had evidence. I had found the bottom, so I knew I could not fall farther.

Courageous enough to take action, but now confident enough to believe in the possibility, I climbed...

Many slips and slides have followed, with hard lessons still to come. As they arrived, and failure seemed imminent, I'd smile wryly. Those were just mistakes. That wasn't the bottom. I had been there. So, I'd keep going.

In competition, larger, stronger, faster, tougher opponents would swarm me, and defeat seemed inevitable, but the worse it appeared the more I would smile, and my opponent's confidence would waver slightly. "Why's this kid smiling? Doesn't he know he's defeated?" I could see the puzzlement in their eyes, and feel doubt creep into their tactics.

No, I wasn't defeated. I was only behind.

You don't know how far down I've gone. This is nothing.

My foot would dig in, push down, and I'd press up.

As J.K. Rowling told a Harvard University commencement audience, *"And so rock bottom became the solid foundation on which I rebuilt my life."*

Hitting bottom can become the firm bedrock of your growth. When you feel that nothing else can give you confidence, when you've depleted all of your energy, resources, and options, find that safe place to release, restore and begin to heal. ... Then, gain confidence that you've found your footing. You've seen the worst. And now you can climb.

You may slip to the bottom again, but you KNOW how solid it is. You KNOW you can stand on it. The bottom isn't the problem. The fear of falling farther is. Let the bottom become your bedrock, as you can't fall any farther. Put your foot down. Dig in. Stand up. And climb, brothers and sisters. Climb.

# TURN LIABILITIES INTO ASSETS

In the ambulance, I could only see the paramedic mouthing the words, "Scott, can you hear me? Can you tell us your name?"

I mumbled back, "Um... Is it Scott?" They didn't think I was funny.

The memory of the collision returned. As the "heavy kid" on the football team, I pushed through the line and saw the quarterback fading back to throw. As I dropped my shoulder to sack him, he faked the pass and handed off to a running back who had remained invisible to me, and me to him. We hit helmet to helmet with a thunderous peal.

I awoke en route to the hospital with terrible pain in my neck. It had always been the most injured place of my body, as far back as the day of my birth, when the doctor exclaimed, "Oh My God, look at its head."

My size 8 head required a special-ordered XXXL helmet for football, earning me school nicknames: fish tank, space shuttle, lollypop and my favorite — push pin.

Recovering from the neck injury, my wrestling coach said to me, "You must become mentally strong before you can become physically strong. You've got to believe in your mind that your neck is strong and your head is an advantage. USE your head, Sonnon!"

The health modalities I've learned—Alexander Technique, Feldenkrais, Somatics, Yoga, Zdorovye, Zurkhaneh, Qigong and others — taught me to balance my head upon a whip made of pearls; to "use my head" even in fighting, where my '5th limb' strategy in grappling became known as "Sonnon head."

Your darkest trouble can become your greatest asset.

I didn't have the time to practice my exercises but I made the time.

I didn't have the knowledge of how to do it, but I did what I could.

I didn't have health insurance or education, so I educated myself to insure my own health.

I didn't have confidence that what I did would work, but I gained confidence from even very slow results.

I had a tremendous amount against me but I had my heart going for me.

I had plenty of excuses but I didn't allow my recovery efforts to be excused by any of them.

When you allow yourself to be mentally weak, recovery can remain a closed door. But when you have the courage to do it all alone if you must, you open the door to recovery and step through.

You are not what has happened to you. You are what you choose to become from all of the aspects in your life. If you're looking for the one person in the world who can help you, take a look in the mirror. That person looking back at you may look like they're facing a lot of troubles, but they're your greatest asset.

# STRENGTH CAN BE CONTAGIOUS

When I was a kid, like most kids, I was often not so smart. Once in junior high school, several meatheads were pushing a classmate of mine around in the parking lot. They were seniors, and the guys who terrorized most of the students as well as some of the teachers.

Without considering the foolishness of my actions, I ran over and told them to knock it off and go pick on someone their own size, to which they responded, "Oh really twerp? That'd be you?" I remember those words vividly, because they were all I heard before unconsciousness.

When I awoke in the infirmary, the nurse asked me what had happened, since a student had found me lying on the parking lot. I shook my painful head and lied that I didn't remember.

When my step-father arrived and saw me, he was furious. He dropped me at home with my grandmother to watch over me, and he returned to work.

She asked what happened, and I told her the story, and how I was afraid of what would happen when I saw them again. She said to me, "Sometimes God knocks you down, not to teach you submission, but to show you your courage; not to see if you'll stay down, but if you'll get back up."

I protested that I didn't want to get beaten up again, and that there's no way I could possibly win. Putting her hand on my head and hugging me, she comforted, "Nobody wants problems. But when they happen, showing yourself that you're willing to lose a fight rather than lose your principles is the biggest victory."

I saw those kids again, and got pummeled several more times. Never won, obviously. But the classmate who had originally been tormented by them once came to me in private and said, "Sorry they got you when you said something to make them stop. Why'd you do that?"

I replied that he'd do the same if he had seen them torturing me. And his words have rung in my ears since, "Not until I saw you stand up to them, I wouldn't have. Maybe now I would."

Maybe that's why we are given opportunities that don't have any possible immediate success: because the impact of being willing to lose on principle is a victory for our virtue.

# ATTITUDE SHAPES OUR BURDENS

She laughed in my face, saying, "You thought I was serious? What a joke!" Then she slammed the door.

At 14 years old and still very overweight, I had ridden my bicycle 24 miles down the highway on a flat tire to get to her house. After speaking with her on the phone that morning, she had said she would like to see me again so I had asked, "What about today?" She replied with a chuckle, "Sure."

I hadn't clued in on the levity. Now, I had another four-plus hours of riding back to my house on a bent rim, emotionally as deflated as my tire.

I had met her the day before at the amusement park. We stood in the long line together for the Super Duper Looper, and I dared a conversation with her and her friends. They all giggled at my awkward rolls and dumpy posture, and pushed her toward me. She reluctantly complied to her friends' dare. After the roller coaster ended, under the continued dare of her friends, she pulled me behind one of the rides, and kissed me. Writing her phone number on my hand, she ran away.

My first kiss.

Of course, never having had a girl even look at me twice before, I was instantly in love. So the next day, I called feverishly. Riding to her house with a flat tire, those long hours of anticipation were the best and fastest moments of my life to that point. A girl had actually LIKED ME! Who cared how far it was, how long it took or how hard it was? I grabbed my broken bike and sneaked out of the house, disappearing down the highway.

Biking to her house felt like only minutes had passed. POOF, and I had arrived elated, excited and energized. In contrast, the ride home dragged on, minute after minute, like days of agony that would never end.

Returning finally home, exhausted, expelled and depressed, collapsing in bed, I lay there, tears carving paths down the sides of my dust-crusted eyes, considering the contrast between my ride there, and my return.

I was so happy going there, the time passed quickly, and my body actually felt great during the unusually long and difficult physical exertion. Heartbroken upon my return, time dragged and each mile pained my body like torture.

At first I thought in self-pity, "If only she would have liked me, the ride home would have been just as easy." But then came one of the most important realizations of my life: "I wish I could have just pretended she liked me so I could have gotten back here quicker."

Immature and unrefined, this seemingly casual thought, borne from humiliation, would become the basis for much of my later university study and professional research.

Life isn't a problem. Only our attitude toward it is a problem.

As Helen Keller, with her amazing insight, once challenged us: *"Life is either a daring adventure, or nothing at all."*

I chose my attitude toward those two 24-mile journeys: one uplifting, the other down-trodden. Certainly at 14, I was not capable of mature, attitudinal shifts in perspective, but I did sense the contrast between the two trips. That immediate disparity allowed me to realize that we control our perception and experience of the world. Nothing changes between the two: the same duration, distance and difficulty. But our attitude carries us to heaven, or makes it a highway of hell.

Since then, I program my attitude with each challenge; during my workouts, projects or presentations, my relationships, meetings and proposals. When enormous work lay ahead, nervous and anxious about my ability, I recall the disparity of those four and a half hours riding my bike as a child; one great, one awful. And I decide not to feel awful, but be great instead. No matter how many insistent little gremlins seek to burrow negativity into my attitude, I steel my will, and remain positive.

W. Clement Stone wrote, *"There is little difference in people, but that little difference makes a big difference. The little difference is attitude. The big difference is positive or negative."*

Attitude takes no physical effort, but immense moral power to alter. It demands our daily practice in the tiny, insignificant events, like spilling coffee, bumping our heads, or forgetting where we placed our keys.

Whenever possible, practice laughing at these experiences: you'll feel better, lighter and more energized by the Game of it all. And when the big events come, and they will, you'll have deposited in your attitude bank a lot of little differences.

And those will make a big difference in shifting your attitude amidst those big challenges.

# YOU MAY NEVER KNOW YOUR IMPACT

A touching message appeared in my browser from a former childhood classmate.

Thoughtful, selfless acts can transform lives, and I suspect this message will impact me with as dramatic a result, once I integrate it into my perspective.

"Scott, I've quietly watched your career since you popped onto the radar in the early 90s. Twenty years later, you've climbed from obscurity to notoriety as an undisputed top leader in your field. Even detractors you've had in the past concede your success. Have you paused in your incredible momentum to reflect on how far you've come? It's remarkable.

To the brass tacks, I write you to say two things:

1. I may not have been one of the individuals who maligned you back in school, for your weight issues, for your family's financial difficulties, or for your educational challenges, but I watched those who did.

I regret not having said anything to anyone. Honestly, I was afraid of getting the attention directed at me, if I spoke up against what was being done to you. Both the teachers who humiliated and neglected you, and the students who mocked and abused you, intimidated me. I was too frightened that if I objected, that I would receive the treatment you were. I'm very sorry.

Ever since reading about you twenty years ago, I've felt like that sin of omission was too heavy, so I'm firstly writing for you to forgive me for not helping you in those long ago years at school.

2. Secondly, [please exclude any personal details of this story if you share these words.] It may be painful for you, but it was transformative for me. I will never forget it. I remember in school when you had [three upperclassmen] knock all of your books out of your hands, and [one] picked up your journal, laughing at what he read aloud from inside.

He read to everyone in the hallway your personal words, "No matter how many of these kids hate me, I will never give up. Never, ever!" Everyone but a few laughed. Those of us who didn't, nervously fidgeted at the public humiliation they continued to perform. I saw them push you, slamming you against the lockers, mocking you for your private thoughts. I saw you fight back. I saw them crush you to the ground with their kicks and punches. I did nothing. I fled to class.

You never did, though. You never gave up. Time has passed for all of us, but for you, time has been well-invested. Do you remember when [our English teacher] did the section on Earl Nightingale and we read aloud our reports? In yours, you got choked up in front of the class, and I still can see you reading, "Earl Nightingale said we should never give up on a dream because it will require time. Time passes anyway. I won't let time pass by giving up on my dreams."

Time did pass for both you and I, but because in the past I lacked your courage to speak up against injustices and stand up for myself like you did, it took me a lot longer. I was too slow in my decision to take action in my growth. I won't make excuses.

But in the past few years since your career exploded, you've become a globetrotter sharing all of your stories and strategies for personal development. I realized that no matter where you are in your age, you can still become courageous, grow, and take back control of your life and invest your time productively, rather than passively letting time pass.

Another passage of Nightingale's you read was, "Your world is a living expression of how you are using and have used your mind." Scott, I just wanted to thank you for never giving up on the world you wanted to create and have now created for yourself. You've made my world and probably for many of your readers so much wider. I'm working to express my mind and use it in effective ways to expand my own world. Thanks to you."

My dear friend, thank you so much for your message. And thank you for permitting me to share your words. They will affect more than just me, but they already have affected me beyond my own comprehension, I am certain.

No child is responsible for facing the madness of those past events. I didn't, and it was directed toward me. You recall only the moments where I occasionally outwardly rebelled, and may have clouded the many more times I collapsed upon myself. You recall the good moments, for no other reason than that you have such strong character.

How courageous of YOU to remain thoughtful of the plight of another, rather than be washed away by the mob mentality.

You CHOSE to not participate in it. Though you judge yourself (without warrant, in my opinion) for not acting out against those events, you do not credit and celebrate how strong you were for not taking part in them.

Refusal to participate takes a brave spirit. It may not have been the active tactics that you later have imagined you wished you had taken, but how much more difficult would the situation had been for me, if you had forfeited your conscience and jumped into the fray? Thank YOU for your moral courage. My life has been easier because of you.

Several years ago, I was given a private tour of the Da Vinci exhibit in Milan. The security measures were all the highest caliber, as I was there with the unit protecting the Prime Minister's family. They escorted me to one exhibit in particular, where I read these words by Leonardo, "Once you have tasted flight, you will forever walk the Earth with your eyes turned skyward, for there you always have been and always will long to return."

Your eyes have never left the skies. You dared to imagine what your world would become were you to take flight. That audacity is the only virtue that transports us from the sandbags of our current reality, to cutting loose and rising in our hot air balloon to our dreams. You never gave up on yourself, by gazing down at the Earth as a prison sentence.

My first Chinese martial art teacher used to chide my impatience of training 3–4 hours a day. He would laugh at my ambition, when I'd tell him that I couldn't afford to develop slowly. I needed help NOW, I would protest. He would smile and say, "Be not afraid of growing slowly. Be afraid of standing still. You are growing at the exactly perfect speed. As long as you do not stop, you cannot fail."

You cannot understand how transformative for me reading your words has been. That powerfully courageous and selfless act of sending out your positive attitude into the world has helped me redefine my early childhood, and as a result, my entire world. How many others of us were out there resisting the mob mentality of abuse and humiliation? So many.

Because of your strength and resolve, I intend to reach out to them, and allow your bravery to avalanche into us all.

# DARE TO EXCEED EXPECTATIONS

My high school counselor chided me for setting my expectations too high, saying, "it's good to have big dreams but you're continually crashing because your goals are unrealistic. You just can't do certain things."

She then read me a quote by Albert Einstein: *"Everybody is a genius. But if you judge a fish by its ability to climb a tree, it will live its whole life believing that it is stupid."* She concluded, "You have several disadvantages working against you, so if you set more realistic goals, you're going to be more successful and happier."

Young, I both took what this "authority" said to a heavy heart, yet emotionally rebelled against it. Being told to lower my expectations felt like a hatchet to my knees. So going back to the library (the only home I really felt safe in), I started flipping through one encyclopedia after another, absent mindedly. And once again, I fell asleep amid my fortress of books.

On awakening with sudden energy, I ran to the copy machine with the book I had used as a pillow, and feverishly copied the page I had opened.

The librarian yelled for me to return all of my books before I left, but I was already running down the hall toward the guidance counselor's office. Rushing past the secretary's objections, I threw open the door and slapped the copied paper down onto her desk.

"Gourami," I panted, undoubtedly mispronouncing the unfamiliar word. She looked down at the paper, then back up at me, and shook her head in confusion.

"The Climbing Gourami climbs trees," I exclaimed. "I don't think he believes he's stupid. HE wasn't told he couldn't, so he did."

I turned and left her office with a sense of vindication and a vision that has extended throughout my career as an athlete, writer and businessman. Anyone who tells me that I "cannot" is met with a sense of skepticism toward themselves, rather than toward the goals that they object I could never accomplish. I found my Gourami.

My goals remain unrealistic to this day, and still people object. I continue to fail to achieve many of them. However, as I discovered over the years, it isn't the achievement that is the benefit, but the struggle. I have learned so much more from my passion even amid my failures than I have from the realization of any one success.

Do not doubt your unreasonable dreams. Reason fails to comprehend them, which is why they're called 'dreams.' Instead, doubt the resistance to them, because succeed or fail, you will be better from pursuing them. Be the Gourami fish, and climb that damned tree anyway.

# WRITE YOUR OWN DEFINITIONS

I heard from a young girl who wrote that my gardening photos were not "sexy" and that I should stick to photos of my abs and return to fighting MMA, because it was "sexier" than putting my hands in manure. It reminded me of story from my youth, where I was nearly arrested for a crime I hadn't committed.

When I was 17, a detective walked into the bank where I worked evenings, and asked me to accompany him to the police station. Paranoid, I started asking all sorts of questions because I couldn't understand what I could have done wrong. He evaded each of them until we arrived at the station, where he asked me about a diamond I had sold the week before.

Telling him of my second job as a lifeguard, I explained how I had found the loose diamond at the bottom of the pool while inspecting the drain after closing time. He asked if I had heard about a robbery at the jewelry store a couple of weeks earlier. I hadn't, but inwardly cringed as I pieced his story together.

Explaining that police had been watching me for a week, he asked why, if I had honestly found the single diamond as I described, had I been trying to sell jewelry at stores in several nearby towns. Worried and confused, I said, "That's impossible, as I work nearly 16 hours a day between my two jobs at the bank and at the pool trying to save money for college."

He chuckled wryly, thinking I was lying, "Why do you look so worried then?"

"Well," I replied, "You think I robbed a jewelry store for one; and two, I'll probably lose my job even for the suspicion of it." To his challenge of whether I could prove my whereabouts on the date of the robbery, and of the attempts to sell jewelry, I said, "Absolutely. I worked all of those dates."

It was his turn to look confused.

He snatched up one paper very closely, and then another and compared them with earnest. "Spell your last name, please." I did, "S.O.N.N.O.N." He dropped the papers to the desk and sat back saying, "I am very sorry for the confusion, Scott, but it seems that we've made a mistake. The individual attempting to sell the stolen jewelry is a Scott Sonnen; with an 'E.'"

My initial reaction was total relief, but then, I thought about my job. Who in the world at the bank was going to believe this story? As predicted, I ended up losing both jobs the next week, though the managers claimed it was unrelated to the allegations.

The detective called me to apologize again, "Scott, we had made a major mistake. We know that you were fired from your jobs because they weren't comfortable with the rumors of your involvement in a crime, despite our insistence that you were innocent. I take full responsibility. You seem like a good kid working hard, and now you're only going to need to work harder because of our actions. I'm sorry. When you need a reference for a new job, please let me know. I will do whatever I can."

(Ironically, I now work with law enforcement agencies around the world, most likely because of this one man's incredible character to accept full accountability for a mistake and offer to help make up for it.)

At 18 years old, I had made a lot of blunders, and I was going to make many more before I got older. But at that frightening point of nearly being arrested for a crime I hadn't committed, and regardless of my innocence losing two jobs that I believed to be critical to my future, I realized a stark reality: Who you are and what others think of you are often disparate, and sometimes opposite each other.

Ralph Waldo Emerson wrote, *"The only person you're destined to be is the one you decide to be."* Others may think they know me, but they have no idea who I really am. Not even I do. I AM whomever I decide to become, no matter what others think. I've reinvented myself many times, because I've repeatedly outgrown the husk that restricted my growth. I've also kept fighting for my development when others typecast me as a failure, with a flawed mind and defective body.

When I overhear or read the words of others pigeonholing someone with negative definitions, I think to myself how much harder my life had been because of such definitions upon me. How much farther would I have been able to travel in my journey, or at least how much less painful and more enjoyable would my journey have been to this point, had others not proclaimed such low and negative expectations of my potential?

You may never be "understood," even by those closest to you. But those who really love you and belong in your life will accept you for the changes you will continually make over the course of your life. ... Because who you are is so much more than we can fathom, and even in several lifetimes, due to its immensity, you could not unearth ALL of your potential. It's bottomless, limitless.

No matter how others define you, only you can define yourself. Despite all events that seem to destroy your reputation, keep working, keep going. Your reputation is only what others think of you. Your character is who you really are. Be true to your character, and nothing can stop you.

*"Character is the one thing we make in this world and take with us into the next. The circumstances amid which you live determine your reputation; the truth you believe determines your character. Reputation is what you are supposed to be; Character is what you are. Reputation is the photograph; Character is the face. Reputation comes over one from without; Character grows up from within. Reputation is what you have when you come to a new community; Character is what you have when you go away. Reputation is made in a moment; Character is built in a lifetime. Your reputation is learned in an hour; Your character doesn't come to light for a year. Reputation grows like a mushroom; Character grows like the oak. A single newspaper report gives you your reputation; A life of toil gives you your character. Reputation makes you rich or makes you poor; Character makes you happy or makes you miserable. Reputation is what men say about you on your tombstone; Character is what angels say about you before the throne of God."*
~ William Hersey Davis

# BREAK FREE FROM THE PAST

Another Facebook post (uncorrected) chided:

"Still remember you from jr high school, sonnon. you havent changed. still pretending your bigger than you are. no matter how rich you got by your fancy word your nothing but the fat four eyed retard we all kicked the sht outta."

This poster may or may not have been someone I knew in school. Unnamed fake accounts have zero credibility.

However, the veracity of his claims remains irrelevant; only the rare gift of being able to learn from him matters.

I feel very grateful for the opportunity to revisit old associates through the modern marvels of the Internet. Imagine being given the chance to return to your past and rewrite old patterns, heal old wounds, and create new possibilities for growth.

I have had to reinvent myself many times from the definitions I had accepted from others, from teachers, doctors, peers and family. Each reinvention comes with great resistance, for to grow, you must proclaim to be more than you've past displayed.

Uttering the words, "I AM…" awakens a before-unseen depth of your potential, and that emergence creates a wake from the uplifting. It can be very frightening to others, who do not realize the fathomless reaches of their own untapped potential.

They may think we are the tiny tips of ice floating the waters, when we are the massive mountains lurking under the surface.

You may encounter great resistance from those from your past, even those closest to you, as you commit to expanding your current definitions of who you are. But you do them a wonderful service by insisting upon your new growth over contentment with past limitations. For as you evolve, as you powerfully proclaim a new, "I AM…" you remind us that most of our own potential remains unexcavated.

To the original poster, I reply: Stay awhile. Let us remind you of how much more you are than you've allowed yourself to believe.

# CHANGE YOUR MIND, CHANGE YOUR WORLD

We are the only creatures that we know for certain can think about thinking. Philosophers call us "second-order" intentional beings, in comparison to others that can only react to what happens, which are distinguished as first-order. This incredible capability — to think about our thoughts — can either dominate us like a cruel torturer, or aid us as an invaluable mental navigator, providing the map location, travel hazards and plotted course of our thinking.

When I was an early teen, on the road to obesity recovery, my mind was mad with threat fixation; my imagination sprinted uncontrolled from one danger to the next, as frequently happens with those abused or terrorized too long. Hypervigilant, with broken alarm systems, everyone and everything became a potential threat, and no one and nowhere was safe.

I learned to escape my situation by running out into the forest with a boken, a training sword that was given to me as a gift. What marvelous adventures I had battling ninjas, pirates and goblins in those woods. Dodging and slashing through the branches, I'd reflect upon the events of the day, and weave them unknowingly into epic fantasies played out in my boyish battles. But instead of merely converting them into a tragic storyline, I changed my stories to where I overcame the villains. Instead of being the victim, I would become the victor.

This activity, I later learned, is used in behavioral psychology to "change state" when encountering a destructive mental pattern: Play out the memory, interrupt the story line, back it up to where you could alter your choices, and replay it with a new, productive ending. My fantastical odysseys in my forest campaigns contributed to my emancipation from the victim mindset I suffered. Inadvertently, I had developed on my own a clinically effective strategy for changing my own state, and thus ... changing my world. It carried throughout my development, and became part of my way of being.

Whenever I encounter a fear, frustration or anxiety, before it becomes terror, rage or panic, I would insert a storyline I wanted to happen. Holding my mind there, I would then exercise. Of course, my exercise is much more regimented and disciplined now, not the fantasy of my youth, but the physical effect is the same. This approach acts in the same way as the shuddering deer: physical movement to release preparatory threat arousal as a relaxation response.

I practice fitness and martial art at certain periods throughout my day, but unlike my early years in the discipline, I do not allow it to mentally run unchecked. Now, I imagine the technique I want to practice, the tactic to apply it within, and then when I train, I mentally rehearse its successful application, or my ability to recover rapidly from its unsuccessful application back to my plan.

We can either be victim or victor by such "what if" debugging of technique and tactic. We can allow paralysis by over-analysis, or we can search for gaps and holes to fill. We must be error focused without being failure fixated.

This became a life skill, exported into my career, my family, friends, and colleagues, and especially my personal finances.

When imagining a potential threat to my project, my relationship or my budget, I interrupt the pattern, insert the choice that would weave a positive, productive conclusion to the event, and play out the rest of the film to its happy ending. I do this while exercising, remembering to exhale through the effort phase of each movement, on the lift, on the jump on the push, on the swing. And it intertwines with the mental rehearsal. ...

Exhalation not only provides our greatest internal power, but it also enables the stress-relief response. As one of our greatest attributes as humans originates from our ability to think about our thoughts, we can choose which thoughts to play out.

As Gandhi advised,

> *"Your beliefs become your thoughts,*
> *Your thoughts become your words,*
> *Your words become your actions,*
> *Your actions become your habits,*
> *Your habits become your values,*
> *Your values become your destiny."*

And as George Bernard Shaw cautioned, *"Those who cannot change their minds, cannot change anything."* Don't limit yourself to merely mentally trying to stop negative thoughts. Get out and MOVE! The exertion holds the key; for once you are acting, your willpower is given a wooden practice sword to begin chopping away at those mental ninjas, pirates and goblins. Suddenly, you will find yourself knighted into a changed state of mind, with productive conclusions to the troubles you once had, with opportunities rather than obstacles, and possibilities rather than problems.

As William James wrote, *"Our greatest weapon against stress is our ability to choose one thought over another."*

Choose.

# MOVEMENT MAY BE YOUR 'RAGE THERAPY'

My earliest childhood memory was of my father beating my mother. No one, especially his family, understood his post-traumatic trauma returning from the Korean War, and the insidious corrosion it caused in our family. One day, my brother heard our mother crying in pain as she lay in a heap on her bed, and told me to go see if she was okay.

Terrified, I felt like I had done something wrong (an operating system pervasive throughout my life). I couldn't talk. I couldn't say a word. I couldn't move. I don't remember anything else. Just fear.

Pan forward two years; after the divorce, my mother had to raise us on her own. She had just broken up with a man she had been dating, who was now drunk outside our trailer. He kicked the door in and started beating my brother and I. He had his hands around my throat, choking me. My mother, livid and furious, knocked him over and off me.

"Don't you EVER touch my kids!" she screamed.

I covered my head and ran into my room as he started on my mother. I trembled, feeling something large and hard in my throat, unable to get it out. My face red and my fists clenched, I listened to him beat her, my mother screaming back at him, fighting him toe to toe.

The door to our room flew open, then slammed shut and locked. My mother, now inside, broke one of the windows with her elbow and, hefting us out, told us to run to the neighbor's house and call police. I screamed that I didn't want to leave her, as she lowered us out the window in our pajamas. Even as her ex-boyfriend kicked open the door, she looked at me calmly, told me gently that it would be okay, and to run as fast as I could. I don't remember anything after that moment.

Pan forward another three years; my mother was to introduce me to a new boyfriend that afternoon when we all went swimming in a stream up in the mountains. When we arrived, my mother went off swimming by herself. I forget why; maybe I didn't know. I felt nervous. This frighteningly large steelworker said to me sternly, with a low, forceful voice, that he was going to marry my mother and be my father; and that he was in charge now.

Erupting with a rage that I couldn't understand, I began screaming, "NO! You're not my father," but he pushed me underwater and held me there, thrashing futilely. Eventually, he pulled me out, and I gasped for air. He asked me if I was ready to obey. Fury filled me, and I lashed out at him.

He pushed me underneath again as water flooded my screaming mouth. I don't remember what happened afterward.

He became my first step-father.

My rage continued, swelled and at times burst. In fourth grade, a kid in the playground stole from my backpack a coin that my brother lent to me for "show and tell."

When I reported this to the teacher who was monitoring the playground, the teacher accused me of lying. Like an erupting volcano, I was immediately on the other kid, grabbing at the coin to get it back. The teacher pulled me by the arm into the school, to his office and shut the door.

Four years later, I was in eighth grade, new to the different building where teachers unsuccessfully attempted to integrate grades 7–12. I was one of their "problem kids" who "always seemed to find trouble." The leader of a gang of eleventh graders walked behind me, taunting. I ignored him, even though that burning lump in my throat started to form. Not getting the response he wanted, he started stepping on the backs of my shoes, then pushing my books out of my arms, then flicking my ears. …

Explosion.

I turned around and hit him as hard as I could in the groin. He went down hard and limp. His friends were in hysterics laughing and making fun of him for this little, fat kid with horn-rimmed glasses knocking him down. Suddenly, he was up off the ground, holding me in a headlock. I couldn't breathe (again). He drove my head into the concrete wall. I blacked out. I don't remember what happened after that.

These handful of experiences are only highlights of much more graphic events from that time, of being terrorized by many more physical fights, and the much more toxic anticipation of violence. So much rage and fear and feeling trapped and hopeless and at the same time vulnerable and exposed.

What followed from that point forward became an ongoing pattern, repeating this drama over and over throughout my childhood. I didn't understand why the meanest people always seemed to peg me as the object of their animosity.

Incapable of understanding why they targeted me, I couldn't keep my mouth shut. I'd explode against them.

As a freshman in high school, I landed in a psychiatric hospital as an in-patient in the children's ward, admitted by a crying mother who didn't understand what was 'wrong' with her child. I learned I had to do what they told me and I would be set free. This discovery compelled me to mask and suppress the rage (so I thought).

When I was finally released, by law no one at my school was supposed to learn where I had been. Of course, one teacher told another teacher, and was overheard by a student … a week later everyone knew. Reinserted into the mainstream population, the negative stigma amplified tenfold.

A senior taunted me for the photosensitive eye protection my doctor had me wear.

He asked me if I thought I was "cool" to wear sunglasses in school. His first strike slapped the glasses from my face. The second punched my eyes and my head bobbed backward several times before I realized what had happened. For some reason, the blow didn't hurt, but actually gave me euphoria. Then the explosion.

When a teacher pulled me off of him, blood pooled beneath his head. Despite the crowd of witnesses – students and teachers — I was suspended for always "bringing out the worst in others" (the vice-principle's words to my mother). My mother drove me home and dropped me there as she returned to work, seething with disappointment in my actions.

When I returned to school a week later, the senior and two of his friends cornered me and held me down, repeatedly punching my stomach so no bruises appeared for evidence. I threw up a lot of blood.

A pattern in my victimizers materialized: If I fought back, they ganged up on me. If I ran away, they found me. If I smiled because it didn't hurt, they beat me unconscious. But, if I rolled with the punches and kicks and pretended as if they really hurt, my would-be attackers would stop feeling successful, their drama played out to conclusion by fulfilling my part of the social contract as a victim. Their group dynamics, posture, movements, expressions, gestures, syntax and words burned into my brain as I studied them through the fog.

I found myself in martial arts, some would say, "obviously." They attracted me for reasons most didn't understand. I saw these martial arts masters with the greatest of composure, minimize harm to their would be attackers, and resolve conflicts without emotional arousal. Asking, "how?" led me on a very long odyssey.

Style after style I studied, some red-faced, arrogant "master" would try to teach me how to 'fight back.' Sometimes I laughed during sparring, as the "master" would beat me senseless and then tell me that I needed to be more "counter-aggressive."

Counter-aggression was counter-intuitive. Experience proved it to be an ineffective approach – force only begot more force. That much was obvious to me, though oblivious to the "masters" teaching how to "destroy an attacker."

Destroy? I just wanted to be left alone.

In university majoring in Philosophy, I gravitated to the debate and rhetoric classes, enjoying most the professors who managed to pick apart seemingly superior arguments with calculated ease and lack of emotion; a verbal complement to my martial arts exploration. But there, I encountered a new martial art, one of yielding and blending with force, one where if attacked you folded around attacks, rolled with the punches. It resonated with me! It would work, since I had already proven it successful intuitively throughout my life.

Years followed as I delved deeply into this practice of yielding to force. I fought around the world, fought some of the best in the world – beat some, lost some. But that wasn't important to me. It wasn't the fighting that made any difference to me whatsoever, but the efficiency of my emotional calm during violence. No freedom comes from escape. You can only be free, if you can stay present in the worst of situations and not be emotionally attached to the excessive stress of negativity.

Martial art allowed me to cathartically release my pent up rage without exploding. Rage wasn't part of me, and exploding wasn't how I needed to respond to threats. Rage is what happens when you suppress how you feel, like a pressure cooker to emotions, which elicits reflexive defense mechanisms. Martial arts (and philosophical debate) took the lid off and allowed me to see that I've always had the tools I needed, if I could keep my head cool under pressure, without the defensive reflexes being triggered.

Martial arts, yoga, dance, and other movement methods became rage-therapy. You don't explode, if you don't suppress. Movement increases your sensitivity to force as it really is, not force as your reflexes interpret it.

Excessive stress, bottled up, triggers defense mechanisms. If you're heavily armored and feel pressure against that armor, it's indiscriminate – it's a threat and you explode. But if you release that tension when you experience force, your body folds around it, like when you press your finger into your skin, perfectly agile and accommodating. In that malleable nature, we become invulnerable.

I stopped fighting. And to prove it to myself, I sought one last time to find the "perfect fight" where I could efficiently perform against some of the world's best and remain emotionally calm. Finally finding my perfect fight by winning the 2010 World Martial Arts Games, I learned that I could and still can prevent accumulating excessive stress without discharge.

Don't put on a lid on the pressure cooker. Move, dance, play. Movement keeps the lid off. Movement keeps you sensitive to the actual events, not the false threats misperceived by excessive stress. Fear can be understood as False Evidence Appearing Real. Excessive stress makes you feel it's worse than it is. Excessive stress builds and reinforces it.

You can't help others until you first help yourself. Being able to recover from and resist excessive stress dramatically changes how you view others; it softens critical judgment and prevents misperceiving threats. Everyone suffers, and if we realize the source of our own suffrage, we can truly empathize with the plight others endure.

This new level of understanding allowed me to look back upon my poorly equipped father, returning from war, and unable to transition to non-combative domesticity. How different would our lives have been if he had been readied with the tools and techniques to recover from and resist excessive stress? His trauma caused him to sacrifice his entire family life.

Releasing my own rage, I now thank him for his sacrifices, even though he didn't choose those.

So, my friends, after decades of trying to discover how to "keep the lid off" of rage, my teachers helped me learn resilience (recovering from excessive stress) and toughness (resisting excessive stress). These tools help us become sensitive again to the world as it really is, not how the defensive reflexes triggered by excessive stress interpret it to be.

Don't fear rage. Rage is the pressure cooker, and if you fear it, it increases, magnifies and then explodes. Let it burn white hot. MOVE, DANCE, PLAY! These three therapies will take the lid off and keep the lid off.

You are not the excessive stress. The primal protective reflexes it triggers do indeed protect you. They're not bad. They're helpful survival mechanisms. But you don't need to rely upon them as your default setting for stress. You can let go. You have the tools, because movement can heal, as it did for me.

I wish you all the best on your own odyssey. Don't hesitate to talk about any emotion, image or sensation, because sometimes it can appear that they are real.

But they are not. They are only biochemical echoes stored by excessive stress. As you move, those feelings, sensations and images may bubble to your brain. They may not. They may just burn off through your movement. Start moving, keep exhaling. … Freedom from excessive stress is now, here. Always.

# LIMITATIONS ARE SIMPLY ARTIFICIAL BARRIERS

"You're nothing special. That's just ABC from XYZ. The Bible says there's nothing new under the sun, so stop pretending like you're doing anything unique, when you're just a normal nobody given a soapbox by the Internet." As posted to my timeline.

I had heard this many times as a child with learning disabilities, facing obesity and impoverishment, but something of the logic didn't quite make sense to me. If I could be facing these challenges and others did not, was I not abnormal, like the teachers and doctors called me? Did not my abnormality make me unique?

This query burned inside my mind for years, before I realized many people had not been given the gift of questioning their normalcy, as I had. Whenever I dared to do something others believed to be impossible, they laughed and said, "Who do you think you are?"

My response was the same, "I don't view what you think you're incapable of, as my limitation. Your beliefs are yours, not mine. That's the only reason we are different. We are equally able to do anything we dream."

(After several very vicious multiple opponent ambushes, I learned to keep this response in my head, and keep walking.)

If you believe in God, then you're absolutely "special" as a Divine creature. What gifts has the dolphin been given, the chimpanzee, the ant, the oak tree? What special talents have allowed them to survive and thrive? And humans? What of us?

I believe our uniqueness lies in striving to be better than we were, the talent potential of conscious growth to recognize a problem and seek better solutions, for ourselves, others and those who come after us. When you read that there is nothing new under the sun, don't see it as imprisonment, but as opportunity for greater flight.

What limiting belief will you begin dispelling today? Start with the uncomfortable, and soon you'll realize you're doing the improbable. Make that a discipline, and impossibility will become your nutrition.

# 'INNOCENT' HUMOR BEGETS CRUELTY

I was nicknamed "retard" for my learning disabilities, and for being institutionalized in a child psychiatric hospital. I was branded "dazer" because I could not speak, write or read as I was taught. I was named "fish tank" because my size 8 head could not balance on the precarious pitch of my brittle neck. I was labeled "bubble butt" for my childhood obesity, "space shuttle" for the thickness of my glasses. I was called many more things amidst the fierceness of fists and boots, and those lingering words hurt much more than the fights.

Though the kids were "innocent" of blame for their behavior, the parents and teachers who chuckled at these names, who perpetuated them and ensocialized them through their silent advocacy, were not innocent.

I tried to stop it all: to fight back, and to be hospitalized, to defend myself and to be kicked out of school. But in the darkness, I saw a pinhole of hope and it whispered to me, "You are not broken. You are not imperfect. They were wrong."

I developed the coping skills to prove them wrong. And I did, becoming a keynote speaker for Mensa, consultant to federal law enforcement and special operations units, a world champion who was named one of the six most influential martial artists of the century by Black Belt magazine, and one of the top 25 trainers in the world by Men's Health. But you see, these things mean nothing, ultimately. They were coping skills.

These things only gained purpose and meaning when I realized I did not have to prove them wrong any longer. They were wrong. I needed to redirect my energies to supporting others who were going through this process, and help each of them to find their own pinhole of hope, help them to gain traction in the darkness, and maybe to throw down a few ropes for them to climb.

And moreover, to take action on these issues in our parenting, in our community, in our schools, in our culture, which institutionalize this belief, "well, that's just how kids are."

No. Incorrect. And the legitimate studies now prove that kids are not born cruel. They're taught to be.

WE are the monsters under their beds. Generational hazing and abuse passes from one to the next, lying innocently under the auspices of "it was just a joke." Humor is the Trojan horse of abuse. The worst bullies in life arise from our own self-judgment, which we carelessly project upon others in the form of "innocent jokes."

# CULTIVATE THE COURAGE TO MAKE MISTAKES

The words vomited from my mouth as I read their confusing disarray, eliciting chiding laughter from the other students in the study hall. As I turned, an upperclassman slammed me into the concrete, pressing his forearm to my throat, his foul breath stinging my eyes, "Nobody can understand you, Retard. Why you even bother? Just shut up."

Shoving him off in rage, I fought back ineffectively; yet another beat-down and, due to school policy, yet another trip to the superintendent. Held by the teacher at the scruff of my neck, I thought, "If I am to get out of this situation, I must change the way I talk and write."

I began writing to clear the storm of confused words, inverted letters and scrambled grammar. Language, to my dyslexic mind, felt like battlefield enemies concealing dangers in smoke and fog. So, I cathartically wrote to unravel my mental chaos. It was not a clean battle, and too often my writing fell victim to friendly fire.

Reading through my articles published in magazines nearly twenty-five years ago, I wished there had been a mental Imodium to my verbal diarrhea. I was reminded of Plato's admonishment, "Wise men speak because they have something to say; fools because they have to say something." In my feverish rush to change my language, I foolishly wrote to convince my audience on every point, rather than sharing the experiences I was too fearful to divulge.

For more than ten years now, since I first read "War of Art" by Steven Pressfield, I have used one exercise with diligence: write every morning on the clock, begin and stop on a deadline. This drill gave birth to a searchable chronology of my evolution: each step of literary improvement paired to a professional development and personal growth.

We think in words, so as I practiced my writing, I observed specific points where my attitudes about life transformed.

In my writing, speech and thoughts, I have sought to become consistent, transparent and authentic. I did not predict that each of these represented an aspect of my life: writing was my professional self, while speech represented my public self and thoughts my private self. By acknowledging that language shapes our world, practicing writing, speaking and thinking changes who you are, like dedication to a martial art or yoga.

Today, some of my articles circulate to millions in a week, I write for multiple magazines each month, and my books have earned top 100 status in their genre. As a keynote speaker, I've presented the vulnerable genius of my handicaps to universities, institutes and conferences worldwide.

The irony of my origins is not lost upon me, and before I speak or write, I can still, with fear and trembling, wonder, "Don't they realize the fool that I am, who they've asked to share his thoughts?"

And then I answer those long-term doubts, "I am the fool who didn't quit. I am living proof that anyone can improve."

In writing, in speech and in thought, you must become courageous to overcome the fear of being hurt by critics; or you'll never learn from your mistakes. Sometimes they point out our mistakes and offer us an opportunity to improve. But often, they just air their own mental noise and our reactions to their careless words distract us from our process. You'll never be successful if you don't put yourself out there and risk professional, public and private failure.

Be the same person professionally, publicly and privately: audacious, bold and brave. As Steve Martin said, *"Be so good that even your critics can't ignore your success."*

# CHOOSING INVISIBILITY SOLVES NOTHING

I was invisible; and the only times I had been seen were the uncomfortable moments of public shaming and violent abuse. Is it any wonder that I began to prefer my invisibility over recognition?

I had been fat. And the differences between how I am treated today with how I had been treated in my youth, I still find extremely uncomfortable.

Please don't misunderstand. I am healthy now, and rarely ill, like I was as a boy. My joints no longer constantly ache. And with a family history of diabetes and heart disease, my path was being carved for the same, had I not departed from carrying so much excess fat.

I remember precisely the day when I had returned home from yet another humiliating beating that I decided I couldn't become any more invisible unless I committed suicide. So, I tried. Calling a friend, I divulged what I had done. She called the police, and I was saved, thanks to her and God.

The next morning, I realized that invisibility couldn't serve me if I were to remain alive, and more importantly, LIVING. That day, the changes in my nutrition and fitness began.

The path that I adopted wasn't the best, as I didn't know anything about how to diet and exercise at the time, but it achieved external results. Within a year, my physique made obvious changes. Within two years, most people no longer recognized me when we passed each other.

As my body changed, so did people's demeanor toward me. The fights virtually disappeared. Many more people began to smile at me, start conversations and even invite me to parties and events. Girls began to flirt with me.

I had thought, "Was this some new type of invisibility? Do they not realize in the same person?"

Guys would slap me on the shoulder and ask me about my exercise routine and ask me to join their team for a game of... anything. I felt enamored with the lavish attention, an extreme contrast with the prior horrifying periods of unwanted visibility.

At first, I held my guard expecting that it would again be one of the jokes pulled on me of pretending to be my friend or girlfriend in order to humiliate me, but it didn't have a punch line. They just continued being friendly and affectionate. Of course, I basked in that warmth. And the more I changed my physique, the more the affection grew. I had become a very willing captive of social conditioning.

But then, I saw the injustice committed against other fat people, and my new "friends" began to invite me into their "humorous" atrocities against them. I became livid with anger. I was ONE of those fat people, even with my bodily changes. Didn't these people understand the terror and depression they were creating?

No, they did not. Every time I spoke out against their mistreatment, they'd turn in surprise, like I had taken off some sort of mask; they realized again that I was one of "those ugly people."

The fights began again as I let my anger take control. But by that time, I had become a champion fighter, and I found myself a vigilante to the bullyism once committed against me.

I came to my senses one day in college. I had pulled two thuggish students off an overweight boy they had been pushing back and forth like a pinball; his carefully prepared papers flying in the wind, presumably lost in those years before memory sticks. Throwing one of the bullies against the wall, I took the other down to the ground, hovering a fist above his face, cocked to unleash my vengeance. The bully flinched his hands over his face, squinting his eyes to avoid watching the impact, quickly muttering, "Dude stop! We were just having some fun!"

I wish that I could write that I had some moral epiphany at that moment, that I realized I had become the thing I had hated. But I didn't. That word "fun" undid me. His nose exploded in a pool of blood, and I stood to check on my fellow fat kid; my fist uncurling from its wrath.

When I saw him, he was terrified. And his words rattled my brain, "What the hell, man!? Do you know what they're going to do to me the next time they see me and you're not around to pull your Captain America routine? Thanks for nothing!" He stormed away running after his still flying papers.

What had I done? I had become the monster; only one of a different breed.

The affection of girls began to lose its luster, as did the members-only guys club of athletics I had willingly joined.

I couldn't hold them accountable for the social quicksand into which even I, with my fat aware perspective, had fallen. There was a very distinct social stratification: fit was SOMETHING and fat was NOTHING.

I was only physically different but mentally and emotionally the same. I had been something before I was fit. I had had dreams, ideas, goals, loves and fantasies. They were dismissed by others because they had learned to define fat as nothing.

Today, when I write about these topics, a few students ask me why I talk about past hardships. They plead with me to stop advocating for severe cases when a coach of my "level" should dedicate himself to "the best athletes." I recognize that they are teetering where I had once stood: inside the door to the cool kids club.

Our culture lionizes fit and castigates fat. But fit or fat is not who we are. It is only how we appear. Myamoto Musashi once wrote, "You can see the shape by which I am victorious but you cannot see the form by which I guarantee triumph."

Our form, who we essentially are, cannot be defined by our shape.

Make no mistake, as I walk down the beach in Costa Rica vacationing with my family, I see the reaction men and women have toward my athletic, tattooed shape. But they don't see my form.

My walk in life may be more visible on the surface now but my thoughts, hopes and dreams for a better future together remain invisible if I allow my current appearance to mask my true form.

I will always have my awareness of the world from a young fat boy. I will take this shape I currently have while others will choose to make it visible, and bring light to the invisible world we are missing by its distraction.

Sharing that awareness might help others realize that they can choose to change their shape, improve their health and enhance their physical capacity, but acknowledge that they are already perfect in form, beautiful and wondrous in nature. And sharing that awareness might also break down the gated prejudice of the cool kids club so that we can improve our insight into the transient nature of our physical bodies, that the world is rich in shapes and sizes, beautiful and wondrous in each.

# PRACTICE THE LIFE YOU DESIRE

We had been discussing on the web site how to educate males to stop raping. This controversial topic caused 900,000 new readers to participate IN ONE DAY! Obviously, I touched a nerve.

As I was on a family vacation in Canada, a few vitriolic comments visitors sneaked under my web team radar. One stated, "Why are any of you listening to this guy? He was a RETARD in school and they put him in an mental ASYLUM for it. Who the hell listens to a retard talk about anything?"

Yes, my learning disabilities had caused me to be placed in a child psychiatric hospital, since the schools at the time did not know how to address dyslexia. I've invested my entire life physically, mentally and emotionally fighting to overcome those definitions, which others had taught me to believe.

Some people try to expose what they perceive as "wrong" with you because they can't handle what they know is "right" about what you are saying. They attack you personally to discredit your cause; a logical error called "ad hominem." But they only expose their own error through this fallacy.

As George Bernard Shaw wrote, *"If you can't get rid of the skeleton in your closet, you better take it out and teach it to dance."*

I learned to tango with my dragons. I couldn't get rid of my learning disabilities, but I did flip them into a career transforming problems into challenges and challenges into opportunities. I had to stretch my perspective of the world in the process, though.

My learning disabilities forced me to look objectively at writing, speech and thoughts; how the words we repeatedly select SHAPE our reality, determine our future and bottle or uncork our potential. Words are things; and the more we use them in certain patterns, the stronger those patterns become … whether we 'like' those patterns or not:

1. Whatever you do becomes a habit, whether you prefer it or not.

2. Whatever habit you have created is more easily repeated, whether you prefer it or not.

3. Whatever habit you make more repeatable becomes stronger and more difficult to undo, whether you prefer it or not.

Therefore, I have learned that whatever I'm doing right now —writing, speaking, thinking — to make sure I prefer it, as I'm in the process of making it at least semi-permanent.

When people attack you for a problem you've faced, you know from their words that they're trapped by patterns of thoughts they've repeated the most. They don't define your prison of potential, but their own. How they perceive you is merely a hologram they've projected on how they perceive themselves. No matter how awful the words they project toward you, imagine how awful it is to live even one day trapped into suffering those words everywhere you look. Those bars have formed their invisible jail cell.

Dance with your dragons. Others' fallacious perspectives cannot define you, confine you, malign or outshine you, because you can choose to put them behind you and instead … refine you. Today, stretch your mind by selecting new, positive, productive words to write, speak and think. And tomorrow, your world will be forever, irrevocably transformed.

# BUILD YOUR STRENGTH, DON'T WAIT FOR IT

I had once imagined that I could help other kids with their learning disabilities, and the parents who struggled to support them while feeling helpless themselves. So I would go to the library and read everything I could about my condition.

When other kids would see me scouring the scant books on the topic, they'd laugh. A classmate once yelled across the library, "Hey Sonnon, don't worry. You don't have to study to be stupid. You've already got it right."

Self-education doesn't mean that you were stupid to begin with, but that you're aware enough to overcome your ignorance of a subject, and to realize you haven't lost by failing; quite the contrary.

When I worked in a neurobehavioral clinic for brain damaged and mentally ill children for two years, I would do everything I could to create bridges to them, to reach the place they were locked inside. Each time that I would reach out with a new approach, it would fail. But magically, whenever I tried something different, a small nugget of insight and connection was wrought from the failed attempt.

Failure is like muscle, when torn down by effort, will, persistence and compassion, it grows back stronger; the same is true in all things.

Oliver Wendell Homes wrote, *"Man's mind, once stretched by a new idea, never regains its original dimensions."* My ideas at the time never held water individually, but they kept expanding my understanding of what I could continue to try; each attempt gave me a larger vision and reinvigorated my purpose.

Daily now, people contact me with incredible stories of their failures and the inevitable triumphs that come after and from them. Often they cry from having been too strong for too long. Some don't know how they can continue, in their perceived helplessness to support their loved ones through hardships.

But crying is the muscle of the heart growing. Greater clarity comes after.

I feel humbled by their courage to reach out to those who will honor them for it.

If you wait until you're strong enough, you'll be waiting for the rest of your life. Strength comes from having failed ... and grown. Courage is not living without fear of your weakness, but rather the ability to unwaveringly accept that your strength comes after and from your failure. Like exercise for your willpower, you get back up the next day stronger.

When you encounter a temporary failure, you may not be able to change your destination overnight, but you CAN immediately change your direction.

When you stumble, make it part of your choreography; a more honest, alive dance of your humanity. You have become stronger from incorporating your fumbles. Let it out. Let it go.

Now get up, for you have grown.

# H.O.P.E. — HANG ON, PAIN ENDS!

Born on a ranch and farm, both sides of my family were familiar with hard work from a young age. But when my family disintegrated into divorce, we suddenly found ourselves in a trailer court, with a single mom working two full-time labor jobs trying to get enough money to pay the bills and buy food. Our diet changed to whatever we could conveniently purchase, and when we got a special surprise, it came in the form of a sugary dessert. These circumstances created my relationship with food, so from this the onset my childhood obesity.

When my mother was laid off from a job, we found ourselves on welfare food stamps. The assistance got us through hard times, but the food was again of the types and qualities for subsistence. So even though we had very little, all of my family members began gaining size, myself included. We considered ourselves lucky that we had "extra" fat rather than starving thin, and this reinforced my relationship with food. No one understood the connection between food type and quality with the storage of fat in the 1970s.

As a teenager I began to spend more time away from my family, unleashed to make my own choices, but my relationship had already been cemented, so I only made selections between poor choices. So when I dedicated to transforming my obesity, my first response was to eat less, restricting snacks, second helpings and desserts. My size began to change, but my thinness produced greater aches and pains, and often injuries.

I looked better thin, but didn't feel healthy. After research into nutrition, I slowly introduced the practice of switching to a simple vegetable or a simply prepared piece of meat or fish. I learned as I went along, maturing into young adulthood.

When life became confusing, overwhelming or difficult (which was most of the time), I would resort to my original relationship with food: comforting myself with sugary desserts, breads, pastas, all of the simple carbohydrates that would trigger the emotional responses of safety and security. I worked so hard at my physical life, training 6–8 hours a day, that when I needed to cut weight to make a weight class to fight at a championship, I'd simply stop eating for a couple of weeks and drink only juice. And then bounce back to my normal skinny, fat self after the competition. Illnesses happened frequently.

As I continued to research nutrition, and moved to the West coast to marry my wife, a yogini and nutrition student, the various healthy choices diversified, but more importantly, my relationship with food changed. I needed mental clarity to overcome my learning disabilities in order to work as a writer, calm energy to parent my children with compassion and patience, a stronger body with less aches and pains from my joint disease, and illness-free health from quality food choices, rather than a destructive codependency upon poor choices formed in my childhood. But on long weeks overseas with long days of training in opposite time zones and hemispheres, I'd often make mistakes, and my performance and health would suffer.

When my teammate and brother, Alberto Gallazzi, and I began working very closely together, we realized that all of our travel, long hours of teaching, and physical challenges from fighting demanded a precision discipline to eating. He shared with me his approach to meal timing, macronutrient combination and food planning and preparation when on the road and on a budget. And the final puzzle piece arrived for me.

I once believed that when I made a poor choice in my diet that I had made a mistake, an error, and fell "off the wagon."

But now I realize that each time I made a poor choice, I had fallen down in order to redefine my relationship with food in a productive, generative way. I've fallen many times over my journey, but each time discovered something very important. Much like martial art, you learn the most when you get thrown to the ground, so now I look forward to it.

Sometimes you fall because you have something important to learn that you've missed. Don't derogate yourself for falling down. Take a moment to investigate. Grab the flashlight of your experiences and illuminate the new, more productive concept you are calling yourself back to rediscover.

# LOOK TO THE MASTERS FOR INSPIRATION

I had been a failure at exercise, though not for a lack of good family examples. Often marveling at my grandfather's strength, "Toned" didn't capture how he looked; he appeared to have been chiseled. Though he wasn't abnormally muscular, he was ridiculously strong. Once while working together, he lifted an engine block out of a car, when the chains securing it had broken and threatened to crush me were it not for his agile and powerful grip.

To my knowledge, he had never attended a gym, other than in the military. He didn't play any sports, but I found him constantly at some form of labor, working on his old pickup, fixing the barn, or digging a posthole on his farm. For as long as I remember him alive, he had maintained that work ethic every time I visited. I only ever saw him doing any sort of exercise in the mornings that I slept over at the farm. He'd be out doing odd swings, twists and stretches. Though he had never told me what it had been he was doing, the memory though remained.

My mother inherited her work ethic from her father, becoming the first female steelworker in Pennsylvania. She had to work twice the job as any man in order to justify her presence in a male-dominated labor field. Every morning I'd see her out in the field, practicing her kata from her martial art. Swinging her body, stretching it, jumping into her stances, walking around in circles and then lunging with her arm strikes, forward and backward, side to side. She did all of this in her regular clothing, and finished in 20 minutes or less; short enough to keep my childhood attention span.

Because of a series of childhood issues — learning disabilities, joint disease and obesity — conventional exercise often left me with debilitating pain. I would hurt myself and then quit. The emotional impact of quitting resulted in more detriment to my health than the injuries I had created. I had felt more than frustrated. I had been humiliated.

Then, I recalled my family of do-it-yourself gumption. My mother suggested that I do whatever makes me feel best. She didn't talk about my looks, size or weight, but about what made me feel great. I'd ask my mother, through my tears of joint pain agony, why I couldn't exercise and play sports like other kids. "What makes you feel great WILL make you look great, but the opposite isn't always true," she would say to me as she rubbed my legs with liniment at 3:30 a.m. day after day when I woke her with my moans.

Searching through the library, I found vintage images of loin-clothed athletes, and exercise programs that promised to transform my overweight weakling self into a Greek Adonis in only 20 minutes a day. Men like Friederich Muller, aka "Eugen Sandow," my grandfather would remark as "snake oil salesmen," but if conventional methods didn't work for me, I had no choice but to explore these vintage methods. So, into them, I journeyed. ...

Those early years, late in the bookshelves, mimicking movements from bygone eras, led me on a trek across the world many times over. I cannot say that I found the fountain of youth. I dare not claim that these methods have made me injury proof and forever rescued me from my unending pain. But I can tell you that I don't FEEL 44 years old. I did become the world champion everyone claimed would be impossible for me to attain. I can tell you that I am no longer injured, and have become free from the prison of pain within which I was once trapped.

I'm not a massive bodybuilder, but I'm healthy, still feel vibrant and powerful and still step up on the mat with athletes half my age, and win with my conditioning and skill.

Like my grandfather and my mother before me, I can now do my diligent work throughout the day without many hours in the gym, but if I need to roll with a martial arts team, train a special unit or prepare an agency for their academy test, I can do so without pain and injury, without siphoning off years from the end of my life.

The masters did not know each other's methods, and with all due respect to their contributions to my life and health, each believed their own method was "best" — and the only one needed.

However, that did not prove true for me. My body could not sustain any one type of movement for very long. Where most people adapt to intense exercise, I was destroyed by it ... initially. Now, I can do intense exercise more than most people.

It's taken patience and compassion to prevent injuries and avoid pain.

Traditional methods won't make you an elite athlete, but if you've been over-training, or consistently over-reaching, then even elites could benefit. Traditional methods are mostly for folks who want steady gains, manageable fat loss and functional muscularity. People looking for the hard-core "Get Huge and Ripped Fast" schemes won't necessarily appreciate traditional approaches. They're very basic, unconventional movements. Anyone can do them, even folks like me, swimming upstream from the shallow end of the gene pool.

Duke Ellington said that a problem is a chance to find your best. The problems of my youth compelled me to find five of the best classical methods ever created for sustainable, healthy fitness. Enjoy them in good and long health!

# BLAME IS AN OBSTACLE – REMOVE IT

It was my parents' fault, my teachers' fault, my neighbor's, my boss' fault; it was my enemy's fault, my government's fault, a leader's fault, a religion's fault, a corporation's fault. ... Why does God do this to me? He must hate me. Satan surely possessed me; he must control me.

When I was obese, I blamed those in charge of my food preparation or those providing nutrition education. When I was considered learning disabled, I blamed others for my unfair labels, unethical misdiagnoses, and wrongful institutionalizing.

When I was homeless, I blamed the government, society, civilization.

When you see others lie, cheat, steal, deceive and conspire, do you blame them for their ignorant hurtful drama? Even if some injustice calls you to action, blaming them will not alter your situation. No one is to blame, yet only one person is in control of re-charting your life.

The herd runs off the cliff blaming others for their stampede, and the crazy ones are those who accept personally responsibility, turn around against the shoving mob and walk away from the immoral demise.

It can feel very hard to accept the truth that only we can change our course, when we so desire to believe the great lies of blame, entitlement and self-righteousness. But we are not in charge of them. We are not their judge, though they will be judged, as we will be. We are only in charge of our responses to the events and actions of people in our life. When things happen, and attitudes grow sour, only we can change our own mind, and take responsibility.

Lao Tzu wrote, *"If the mind is correct, all will properly fall into place."* So while others may behave without scruples, do not reduce your actions, diminish your energy, or divert your attention from the positive growth and abundant service to which you have devoted your life.

While others acting with less than moral intent commiserate against their fates, stay free from their emotional corrosion.

Stay aligned to your values. Stay true to yourself. Don't underestimate your innate potential to change your mind, and all will fall into place. Just so.

# BEFORE YOU APPLY, ABSORB

As a child, repeatedly under the dog-pile of fights, I had no interest in "defeating" my attackers. I merely wanted the violence to end. My teachers, in unknowing concert, taught me a method for ending violence without counter-violence. Some, still in the same process, may, as I did, lose faith that it's possible, so I feel an obligation to share what they elegantly orchestrated through my life.

My love of physics could not help me apply sufficient force against superior numbers and size, though my physics teacher insisted that simple machines could multiply effort to overcome larger forces. If I used these levers and screws, wheels and axles, pulleys and planes, I ought to be able to neutralize the forces against me, I thought. Use the right machine, and these attacks would be reduced to zero, impotent of doing me (or anyone) more harm. So, I'd psyche myself up, and as soon as they began shoving me into the walls for my lunch money, I'd lunge after them … and be crushed under their mass of blows; over and over, again and again. Each time I sought to overcome my attackers, I felt more heavily beaten down.

Shouldn't simple physics reduce their attacks to zero effect?

My first martial art instructor, through a variant of Baguazhang, watched me charging after my sparring partners, and stopping me, admonished, "Let your mind flow like water, reflect like a mirror, and respond like an echo."

Years later, my Aikido instructor advised, "Calm your spirit and return to the source. When centered, you can move freely."

My Systema teacher, due to our language barrier, would draw engineering diagrams, pointing to the moment where I could absorb and dissipate his attacks more efficiently.

I had been trying to use advantage "against" my attackers. My force would always be inferior to numbers and size. But when I centered, I regained the greatest freedom of (mental, emotional and physical) movement, and could flow like water, reflect their forces like a mirror, and defuse them as an outwardly rippling echo. If I had the calm awareness to act during this decisive moment and revolve around it, I could guide a more optimal resolution to the conflict.

Over many years of facing resistant partners in competition, applied into business, relationships and travel, I began to feel these spirals of force, so I stopped trying to attack, withstand or retreat, but instead revolved around, married to, and redirected their forces … to zero. The "zero point" is the exact moment when all of the various forces acting against you suddenly cancel out each other. My teachers had shown me and my practice realized that I didn't need to defeat my opponents, but only needed to flow with the blows and guide the forces into each other until the spirals reached zero.

For over a decade, my yoga teacher has been helping me own a new level of this understanding: that I COULD apply my own intention into these blending forces, ONCE I had reduced the aggressive forces to zero. After neutralizing the downward spiral of negative forces, bringing them to zero, I could add powerful intention of positivity and "uplift" them. I could transform situations with positivity.

But she cautioned I should not become romanced by this and dreamily doe-eyed into ignoring my responsibilities. If forces threaten to bring harm to innocent lives, and we have the skills and awareness to neutralize those forces, we have a duty to act to protect them from harm, even if it offends our spiritual aspirations to non-violence. First, find the zero point, then add your own intention to uplift the energy of the situation:

First prevent harm, then add help.

We can expedite the zero point in a confrontation with practice; sometimes find and hold the center, and add positive force to resolve the situation. But only if we practice compassion. Only when we get out of our own way. Only if we remove the ego from intervening, opposing and exploiting. …

If you'll allow me to adapt Hemingway's words,

Before you act, feel. Before you react, blend. Before you apply, absorb. Before you oppose, redirect. Before you neutralize, forgive. Before you conclude, build.

# AIM HIGH, KEEP GOING

When I was a kid, a guidance counselor asked me what I wanted to be when I grew up. "A martial artist," I quickly replied.

She chuckled, "That's just something you think would be fun; not an actual job where people will pay you money for a service. Considering your learning disabilities, consider working at the local chicken processing plant."

Soul-crushed, I took the job that summer; working graveyard shift, snapping the necks off of fowl hanging from a conveyor belt. A week passed, a month, the season. School restarted, and I met with the counselor again, and she asked if I had taken her advice. "Yes, I worked the Summer there," I replied.

"See? Good job. It was something even you could do. So, what do you think you want to do now as a career? Eventually floor manager at the plant?" She asked.

"No, I'm going to study martial arts, and now I have enough money saved to pay for training, and the car to drive me there."

My response left her silent and mouth gaping. I left her office, and never returned for her advice again.

I've done many crappy jobs since then, but never took my eyes off the ultimate goal of studying with great masters, practicing daily what they taught, and sharing what I uncovered. Recently, Black Belt Magazine awarded me with the honor of being "One of the Six Most Influential Martial Arts Teachers of the Century" for distilling what my teachers have shared with me, and sharing it around the world.

Do not fear failure, but low aim. If you aim high and miss, you'll still be among the stars. If you aim low, the worst could happen: you could hit your target. Keep your feet on the ground, but your gaze high up among the canopy of your great potential.

Dale Carnegie said, *"People rarely succeed unless they are having fun in what they are doing."* People often misinterpret this to mean that everything required for success will be fun. It won't. In many cases, it will be the opposite. This isn't because it doesn't require discipline, but because unless it's what you love to do, you may not find the motivation to endure the daily, mundane repetitious practice necessary to master your craft.

It's because mastering the craft is not enough. You also must create the opportunity to study and practice your craft. Like the job on the chicken refinery conveyor belt, it may be a highly unwanted means-to-an-end, but if you want to achieve your dreams, sometimes you have to get it done, and keep your eyes on the long range goal.

"Don't be disappointed if people refuse to help you," as Einstein cautioned. "I'm thankful to all those who said 'NO'; because of them, I did it myself."

Don't be discouraged. This is temporary. Aim high, keep running. When you trip and get discouraged, get up, smile and realize you're closer now even having fallen, than when you began.

I wrote of how my school guidance counselor advised me to pursue a career in chicken processing at the local plant, since pursuing my dreams would be impractical due to my learning disabilities. Not only did I realize my goal of becoming a martial artist, but also became a multiple time world champion and USA national team coach and honored by Black Belt Magazine — the world's oldest self-defense publication — as one of the most influential martial artists of the century.

The story regards persevering when all "experts" set their expectations on your potential low.

A young man commented on my story that, "Martial art careers are short. Hope you like chicken."

Though he misplaced his snide remarks toward me, they're an outward hologram of the low expectations, and ultimate failure we can expect in our lives when all we see everywhere is failure.

Be very leery of low expectations, for you may just achieve them.

As Shakespeare wrote, "Expectations are the root of all heartache."

When we are blind with desperation and hopelessness, and hear of those who triumph over adversity against all odds, we can lash out, externalizing a rationalization for why others have succeeded, and we have not.

But secretly, quietly, we hope to be proven wrong. We hope to hope in anyone's possibility, for we intuitively know, if one can do it, anyone can.

When you see others succeed, celebrate and you enable a virtuous, not a vicious, cycle.

Don't ever let anyone turn your sky into a ceiling, or your dreams into a cage; especially yourself.

Errors teach us how to improve

I fumbled over my adolescent feet, like a cow on ice, as my martial art teacher instructed my "circle walking."

My coordination suffered greatly from the disruption of my joint disease, so I incoherently wobbled through most steps. Not being able to make me understand the verbal directions because of my dyslexia, he broke down movement into digestible components.

I'd get the drill correct for just a moment, and then it would fall apart. I'd find the groove again for a second, and then face another coordination meltdown. Repeatedly frustrated, my instructor stopped me and placed his hands on my soured, contorted face, pulling my cheeks into a fabricated smile.

"Scott, why are you so upset? OF COURSE you're getting it wrong. That's your job as my student! A bad student practices until he gets it right; a good student practices until he gets it wrong; but a great student keeps practicing until he can't get it wrong. What are you here to learn?"

Becoming highly error-focused, I sought out where I couldn't move, and more importantly where I couldn't THINK to move due to the brain-body disconnect my conditions had severed. Later in my University studies, I learned that the nervous system repeatedly manifests the same motor problem until you can pay attention to, correct, and reintegrate it.

My entire life became infused with that awareness on a macro-level, as Pema Chödrön so elegantly states, *"Nothing goes away until it teaches us what we need to know."*

Stop viewing what repeatedly happens to you as a self-sabotaged setback. You aren't repeatedly failing. You're actually consistently returning to a discovery and deepening your understanding of its lesson.

When you repeatedly experience a pain in your body, feel grateful that it calls you to awareness of something that you've been missing, a gap in the connection between your mind and your movement. Don't ignore or lament it! It draws your attention to the lost mobility surrounding a stable joint, forcing its tissues into movement, and begging you to restore its neighboring lost function so that it can restabilize. It SERVES you!

When you repeatedly experience a craving, a crash or a collapse into impulse with your nutrition, don't guilt yourself with shame! It's happening for a reason, secretly serving your awareness of a gap in your biochemistry. Celebrate your victory of increased awareness, because the more it happens, the more clearly you realize where you must increase good food early to displace the later crave, crash and collapse.

Modifying Isadora Duncan's words for this purpose: BE WILDLY BOLD! Don't let frustration tame you! When you find the problem, fight to keep your awareness of it, so that you can benefit from the service it conspires to bring you. Wrench every drop of lesson out of it, so that it no longer needs to return repeatedly for your attention. Be grateful that you live in a body, in a universe, where every situation, event and experience silently serves your growth, success and awareness.

# EVEN DISBELIEVERS GAIN FROM YOUR SUCCESS

"Why are you even wasting your time with this hobby? It's not like you're ever going to become a champion. You don't even have enough money to get a real teacher. You're not going to figure it out on your own reading books and practicing by yourself. And let's be honest: you're not the most genetically gifted person. Shouldn't you just accept what you're really capable of and make the best out of the hand you've been dealt?"

The words of a former close friend burned deeply, as I stood at my beginning. In his mind, he was being a critical realist because he cared. And I truly believe that he did have my best interests in mind. He was wrong to let his fears cloud his words, but he did care.

Twenty-five years later, I'd be voted one of the six most influential martial artists of the century for sharing the lessons learned from great teachers who allowed me to see my true potential in the clear reflection of their lucid waters. If I had never started, if I had given up anywhere along the way, I would not have been able to surround myself with those who would lift me up toward my own dreams, rather than hold me down under their own fears. More importantly, I would not have had the opportunity to let my teachers' insights influence so many through my writing and speaking.

Don't let someone make your sky into a ceiling. Climb and soar. You are only confined by the walls you have been building for yourself. You decide when you've had enough growth, success and abundance. Only you. Don't let others blame your situation on family, friends, genetics, government, enemy, job, boss, skills, money, geography or condition.

Blame darkens. Accountability illuminates. Don't dim your light because someone else complains you're shining in their eyes. Ignite. Set your soul on fire.

The more, through their choices, others drift from their own truth, or the longer their fears keep them ignorant of it, the more they will hate you for speaking yours; the more they will try to hurt you for doing what they're afraid to do; and the more they'll try to climb over each other, like crabs in a bucket, when they see you escape your self-imposed limitations.

Others will broadcast your failures yet whisper your triumphs. Listen to your internal signal, not the external noise. Live by choice, not chance. Make changes, not excuses. Be motivated, not manipulated; useful not used. Have self-esteem, not self-pity. Share autonomy through accountability, and freedom through personal responsibility, not confinement by blame and enslavement by self-entitlement.

Don't let others ensnare you into wearing the cynical countenance with which they've insulated their perception of their own potential. Emancipate yourself with the courage to go ALL the way absolutely alone, if you must. And everyone will benefit from your example; for the success of one us realizing his or her dreams benefits all of us realizing our own.

# RELEASE THE PAIN TO START HEALING

"You're just not good enough ... for me," she said; a spear which penetrated into the weaknesses of my spirit, a fanged gremlin which devoured my self-confidence, when the girl I had been dating verbalized what I had always feared most.

Simon Peter Fuller suggested that what angers us in another reflects an unhealed aspect of ourselves: *"If we had already resolved that particular issue, we wouldn't be irritated by its reflection back to us."* If we didn't believe something to be true, it would not hurt us so deeply.

From my childhood calamities, I had adopted the belief that I wasn't good enough, so I developed a lifestyle of overcompensating for that feeling.

The mind replays what the heart doesn't heal. Throughout my life, I placed myself repeatedly in situations and relationships that would result in my not being good enough. I'd work feverishly to build myself, and improve myself, make myself worthy, until finally an incredible coach came along and said to me, *"You can choose to expand your capacity if you wish, but you're perfect right now. Allow 100 percent of your capacity to be utilized by letting go of this limiting belief that you're imperfect."*

You won't find the right attitude, if you won't let go of the wrong one. I had to flip my perspective, and see that my fear of not being good enough actually involved an intense passion for self-betterment: Whenever I observed others striving to utilize their full capacity, and expand it, it appeared to me as "beauty." I see it everywhere in the world, and it inspires and sets me ablaze with motivation.

Certain attractions may catch the eye, but pursue only those which heal the heart of ugliness. Whenever I see ugliness in the world, I realize that I am projecting my own unresolved fears outward. As my philosophy professor said, *"Enlightenment is a destructive process. It is the destroyer of untruth, like a flame eradicates the darkness."* The very misperception of ugliness signals to me where to illuminate my awareness.

Examining how I feel about new situations, if I see something that makes me feel little and not good enough, I've found within me a choice to reach my full capacity. That little fanged gremlin can skulk up behind me and surprise me with its ugliness, but when I honor that I've been given an opportunity to acknowledge my inherent perfection, I heal my heart of its dark misperception. My gremlin tells me where to cast my light.

Some feel that they've wasted years of their lives with poor choices: years in toxic relationships, years suffering under addictions, years in unfulfilling jobs, years suffering physical agony. But realize, you never waste any time, for good or bad, each choice has invested in you unique wisdom that only your amalgam of experiences could have uncovered. Our choices have given us a reflection, which if we dare to gaze upon, shall allow us to see where we have misperceived ugliness, illuminate our true beauty and heal our heart to grow.

# TRUE WEALTH ISN'T FOUND IN A WALLET

Even growing up in a trailer court, you don't think of yourself as "poor" until in contrast to those who consider themselves as "rich."

I once asked a girl in school to "go with me." A boy overheard and shoved me into the lockers, saying, "She doesn't go with hobos, retard." I didn't understand honestly, but over time, it began to sink in: I was poor.

Despite having been labeled as "retarded" for my learning disabilities, when my first university semester arrived, I strolled the campus, head tipped up, gazing on the tall buildings flooded with the secrets they had held. Some who don't understand the humility of such a beginning may not understand why I had wept, walking through MY university.

My mother kept her second job to help me through college, and I worked as a resident assistant, library aid and a canoe driver to assist, but the student aid ran out. So for two semesters, I lied about my residence, and slept in the library, friends' couches and in the park. It was little inconvenience to be able to continue to unearth the mysteries my professors shared.

Sitting with our accountant, working on our college fund for our children to ensure the financial support to attend the best institutions we can afford, I worried about needing to work harder, speak more, travel more, write more, produce more, teach more. ...

Then, like a salve for my anxiety, I recalled a story my grandmother once told us:

One day, a wealthy father took his son on a trip to the country, so the son could see how the poor lived. They spent a day and a night at the farm of a very poor family. When they got back from their trip, the father asked his son, "How was the trip?"

"Very good, Dad!"

"Did you see how poor people can be?"

"Yeah!"

"And what did you learn?"

The son answered, "I saw that we have a dog at home, and they have four. We have a pool that reaches to the middle of the garden; they have a creek that has no end. We have imported lamps in the house; they have the stars. Our patio reaches to the front yard; they have the whole horizon."

When the little boy was finished, the father was speechless. His son then added, "Thanks Dad for showing me how poor we are!"

For a moment, I had forgotten the humility of my own upbringing. I now actually GET to worry about bringing my children an opportunity to have the best education we can provide. My kids love being out in the woods, identifying plants, tracking creatures, growing food, building shelters, playing instruments and sports, taking care of creatures, helping others, working on their own and as a team to complete tasks. They've already had great education and become determined, compassionate young people.

Some people are so poor all they have is money, and for a moment, I had allowed my mind to empty and become poor.

But like the support I had received, no matter what happens, my children will always feel a wealth of love, be surrounded by riches of support and always feel the abundance of our faith in them. I can continue to work to bring them greater opportunities, but they've already made a fortune in their hearts.

As Norman Vincent Peale wrote, *"Empty pockets never stopped anyone. Only empty hearts have."*

Thank you, Mom.

# MY GRANDFATHER'S BROKEN WATCH

My grandfather was always wearing a broken watch when I would see him. When he wound it, the hands would spin like a roulette wheel flying by, and then stop dead. He'd smile, and we'd go about the day, around the farm, hands in the dirt, or in the garage, heads under the hood. He felt so enigmatic to me, and suddenly, he was gone and nothing felt clear.

After his funeral, my mother gave me a small box of his possessions, and in it was the watch. Immediately grabbing it, I heard my mother say, "Oh, that was the thing he treasured most."

She read my confused expression, and continued, "He used to tell me that he had kept that since the Great War, where it had broken. Wanting to get home to his family, he'd wind it, and it'd spin out and stop. He said it reminded him to not waste any moment, because our most precious possession is time."

When my son walks in to my office because he wants to play swords, when my daughter comes in to tell me a story she's written, or a song she'd like to sing, when my wife starts talking about anything at all, and when my dog places her head in my lap pleading for a game of chuck-it …

While I feel in a rush to finish multiple projects, make several very important phone calls, read through backlogged texts, open a glut of the day's unread emails, make sure I've published my articles throughout all of my social media, get my third training session optimally timed with my macronutrients …

I STOP and remember my grandfather's watch … and step away from all of the perceived urgency of my day, to spend it with my loved ones. The hands of time are spinning wildly by… Don't miss a moment.

# YOU WILL CHANGE, READY OR NOT

Sometimes, we scoff thinking, "I'm too old for that." Then, we are right.

The same with any of the "Terrible 2s" — too fat, too tired, too dumb, too weak, too ugly, too poor, too, too … too late. If you think you're too anything, then you are. However, if you think NOW is the PERFECT time, then you're right, as well.

We battle BELIEFS, not time, not weight, not fatigue, not intelligence, or strength, or appearance or riches. It's not about how far along the calendar you're creeping toward the coffin. It's about your willingness to embrace your change today.

A Sufi master once taught me that there are two groups of people in the world: neophiles and neophobes — those who embrace change, and those who resist it. They're both needed for social stability, but in today's world we're out of balance, with too many who fear change, and they define that reality for everyone else.

My mother once said to me, "I'm too old to change." She said it to me a year before her stroke. She was bored with retirement. She felt she lacked importance, lacked friends and lacked personal power to do anything about it. She was overweight and pre-diabetic; her life was in danger. None of this was leverage enough for her to change. Her belief that she was too old held her imprisoned.

Until the stroke came.

I remember standing by my fireplace when I received the phone call from my sister. Half of my mother's body had become paralyzed. How could she deserve this after the extremely difficult life she had already endured? On my knees, I cried because of the very strong beliefs that had brought this upon my mother. My family and I made arrangements to fly across the country to be of any help we could.

Change was not impossible. Change was guaranteed. You either embrace change, or it is thrust upon you.

After she recovered from her stroke, she radically changed her diet, to which she's tightly adhered for years now. She started doing exercises to her to optimize her health, and kept doing them. She became highly socially active as a commander for the Civil Air Patrol and an event organizer for the Veterans of Foreign Wars medical centers.

She brought purpose into her life again by being of service to hundreds of cadets and veterans, taking them in tours around the country, in addition to her weekly visits to the hospital to volunteer.

All of her changes overwrote her old beliefs. She now feels empowered, alive and vibrant. She loves getting up in the morning, and looks forward to going to sleep so she can enjoy the next day's activities.

If you believe it's too late, it is. But it is as simple as committing to making one different choice each day, no matter how scary or even impossible it may initially appear. Two years from now, I promise that you will never imagine the imprisoned experience as your beliefs might make you feel today.

It is easy to benefit from an experience when we embrace change. But the most important lessons in life often come from our resistance to change. Our lives are like photography: we develop from the negatives.

What moment in your life gave you confidence to challenge a negative belief with a new, positive one? Take a chance to apply that change — everywhere, today.

# PART 2

---

# THE SEARCH FOR AWAKENING

# WHY I GOT STARTED IN MARTIAL ARTS

Doctors claimed my joint pain related to a condition called osteochondrosis, which basically means as I grew, my connective tissue didn't adhere to my growth plates as in normal children, causing conventional sports and athletics to shred me.

Severe learning disabilities — several types of dyslexia — left me with a motor skill acquisition issue, which also prevented me from learning sports that came naturally to other children.

Always enamored with the graceful mastery of martial arts on Sunday morning Kung Fu Theater (and praying that perhaps such study would allow me to defend my right to exist), I realized that this connection between movement and language, and my propensity for devouring the two when they were bound together, would give me an advantage in martial art.

From one teacher to the next, I found nothing but ineffective education (having been well-researched on models of educational psychology from my "situation"). I managed to gain entrance into University to further my study of both philosophy (how to think) and martial art (how to move).

This led me to studying the psychophysiology of the former Soviet Union while simultaneously discovering their native martial art, Sambo, at my University. I had become a sponge, every waking hour investing myself in books or sweat. I discovered in both that my dyslexia was not a pathology, but rather a significant advantage in training, practice and competition. Not bound to directional sense, I could move spontaneously, improvise motor solutions, and respond with uncanny sensitivity that felt like it was bordering on clairvoyance.

My dyslexia had never been a deficit, despite the Pygmalion delusion I suffered due to doctors and teachers who said that I would never amount to anything athletically or academically.

In two years, I qualified for the USA Team and won a silver medal at the World University Games (the Olympics for college age students), as well as winning gold medals at USA Grand National and Pan-American Championships. Other athletes saw my determination and my alternative methods of conditioning, and eventually asked me to coach the US Team as the national coach. Leveraging my successes and position, I petitioned to become the first Westerner to formally intern behind the "Iron Curtain." Finally, in 1996 I was accepted and for the next six years poured myself into their research.

They immersed me in a vast think-tank of professional doctors, science researchers, Olympic coaches, Special Forces trainers, and even representatives from their Cosmonaut program. They sought, as always in Russia, to find the most pragmatic solution to the most complex issues.

As the story goes, whereas our NASA developed a million-dollar pen that writes in zero gravity, the Soviets took a pencil.

So too was the high-minded science expressed in low-tech solutions: more precise training methods would mean a more efficient and economical athlete rather than the USA approach of a bigger, faster, stronger one. This was perfect for me, since bigger, faster, stronger didn't work due to my congenital issues.

They sought to develop anti-aging technologies to allow their athletes — since sport was a political platform — to train and compete longer than their international competitors. And what they developed perfectly grafted onto what I had discovered through trial-and-error as a genetically inferior physiological specimen. I needed every technological advantage to offset my genetic disadvantage.

When I returned to the USA, what I had amalgamated transformed into a systematic formula for addressing any sport, and any individual. It addressed the 85 percent of people who weren't genetically gifted, rather than the conventional fitness approach, which only caters to the 15 percent who "naturally" pick up skills (due to the limited scope in which physical skills and language are taught).

In 2005, to test my research, I accepted an offer to compete in the International Sanshou (Chinese Kickboxing) Championships, since all the proceeds were going to Hurricane Katrina relief. Using my training methods with only six weeks to prepare for a sport I had never competed in, I won the gold medal by knockout.

Later, feeling the quest for the gold once again at 40 years young, as part of the US Martial Arts Team competing at the 2010 World Martial Arts Games, I knew I would be able to translate my lifetime of discoveries into future personal development.

As Musashi wrote, *"The Way is in training."*

And then to take those discoveries and share them with the 85 percent of people out there like myself, swimming upstream from the shallow end of the gene pool … for we may be thrust into circumstances that appear insurmountable, but we may overcome them through training. We may be born to fail, but made to succeed!

# DON'T SEEK MASTERY, LET IT FIND YOU

*"We often miss opportunity because it is dressed in overalls and looks like work."* ~ Thomas Edison

As a child, I watched Sunday morning Kung Fu Theater and awed at their elegant effortlessness of their advanced movements. To lift myself from the toil of constant violence, I began searching for martial arts instruction.

Each class I visited lacked any of these advanced techniques. So, I took entrance exams to be enrolled at University. There, I found champions, and immediately entered their competition training. Compared to my early training, this was much harder, yet again, nothing but basic, mundane repetition.

So, I acquired my passport, visas and (after agreeing with them to stop competing until they finished training me) invitations to train abroad with the direct inheritors and founders of martial art styles.

To my amazement, they offered me nothing but simple drills to perform, over and over again. Assuming I needed to earn their trust as the first foreigner to study with them, I put my nose down and kept practicing, patiently awaiting the "advanced stuff."

Years passed. It never came (to my awareness).

They awarded me with a license from their government as the first American to be qualified to teach. TEACH? But I hadn't learned anything advanced yet. But maybe this was their price: share what I had learned. So, I began teaching what I had learned: simple, basic, mundane, boring drills. Over and over again, I taught them to different people from different backgrounds, cultures, nations, purposes.

I entered competition again, and something strange happened for a few brief moments. I wasn't quite sure of what. I reviewed the tapes; yet it still didn't make sense.

Returning to training, I focused on movements that seemed to come out in performance with a high degree of efficiency.

I didn't know what to do other than practice the same simple drills, just more mindfully, so I could observe and perhaps reproduce the effect.

Back into another competition … even greater efficiency erupted … back into training again, and again. When I returned to competition, at world championships, something miraculous happened. …

Effortlessness happened, and I was fully conscious while it unfolded. It felt non-corporeal. I had to step out of its way.

When I tried to apply something tricky, cunning or advanced, it interrupted the phenomenon each time. But every time that I didn't tamper with the effect, and concentrated on my "basics," it erupted.

Until that time, it had remained a dubious suspicion, but the ostensible proof validated it without doubt. My teachers had ALWAYS been sharing with me the "advanced" techniques. It's just that they were dressed in basics and appeared mundane and repetitious.

# SKILL ALSO CONFERS ACCOUNTABILITY

I did not get involved with martial art to love people. In fact, from the trauma and abuse I faced, quite the opposite.

I fully intended to create firm boundaries on acceptable behavior. But something happened over time, as an unintended consequence of daily training with the intent of becoming a better martial artist.

Morihei Ueshiba, Aikido founder, said, *"Loyalty and devotion lead to bravery. Bravery leads to the spirit of self-sacrifice. The spirit of self-sacrifice creates trust in the power of love."* One of the first and the single most philosophically impacting black belts I earned was Aikido. I still practice the sentiment of the art today, as it has interwoven its approach into even the most combative skills I've learned.

Directly counter-aggressive, anti-ambush combatives that I have been taught, like Gung Ho Chuan — the WWII CQC method of the former USMC Raiders — may not be the best option, but they are the first and most important. Before you can study more deeply, you must learn to feel confident that you can counter the current violence you face.

Our more efficient martial art skills, from Sambo, Muay Thai, Jiujitsu, Boxing, Wrestling, demand higher levels of commitment and longer term dedication to master, and I continue to practice them.

But as you do, you learn that you have greater accountability for your actions, not just legally but morally. With greater training, you CAN do less harm to achieve the same result, so you MUST do less harm. It begins first with the acknowledgment that you're not taking a greater risk by lessening the harm your attacker will face.

But then, a shift happens: a very slight, imperceptible one, where you start to protect your would-be assailant from the imminent jeopardy he faces with his own violent intent. Twisting here, turning there, you blend more efficiently with the incoming forces, because you know the sinew ripping conclusion to his ignorant attack that is the alternative. You try to subdue him, rather than permanently hobble him, or worse.

I resisted this increasing compassion because I was concerned that those I protect would be placed in harm's way because of my actions in decreasing the harm my opponents faced. I did not want to make anyone I protected more vulnerable because I may have "lost the stomach" for stopping violence. But the harder I trained, the faster this shift happened.

I'd get more efficient, and use less force, and in some cases, effortlessly subdue opponents. Then I realized that was the whole point of the process. If you can, you must. If you can use less force, you must and you will.

The gateway to love is compassion. Compassion isn't all rainbows, cuddly unicorns and cotton-candy. Compassion also involves not interrupting a person's process and preventing their opportunity to grow from an experience; including "hard" lessons when they refuse to desist from intending to do harm to others.

Sensitivity produces compassion. As we train, we become more alert, more sensitive to attacks before they happen, more aware of how to defuse, redirect and inoculate the intended aggression. You don't need to try to be more sensitive, but if you train to get more efficient at skill execution, delivery and result, your sensitivity increases irrespective of your intent.

As we become more efficiently sensitive, we develop a level of compassion for the subject who harbors the ignorant aggression. I would not have called it "love" in the past, because of how others talk about love in fluffy, dreamy imaginings. But it obviously ... is a hard earned and learned ... let's say "Care" for those ignorantly meaning me and others harm.

I have not seen anyone in martial art master it because they began with the belief that they should love their attacker. The trials and rites of developing combative skill seem to me more of a catharsis of mastery: as you master the arts, you change with your skill, like satisfying each ascending level of Maslow's pyramid, starting with your right to be free from harm and abuse.

True compassion is sometimes a hard straight jab, or worse. But love does come. ... And the harder we fight it, the more strongly it infuses into every thought and movement.

# AS YOU THINK, SO SHALL YOU BECOME

In the late 1980s, much of my initial martial art training was heavily influenced by Jeet Kun Do, as my direct teacher was a fanatic of Bruce Lee's work. Once, my teacher asked me to go to a bar with him. Not drinking because I was under-aged, I sat as my teacher began verbally taunting one man, in front of his four friends. The situation rapidly escalated, and suddenly five very angered men herded us outside. As I was apologizing and backing away with my palms held up, my teacher continued taunting them.

My teacher pulled out his keychain and loaded one end over his shoulder like nunchaku. Slashing open the lead man's face, he slammed the door shut behind us. I looked at him with surprise! He picked this fight, and now we had no way to deescalate and defuse it.

I looked at the five men, so … I prepared myself, shifted my weight onto the balls of my feet, changed my levels, and shot in a wrester's double leg on my teacher. Now, he was the one surprised, but I was too busy running with him over my shoulder like a sack of potatoes. Cursing, he told me to put him down, that we were fine and could handle them.

Faster than our opponents, we arrived at the car with enough time to hop in before the group arrived. Sirens could be heard, so though he considered running back to the fight, he conceded, and we drove away quickly before the police arrived.

My teacher asked me WTF I was doing, that I was lucky he didn't choke me out. I countered by asking him why he blatantly initiated that encounter. He said he created it as a chance to test out my skills on multiple opponents; and since they were drunk, they were slow, easy targets.

"They're not targets," I yelled, "Those were just regular guys decompressing from a hard day at work before heading home to their wives and kids. I don't need to test my skills fighting. I came to you to STOP FIGHTING, not to do it more often!"

Bruce Lee wrote, *"If you spend too much time thinking about a thing, you'll never get it done."*

Overanalysis leads to paralysis under stress. Hick's law shows us that the reactionary gap widens with each additional option you have, so the fewer choices you must select from, the faster you can respond. My teacher would often quote this, and justify his pugnacity with it, insisting, "You got to get 'er done" (referring to the fight).

His application of this was to slash open the face of the leader of the group. My application of this was to grab my pugnacious teacher and run like hell, since I was sober, strong and fast.

My teacher missed a major point Bruce Lee also said, *"As you think, so shall you become."* If you repeatedly fixate on what you would do when you antagonize someone, you will find yourself constantly in those circumstances.

I didn't get into martial art because I wanted to fight more often. I wanted to end the violence in my life, decrease its frequency, and create more positive solutions.

We can get lost in the beginning of martial art. We can become highly skilled even with a low level attitude. Most people begin training due to fear, in desperate need to defend themselves. But if you don't address the fear, violence will continue to be directed your way because you still smell like a victim. You must shift to radiate calm confidence; that you're not a victim and are not safe to attack.

You will become what you fixate upon. If you see enemies everywhere, you'll find them. Certainly: be prepared, and plan for the worst, but hope for the best.

I found a new instructor after realizing the attitude of the one above was bringing me more violent encounters, not fewer. I found professionals who became invisible to violence, and taught me how to smoothly navigate through potential encounters, defusing, distracting and disarming them when possible. No ego, just de-escalation, evasion and escape.

You become what you think upon most, so before you must choose an action to take, make sure you're shifting your attitude toward the ultimate outcome you seek in life.

# SWAP CONVENIENT LIES FOR PAINFUL TRUTHS

The illuminating flames of truth or the comfortable blanket of protected lies?

Choosing the former caused me great pains in my youth, as I spoke out against my adult persecutors and accrued their disdain. It continues to cause me discomfort today when I see an injustice, take action on my ethics, and attract the ire of those who would prefer peaceful slavery over others rather than dangerous rebellion of truth. But would I really prefer the lie of silence?

My professor, the most intelligent man I had ever met, a former Guest Professor of Philosophy at the University of Vienna in Austria, pounded his fist into my desk and said, "Are you a liar, Mr. Sonnon?"

Dumbfounded, I stammered, "WHAT?"

He leaned in closer, "Did I speak too softly; or did you not understand my question? Are you a LIAR, Mr. Sonnon?"

"No, Dr. Winter, I don't think I'm a liar," I muttered uncomfortably.

He harrumphed as he often did, and continued his advance,

"You ARE not, or you only THINK you are not?"

Unsure of his motives, metallic bile rose in my throat, and reflexively my fists clenched. But why am I angry, I thought? He had not accused me of lying. He had only asked me if I had thought I was.

Instead of becoming further defensive, I replied, "I had not thought I was, but I certainly became angry by your question."

His weathered face melted into a wizened smirk, as he backed off my table. "Precisely, Mr. Sonnon. If I speak to you with polite questions and you perceive them as an attack and become upset, there may be an element of truth to them.

Your reaction reveals a lie you tell yourself. By your courage to look at your reactions, you allow yourself the truth to grow beyond an illusion you may be holding. I asked you these questions to point out the failure of most interaction you have with others. Others will not have my intentions of assisting your self-illumination. How then will you react?"

Philosophy is a catabolic process, we repeatedly discovered in his classes. It had nothing to do with becoming happier or feeling better; quite the opposite. His pointed interrogations into our thoughts crumbled away our armor by eroding our self-delusions. Many students dropped his classes in the first week, because of the nerves they quickly laid bare.

But for those of us who remained, our sensitivity developed through practice, and matured into compassion for our aggressor's plight. When others shoot hateful arrows toward our chest, and I know within me that I am living my truth, then I can remain firmly rooted under their attacks.

Yet arrows still sometimes pierced my flesh. I had not developed a "thick skin"; quite the contrary, as this process stripped off armor rather than thickening it. Other people's words reflect your internal experience; your inner truth externalizes (not the other way around). When things hurt, it can reveal a patch of armored self-lies that had been festering underneath.

Healing ... hurts.

My grandfather once stated with complete lack of adornment, "The stronger you become, the gentler you'll be." I believe he referred to this very process. Most of the time, we are like toddlers in our daily warfare, squabbling at each other with hurtful words and enraged reactions. True strength isn't proven by the domination of others, but in the freedom from the need to defend ourselves against their attacks. We can have a gentle hand, because we have been strong enough to face our self-deceptions.

Life shouldn't be an accumulating snowball, amassing thick, rusting, diseased armor against the weather of attacks.

Naked of lies, we live unfettered. The process brings the pain of self-illumination, but it also sets us free. In your vulnerability to remove your illusions, find your true strength, and the gentle hand to wield it.

# FACE YOUR TRUE SOURCE OF CONFLICT

To move forward, sometimes you must go backward. The larger the challenge to be faced — the farther back you often must travel. I once had misperceived this as regress, but now I realize, sometimes you must back up to get a running start.

When I was young, if I fought back, I'd get beaten unconscious. If I ran, they'd pulverize me when I returned. If I acted like it didn't hurt, they'd continue until I couldn't stop screaming in agony. I discovered if I satisfied them with my pain they'd grow bored, moving on to another target. So I learned to roll with the punches, literally. This discovery diminished the amount of damage.

Most martial art instructors I found laughable when I began training in the '80s, not because what they taught was ineffective, but it was ill-conceived. The mentality of "destroying my attacker" exacerbated my already volatile encounters. I tried that once, hospitalizing one of my attackers. I was pursued and terrorized for weeks until I finally stood my ground, resulting in my own hospitalization. I had needed a better strategy.

In University, we studied Fichte's Position — Opposition — Composition. To any position, there was opposition which would resolve the conflict.

My professor asked me to walk with him to his office. I immediately started, "If conflict results from any position, then why adopt ANY position if we want to prevent opposition?"

He nodded, "But a man who believes in nothing has no purpose. Purpose is the essence of the human condition, do you agree?"

I countered, "Yes, I agree, but then how are we to avoid conflict?"

"With the bruises and cuts you bring to our classroom daily, do you avoid conflict?" he asked. "Your martial art appears to bring you greater conflict than those who aren't practicing it. Shouldn't it decrease your conflict?"

"It's impossible to avoid some confrontation," but I paused ... "Alright, so your point is that I should stop focusing on preventing opposition?"

He replied, rattling my teeth with the implications of his words, "Mr. Sonnon, remember our class on Immanuel Kant: We do not see the world as it is, but as we are. Your fixation on avoiding conflict hampers you from quickly resolving conflict when it happens. Think of Hegel's variation: Thesis — Antitheses — Synthesis. When you encounter conflict in the world, it reflects as much about you as it does your would be aggressor. Many are innocent victims to conflict. That you are awakened to this, what can you do to more rapidly compose a synthesis of the forces outside and inside you? What does your presence bring to the conflict? Whose agent are you: conflict or its resolution?"

Hand on my shoulder, he told me to see him the following week.

At any point in time we hold a position, which if passionately purposeful, inherently holds opposition. Like martial art, any stance can be unbalanced at an angle to it. Fixating on removing any opposition perpetuated it, because I continually sought to conceal my vulnerability.

But ... by accepting my vulnerability, I could blend with the opposition to compose a new synthesis of forces, using my opponent's energy.

My focus needed to shift from retroactively attempting to prevent conflict, to proactively focus on the speed at which I could find confluent resolution.

Years later, my yoga teacher, Amma, pointed out, *"By changing a very common misconception — the idea that your problems are to be found in the outer situations of life — you can remove your problems once and for all. The awakening student understands that difficulties lie with perspective. Once you become awake to this, you can begin the process of changing perspective."*

Rather than anxiously seek to prevent all confrontation, I realign to remain calm when it happens, and to move toward and blend with it, to compose a new solution, and to resolve the issue with a fresh synthesis of the forces within and without.

When I have attempted to flee perceived phantoms snapping at my tail, like a shadow attached to me they chase me wherever I have hidden. What I've resisted has persisted. But when I have mustered the courage to turn and face my fears with an open heart, I've become the agent of change. My early challenges happened so that I now have passionate purpose.

In the coming year, I step upward to much larger challenges than I've accepted in the past, to acknowledge — however reluctantly fearful — my vulnerabilities, which will be attacked, to embrace the opposition which will be faced, to be a positive composer of change and to give a voice to those who, in their isolation from each other, still feel overwhelmed by the victimization of societal labels of incompetence, invalidity and impossibility.

I resolve.

# WE SHOUT FROM THE HEART'S DISTANCE

"My husband screams at me all the time. Why do we get so enraged at each other?" I was asked by private message. My answer comes from my teacher, Amma, an Indian saint who taught me how to bodyguard.

I've been a martial artist for longer than I haven't been, competing at world championships in several styles, and working as a doorman, bouncer and defense specialist for federal law enforcement agencies. So, you'll forgive my arrogance when I say I thought I understood how to control hostility.

But this I came to discover was only retroactive ... a reaction to confrontation.

When my teacher asked me to lead her security team, I was suddenly placed in a situation where thousands of people had traveled to spend time with her. Crowding, the students would inevitably push into each other and strained tempers would flare. What started as whispers between caring students would sometimes become shouting matches.

Asking my teacher how she wanted me to address students when they're angry, she told everyone a story:

A teacher visiting a river found a family on the banks, shouting in anger at each other. He turned to his students, smiled and asked, "Why do people shout in anger?"

The students thought for a while and one said, "When we lose our calm, we shout."

"But, why would you shout when the other person stands next to you? You can just as easily tell him what you have to say in a soft manner," said the teacher.

The students gave some other answers but none satisfied everyone.

Finally, the teacher explained, "When two people are angry at each other, their hearts distance themselves. To cover that distance, they must shout to be able to hear. The angrier they are, the louder they will have to shout to cover that great distance between their hearts.

"What happens when two people fall in love? They don't shout, but talk softly, because their hearts are very close. The distance between them becomes very small. When they love each other even more, they only whisper. Finally, they even need not whisper, and only tenderly, knowingly look at each other, and that's all. That is how close two people are when they love each other."

Heeding my teacher's story, when tempers began to flare in the audiences, I would smile, lean in and whisper. The arguments would soften, and the shouting would quiet, most often to normal talking tones, often to my whispered level, and even on occasion, to a melted smile asking forgiveness of each other.

I've been in many fights around the world. I recognize now where those hardened hearts — mine as well — had exacerbated, if not created the conflicts. Had I only fully empowered myself with this understanding, how many could have been proactively defused?

Certainly my martial art training has helped my confidence in applying this understanding in physical confrontations, but not every argument will become a fight.

I've worked to apply this lesson both in my own relationship with my wife and in parenting my children. I'm not perfect at it but I am recognizing when the tones increase and the hearts separate.

Softening our own voices calls out to the other heart to come close again ... until we can glance across a crowded room and smile tenderly, knowingly.

For no matter how far away, no matter what lies between, no distance will remain between our hearts.

# ACCEPT OTHERS' NEGATIVITY AS A GIFT

I walked into the room but was cut off before I sat down. The proctor pointed to a sign that read MENSA EXAM. She said, "You must be lost. This is the examination room for Mensa candidates. The library reading rooms are down the hall."

When I replied that I was there to take the entrance exams, she looked me up and down, smirking. "To take the exam, you must pass the online pre-qualifier, and then register for this exam. We don't take walk-ins."

Admittedly a bit offended, I suggested she check the list for my name. Even then, she asked for ID.

This is going to be a long day, I thought.

After several hours of various types of examinations, I submitted my test folder to the proctor. It would be several weeks before I learned if I had qualified for entrance into Mensa, the High IQ Society. Though unlikely that I would have high enough score, I wanted to challenge myself, despite feeling intimidated by the scope of these geniuses lining the Mensa halls; such as two authors I've studied all my life, Buckminster Fuller and Isaac Asimov.

Flabbergasted, I received my congratulatory acceptance letter in the mail, with my first copy of Mensa magazine. In the journal was a request for submissions on "Your Story." So, I wrote about my unlikely success, from being institutionalized in a children's mental hospital due to my learning disabilities to becoming a world martial art champion, wellness author and fitness coach.

The phone rang weeks later, and the Mensa magazine editor asked me if I would be willing to be featured in the journal. I was honored to share my story in the hopes it would help others who faced similar challenges. The story grew viral, and the phone rang again, this time, asking if I would be a keynote speaker for the Mensa annual conference.

As I stood behind the podium at that national conference, watching the Mensans from around the country pour in, I reflected on the irony of my journey. I'm not particularly remarkable in any domain, except one. Stubbornness. I refuse to accept others' judgments of my potential. Tell me it's impossible due to some inadequacy you see within me, and I'll do it anyway. Tell me to quit because I'm somehow defective and will never succeed no matter how hard I try, and I'll keep going until I do. Only I decide my potential, and when I encounter perceived limitations on my path, I run them over with the car of my Will (and then back over it again to make sure it stays down).

The proctor had looked at my physique, my shaved head, my tattoos, and judged me to be in the wrong place.

Ironically, the right place to be is exactly where you find those judgments of supposed inadequacy. Despite my appearance, and my genetic limitations, I was named one of the six "Most Noteworthy Mensans" at the 2011 annual conference.

We get negative comments from a few people who want to put others down and keep them down. Their negativity is a gift, though. For the writers, it provides an opportunity to experience a response that is mature, rational and comes from a perspective of committed tenacity. And for us, it serves as a reminder that only we define our fate, only we write our destiny in our daily choices to be courageous, audacious and tenacious.

Never give up. Never give in. Always get up. Always get going. The greater the opposition you encounter, the more likely you're heading in exactly the right direction.

# HEALTHY HABITS APPLY BEYOND EXERCISE

I was too busy. At college, if I wasn't reading, writing, studying or sleeping, I was training or traveling to the next competition. I had been dating a very nice girl, but because I was too busy, I rarely saw her.

One week, she contracted a horrible flu that had been circulating the campus. Fortunately, I had already completed my exams, and simultaneously happened to have been on a recovery week from training, having just finished a competition. The reprieve allowed me to be available to help her, so I brought her various books for her legal courses, ran her papers (in the pre-email era) to her professors, cooked her food and did all of the sundry tasks she could not.

When she recovered, she broke up with me.

Crying, she said, "I'm sorry, Scott. I know you have a lot going on, but having you around this week made me realize what it would be like to have a boyfriend who I can rely on consistently. You're great in a crisis, and that's why everyone goes to you when they need help, but you suck at daily, normal presence in my life. Now that I know what it feels like having you around, I can't go back to not."

She was right.

What you do every day is more important than what you do every once in awhile. And I realized that one of the most important methods that had allowed me to step on the mat facing genetically superior opponents and inconceivably win — through consistent discipline — also applied outside of exercise. It applied to relationships, just as it applied to working on writing my books, studying for my tests, practicing my martial art, and training for my fitness.

# TRUE FRIENDS WON'T HOLD YOU BACK

After high school, college wasn't a consideration. No one in my family had ever gone. Considering how poorly the education system supported learning disabilities, I had barely made it out of high school.

All I could dream about was my martial art training, so that's what I did with any free moment. But with less and less sleep, falling farther and farther behind on bills despite two jobs, I saw any dreams of college slipping away.

J.K. Rowling cautioned, *"One does not do well to dream yet forget to live."*

I needed to live my dream, rather than fantasizing about it. Dreams without action are just wishes. So, two years out of high school, without any money saved, I prepared to take the SAT college entrance exams. Despite teachers advising me that I shouldn't bother, I studied my OWN way for the exams.

My "friends" at the time were toxic and wanted nothing for themselves but partying, and laughed at my aspirations. "Why do you think you're so different than us? Look at you," one said to me.

They would invite me to parties. I'd like to say I was focused enough to never accept, but sometimes I did, and I paid for it. Each night out would equate to less points on my exam. I quantitatively "paid" for my indiscretions in a lower score on my entry tests. Starting so far behind the curve, there wasn't any room for debauchery.

The morning before the exams, I vomited in the bathroom several times. Who was I to take college exams? I came from nothing, and my teachers in high school advised me that I shouldn't have "high expectations" of myself.

The scores returned, and I had done well enough to be accepted into a state university. I sat there looking my scores for a very long time, tears obscuring my vision. There were still student loans to obtain, schools to select, but I had made an important discovery:

Dreams can't be wished. They must be acted upon. Dreams don't come by waiting, nor even by wanting them strongly. The "law of attraction" is heavy iron we hold in our lap as an excuse to not get up and get going. Determination is a crowbar, which pries us loose, leverages obstacles into opportunities and problems into possibilities.

We can go through our entire lives never pursuing our dreams, only to realize, at the end, we've only lived the length of our lives, and not the width. Our words only represent who we want to be. Actions prove who we really are.

Don't wait for the perfect moment; it'll never be perfect. But it will always be right … now. Now is the only moment to act. A great Facebook poster commented on one of my articles that if you stay focused on your dreams, toxic people just melt away. I agree with that comment to a point.

As lifeguards, we painfully discovered that drowning people will climb over you for one last gulp of air, and drown you instead. If you're already in the water, you must restrain them from killing you both. Sometimes, and not for the faint of heart, you even need to knock them out.

Similarly, an emotionally toxic person can be thrown a life-saving device by seeing the life you live as an example. But if you're "in the water" with them (if they're close to you in your workplace, family or home), then sometimes you must ACTIVELY remove them from your space to prevent yourself harm, or from dragging you both down to the bottom.

Every time I thought I was being rejected or disrespected by someone close to me, I was actually being deflected and redirected to someone else who would treat me with the support and care I deserved. Surround yourself with those who make you feel safe to grow, and help them feel the same.

*"Even the finest sword, if plunged into salt water, will eventually rust,"* cautioned Sun Tzu. But there are those glinting blades who are shining in their own lives, and as Proverbs 27:17 suggests:

*Steel sharpens steel, and one friend sharpens another.*

# WAKE UP TO YOUR PURPOSE

As I fell asleep at the wheel, my tires rolled over the rumble strips, onto the shoulder, and over the embankment I drifted.

Flipping, I awoke with a sharp inhale that froze my lungs as something shattered my windshield and the falling blizzard invaded the lullaby of warmth which had nestled me to sleep while driving home.

Why would I take such a dangerous chance, driving four hours with bald tires through a terrible snowstorm at 2 in the morning?

Pre-cellphone era, I climbed out of my car and walked the trail of my dream back to the vacant highway. Waiting for a car to rescue me, it dawned on me that I kept facing these same sorts of poor judgments.

I was in real danger. What could I do to make the most of my situation, since I was freezing, hungry and alone? So I began some jumping jacks to warm myself.

A pair of oncoming lights slowed to a stop, inviting me into the warmth, and the driver offered me a ride to the next truck stop to call a tow. The driver remarked, "That's a heck of a way to stay in shape," as he chuckled, "Sometimes, I need to pull over and do some exercise just to keep awake so I can see the road clearly and remember where in the hell I'm going."

Those literal comments echoed for a long time. Overcoming my problems, recognizing my challenges and understanding my chances to stay on course would take some disciplined attention. A slumbering mind sees only random problems. A stirring mind sees unclear challenges. But an awakened mind sees intentional opportunities. Our level of awareness changes with the circumstances; in some aspects, we remain fast asleep, while in others, we have become lucidly awake; in most, we exist somewhere in the continuum between the two.

Sleeping, our life takes on the facade of a pointless game of chaotic misfortune. Disciplining our minds to alertness in our behavior, actions and thoughts, we can only hold faith that the challenges we face hold a rationale, some reason that will bring growth, but it still remains unclear. Yet in those fleeting moments when we hold the grace of an awakened state, our murky vision settles to a penetrating clarity of a life on purpose. We back away from a mosaic and suddenly recognize the elegance of our life's masterpiece.

Awareness determines our quality of life, for only when we live with Purpose does it all make sense. But regardless of the level of awareness we bring to a situation, when we are in it, it requires Will. It requires courage to face our problems, faith to embrace our challenges, and alertness to act upon opportunities.

As Albert Einstein wrote, *"in the middle of difficulty, lies opportunity."* We cannot awaken our vision if we do not begin, and if we do not continue. It will take time for us to wake up to the conscious potential in our once-perceived unconscious problems and subconscious challenges; and yet as we do, we often fall asleep to our attention in other things.

It takes time, patience and compassion, but most of all it takes Will. We often grow slowly, but we only face danger when we allow ourselves to become paralyzed by our problems, overwhelmed by our challenges, or enamored by our opportunities. Those are merely mental reflections on life, and call us to deeper sleep. The action of the will awakens us to purpose; even when that action involves resisting superfluous "busy" behavior, when we must remain still to refocus.

But by courage, faith or awareness, it always takes Will. Let us all ... Wake up to a life "on purpose."

# MONEY IS A POOR SUBSTITUTE FOR VALUE

While trying to save money to go to college, I worked selling time-share vacation memberships, which felt like a soul-less job to me at the time, because everything we said, everything the prospect replied, had a prepared, canned response.

Each argument had been flow-charted in a specific sequence of predicted conversations. It was so thoroughly planned that when the prospect arrived to claim the free gift they had been notified by mail to have won, almost all left with a signed membership contract in their hands. It felt like stealing, because most of these people did not need or want these offers, but the arguments were so persuasive, that they inevitably purchased, even when they couldn't afford it.

I brought my concerns to my supervisor. He shushed me out of the door. But at the next morning's "pump" meeting, he called me to the front of the team. Pointing at me he said, "Scott here is a dreamer. He doesn't believe that these people should be sold something they don't want." Then, he looked at me and said, "Scott, you, like every one of us here, will never be a world champion and never get in the Hall of Fame, but what we can do is become millionaires and then we can truly enjoy life's pleasures. But you, like every one of us, need to get over your little weak voices talking about unrealistic dreams. Now, all of you get out there and make some big sales!"

I quit that day, and took a lesser paying job doing honest work.

On the side, I'd train every day after long hours of labor. An individual once laughed, "You work too hard and are never going to be successful at this, because you love it too much. If you want to be successful, find something that you hate to do but can tolerate long enough to fund what you love."

He would make suspect choices claiming that he, "didn't have a conscience, and didn't need to live by other people's ethics."

In the hope of making a final impact upon him I said his approach could potentially work for him, but could never work for me; I had already found a difficult but simple way to be successful at what I love to do.

Another individual later said his marketing advisor told him to, "Monetize every action, make his relationships into transactions, so each becomes a revenue stream." So, when he would ask me if he could apprentice with me to learn one of my approaches, I'd later receive an invoice in my inbox. I would create joint venture opportunities for him; only to discover that he'd changed them so that he kept all of the profit. I had to let him go.

There will always be aspects of becoming successful at what you love that are mundane, tedious and repetitive. Every discipline has these necessary practical steps.

But performing a task so vile to your conscience that you cannot look at yourself in the mirror at night without contempt will not lead you closer to fulfillment, no matter how much money you amass.

If you find a way to monetize your activities so that the value contributes to someone's growth, development, or satisfaction, you'll find small rivers of revenue begin to converge into a torrent. But not everything you do, nor everyone you meet, should be viewed as transactional.

Jack Canfield writes, *"The most successful people I've met love what they do so much, they would actually do it for free. But they're successful because they've found a way to make a living doing what they love to do. If you're not skilled enough to do the work you'd love to do, make time to educate yourself so you are. Do whatever it takes to prepare — working part time in your dream job or even volunteering as an intern — while still maintaining your current job."*

Go the distance with persistence AND integrity. Attack your dreams with courage AND honor. Tenaciously fight for a noble cause, and have faith that the universe will flood behind you to support your mission. Keep tremendous belief that every event silently conspires to your success, if you view moral character as your most important asset to be protected.

Stay strong. Sometimes you face difficulties not because you're doing something wrong, but because you're doing something right. Keep going.

You're almost there.

# BECOME CRAZILY SANE

When I entered University, I went crazy for a few years.

Though I now write about my childhood with gratitude and clarity, those mentally formative years in university where I learned the difference between normalcy and insanity exhumed memories that I had pushed way down into the catacombs of my psyche.

When you first begin intense exercise and nutritional transition, you can experience similar extreme emotions as the biochemistry of past feelings burns free, re-enters circulation and is discharged. Research developing psychoneuroimmunology allowed us to see clearly these "Molecules of Emotion," thanks to authors like Dr. Candace Pert.

Similarly, when you mentally unearth suppressed memories, you may re-experience entire events as the images, thoughts and feelings reintegrate into your psyche. You often cannot shift from a negative attitude to a positive one without a temporary increase in psychological discomfort.

So, I went a little crazy for awhile as I confronted my denial of the time I had spent in a childhood psychiatric hospital.

Confiding in my teacher, Dr. Jonathon Ellsworth Winter, of my difficulty processing the event, I said to him, "As we study Pirsig's Zen and the Art of Motorcycle Maintenance, I feel WORSE digging within the terrors of the memories, hospitalized for my learning disabilities. How could I possibly admit to anyone, even to myself, such a blight in my history? Everyone will surely think me insane. Wasn't I?"

He replied, "After I share this story, Mr. Sonnon, I shall ask you to define normalcy." And so he began…

In a far away city, a wise king rules his people with justice, mercy and kindness. At the center of the city is a well of fresh, clear water: the city's only water source.

All the residents, including the king, drink from the well.

One night an assassin, sent by the king's enemies from a distant land, poisons the well. All who drink of the poisoned water will be overcome by madness. As he slips away, he is seen by the watchman who guards the well.

The watchman reports the assassin's actions to the king. Morning soon arrives, and before the king has made a decision, the people of the city begin to drink from the well. By noon all of the city's residents, apart from the king and the watchman, have turned mad.

Still the watchman and the king do not drink from the well. People begin to whisper to one another — the king is behaving strangely lately. Rumor spreads the king has lost his mind.

"We cannot be ruled by a madman," they say, and come together to overthrow their ruler. As the rebellion begins, the king orders a goblet of the well's water to be brought before him. He and the watchman drink from the goblet. When the mob reaches the hall's of the palace, the rebellion is quelled and the people rejoice: They see the king has regained his wisdom.

"Now, Mr. Sonnon, explain to me the difference between normalcy and insanity," Dr. Winter concluded.

I responded, "You'd be crazy to drink from the well, but you'd need insane courage not to."

He smiled, as he so infrequently did. He continued, "Then, be courageous, Boy, for you can either suffer a lifetime in the insane lie of normalcy, or exalt in your moment of crazed truth. Conformity incurs a terrible price upon your psyche. You access your absolute best, only when you embrace completely and utterly your unique craziness."

I left his office raw yet unfettered, a strange blend of knowing that many years would be required to internalize what he had taught me, with the odd sense of elation that if I were courageous enough, I could be liberated from the perceived threat of sharing the truth of my history.

As time passed, I failed in my courage many times, and drank from the insane well of denial. I disguised myself in the trappings of normalcy, yet repeatedly would find the rusty armor to be uncomfortably ill-fitting. So, I would set it aside, and stand exposed to the world in my truth. Only to retreat again to the painful protection of my armor.

Other individuals began to appear as I shared my stories ... a legion who had suffered their own poisoned wells. With each new voice, the strength of the poison wears thin, and more come forward with the courage to shed the lies we have believed for so long, that we are inadequate.

We are, each of us, perfectly adequate right now. Embrace life's constant changes, but know that nothing need change to conform to the perceived demands of others' definitions of normalcy.

Be crazily you, and you become truly sane.

# TRADE DREAMS FOR ACTIONS

"Just because you're thinking, doesn't mean you're alive. You may exist, but ARE YOU TRULY LIVING?!"

Dr. Winter slammed his meaty paw down onto my desk, jutting his chin over a barreled chest. My breath held.

We had been discussing Cartesian dualism, the still mainstream belief that we are a "ghost in the machine" — a body split from an operating host. The author of this philosophy, Rene Descartes, couldn't imagine any way to prove that he was anything more than a grand deception by an evil genius, "What if the world were all a carefully imposed dream by a madman, how would you know it is not real?" Descartes' response was, cogito ergo sum — "I think, therefore I am."

But is thinking enough? Are thoughts really sufficient existence? I spent years trying to think my way out of a predicament: the shame of my learning disabilities, the guilt of my obesity, the terror of abuse and violence. But thought formed a permanent prison sentence: The more my thinking ruminated over the injustice of my circumstances, the more frustrated and hopeless I felt. Why wouldn't anyone help me? What wasn't I being saved from this situation?

Dr. Winter grabbed the sides of my desk and leaned in, "Are you in there Mr. Sonnon?!"

Muttering a nervous chuckle, "I think so."

He harrumphed, "THINK? Prove it! Prove that you're nothing more than a great deception. Show us your ghost." He poised. Waiting.

Stammering, I asked in reply, "How could I prove to the outside world that my thoughts exist?"

This gained an approving nod as Dr. Winter moved back to the front of the class, resulting in an audible sigh of relief erupting from my lungs.

"Indeed, Mr. Sonnon, how can you? You think you're breathing, but are you truly alive? Descartes would say that because you think you are, you are. But that is utter sophomoric confirmation bias. Is a dog not alive, a spider, a blade of grass? They do not think, yet they're living creatures who need not prove their existence. Humans suffer because they can think about their existence. We do not prove that we are alive because we can think. We only prove our reflection upon life; and a vain, self-consuming shade it is.

"The privilege of the life you've been given exceeds the pale shadow of reflection. Your thoughts are not the end of your potential existence, but the MEANS for it! If you want ALIVENESS, then command those thoughts to animate your energy into that which inspires you to thrive! Now get OUT of here!" he commanded, pointing to the door.

We all looked at the clock's fifteen remaining minutes until dismissal and remained confused and motionless.

Then, I laughed. Here my greatest teacher of my life was telling me to go out and MAKE my life, and we sat here frozen, thinking about what if he was being literal in commanding us to get out. So, I picked up my textbook and backpack and left; a trailing room full of frozen students in my wake.

The words echoed again through my mind: Just because you're thinking, doesn't mean you're alive. You may exist, but ARE YOU TRULY LIVING?!

That's when I realized that to think about my existence — the injustices of my troubled circumstances — could never alter the doom of their imprisonment. As Ralph Waldo Emerson wrote, *"The only person you are destined to be is the person you decide to be, and act upon."*

Dreaming wasn't enough. I needed a deadline, and a strategy to make it happen. And then I needed to act upon it. There were only two true mistakes I could make: stopping along the pursuit of my dreams, or never starting. It's the starting that stops me most often. No more.

Be a doer. Awaken within to the necessity of your passion, and then let it strap on your shoes, don your coat and run into the world... creating.

# CHALLENGE WHAT YOU 'KNOW'

Dr. Winter leaned far across the desk of yet another freshman, very convinced that he understood the world, and said to the student, "Tell me, young man, how certain are you that you know that is a desk you're sitting in."

The student replied, "Very certain, I can see that it is a desk."

"Truly, you believe your eyes see a light illuminating an object, bouncing to the back of your eyes inverted, interpreted by your brain to flip, processed to associate with other similar images observed in your past. Despite all of these various processes, each one containing inherent error and miscalculation, you still believe?"

The student nervously nodded that he still believed.

"Young man, I challenge you to question if you see the desk as it truly is. You only believe you see light reflecting off a surface. What is the true surface that the visible spectrum of light does not reveal? What of the ultraviolet and infrared? But in your current perception, if you turn off the lights, the desk disappears."

"Close your eyes," Dr. Winter compelled. "Press gently on your eyes with your palms. Tell us what you see."

The student replied that he saw flashing lights. Our professor resumed, "The lights you saw are products of your brain interpreting the pressure to your eyes as light. We know that you have not seen these lights, for they do not exist 'out here' with us, only 'in there' with your perception. Despite that a surgeon can prod areas of your brain and create these sensations you experience, you still believe that you KNOW the world you see? You cannot 'know' it, or anything, from your sight, or from ANY sense."

Leaning back, he addressed us all, "You cannot know the world, as you see, feel, hear, taste, or smell it. You cannot know anything 'out there' for certain. You can only know what is 'in here,'" returning to rap a finger on the freshman's forehead.

"The world, for all you know, could be merely a very convincing deception crafted by some evil genius who has extracted your brain and placed it in a nutrient fed container, giving you electrical stimulation."

Pausing, he scanned each of our eyes, and resumed, "Take from this uncomfortable realization that you now know what you perceive of the world will be, and has only ever been, what you have elected to believe. You do not see life as it is, but as YOU believe."

I had grown a distrust of my senses due to my learning disabilities. As simple as reading and writing are for most people, something a 7-year-old can do with relative ease, I found them painful. While reading, letters would move, switch, and reverse. Writing, words would invert into mirrored reflections, and jumble their order. Speaking, words would evaporate from my vocabulary, remaining inaccessible as my brain would seize on their disappearance. No, I did not trust that I even knew my own experience of the world.

This can be misunderstood as a dysfunctional sense-related condition. Doctors presumed that I had faulty senses; and if they could merely explain and convince me to see the world through their eyes, I would be able to read, write and speak correctly. Or never at all. My doctors didn't realize I merely think differently than they expected me to. Instead of a dysfunction, my process revealed itself as a talent. My way of thinking allows me to instantly see events from an alternate angle, reversed, inverted or reworded. (And as movement is a series of thoughts, I moved differently too.)

We must learn the way WE individually perceive and think. When you face a challenge, make sure your worst enemy is not living between your two ears. If you face one obstacle and doubt yourself, you'll be outnumbered. Why raise the hurdle when you can lower it by becoming your own ally?

Only you can choose to believe that you remain entirely incompetent, under-resourced and disconnected. You can also choose the opposite: that you are entirely competent, with unlimited resources and perfectly plugged in to everything you need to grow and help others do the same.

# CONSIDER THE PEBBLE IN YOUR HAND

When I was younger, I doubted the impact of my thoughts. I did not see my thoughts become my words. I did not notice my words become my behavior. I did not recognize those behaviors evolve into habits. I did not realize that my habits transformed into my values. And I could not comprehend my values determined my destiny.

It took many more years for me to observe this process objectively, but as I aged, the swiftness of this process appeared, undeniably. And my awareness created both responsibility for it, as well as excitement at the empowered choice to co-create my existence.

Dr. Jonathon Ellsworth Winter accelerated my awareness of the process when he and I walked across campus during one of our weekly meetings. They were more like Socratic lessons, and I recall fondly each of these moments that I had with one of the most significant teachers I have ever known.

On one such walk Dr. Winter noticed the scowl upon my face, and remarked. "On such a beautiful day, it must be difficult to stay so serious."

"Is it? I hadn't noticed," I said, turning to look around at my surroundings. My eyes scanned the landscape, but nothing seemed to register; my mind elsewhere, upon my training preparation for competition.

Watching intently, Dr. Winter continued to walk. "Join me if you like, unless you are too busy today with your thoughts."

We walked to the edge of the University pond where our two swans Miller and Seville, swam effortlessly.

"Please sit down," Dr. Winter invited, patting the ground next to him. Looking carefully before sitting, I brushed the ground to clear a space for myself.

"Now, find a small stone, please," my teacher instructed.

"What?"

"A stone. Please find a small stone and throw it in the pond."

Searching around, I grabbed a pebble and threw it as far as I could.

"Tell me what you see," Dr. Winter instructed.

Straining my eyes to not miss a single detail, I looked at the water's surface. "I see ripples."

"Where did the ripples come from?"

"From the pebble I threw in the pond, obviously."

"Please reach your hand into the water and stop the ripples," Dr. Winter instructed, with his usual barrel-chested German grin.

Like an ignorant child, I stuck a hand in the water as a ripple neared, only to cause more ripples.

Once again around Dr. Winter, I was completely baffled. Where was this going? Had I made a mistake in walking with Professor today? I had training to do, and important preparation for my championships to make. Puzzled, I just continued to wait.

"Were you able to stop the ripples with your hands?" Dr. Winter asked.

"No, of course not."

"Could you have stopped the ripples, then?"

"No, Professor. I told you, I only caused more ripples."

"What if you had stopped the pebble from entering the water to begin with?"

Dr. Winter smiled with that big booming silence that only his students could appreciate. I could not be upset.

"Next time you are unhappy with your life, catch the stone before it hits the water. Do not spend time trying to undo what you have done. Rather, change what you are going to do before you do it."

Dr. Winter smiled, smacked me on the back affectionately, and advised me to stop worrying about my preparation for my competition, and just prepare.

"But Dr. Winter, how will I know what I am going to do before I do it?"

"Take the responsibility for your own training. Like if you're working with a doctor to treat an illness, you ask the doctor to help you understand what caused the illness. If you're going to train with your coach, you do not ask your coach what if my opponent beats me here, or defeats me there. Train hard and train well in your strategy and stick to it. Mentally rehearsing things going wrong is like trying to grab the ripples in the pond. You only create many more ripples."

Positive thinking became this for me as a result of Dr. Winter's lesson: not an affirmational prayer for things to not go wrong, but an active focus on my preparation, and a letting-go of mentally catastrophizing, to enjoy life. Stillness isn't passive. Positive thinking isn't a wish. Mental stillness and positive thoughts are like my teacher's lesson at the pond.

Dr. Winter continued with some of the most significant education I have ever had in mental preparation.

"Focus your mind on your plan. Practice it perfectly mentally before you arrive on the mat. Then, step away confidently from your training, and respect what you and your coach have prepared. Keep your rehearsal like a still pond surface, and don't chase ripples."

# FIND MINDFULNESS AMID THE NOISE

Dr. Winter gave us the assignment to be as silent as possible in everything we do for one week.

It was one of the most excruciating challenges I had ever faced. Unaware of the cacophonous lifestyle I had mindlessly developed, as I tried to be quiet in my steps, in packing my backpack, in turning a page of my book, in setting down my glass, I realized that I had become a foghorn of unconscious noise.

By the fourth day, I felt as if I would go mad and suddenly burst out in a scream.

But eventually, the anxiety subsided, and by the following Monday, I had regained some awareness of my mindless collisions with the world.

Dr. Winter told us, not our noisiness, but rather our lack of conscious awareness of it, was what the assignment had sought to reveal. He then taught us a mnemonic for mindfulness:

*Moment to moment attention*
*In the here and now, with a*
*Non-judgmental attitude;*
*Detach from negativity, and*
*Forgive yourself and others with*
*Unconditional acceptance;*
*Listen with a beginner's mind.*

I have brought Dr. Winter's lesson with me, throughout all of my career and life.

Nowhere have I found mindfulness more crucial than in my nutrition. Bring mindfulness to your cravings and impulses, desires and needs, and suddenly you hear the unconscious roar of your damaged biochemistry.

What are you feeling right now? Why does your body feel that way? What did you eat and drink earlier that could have resulted in this feeling? Removing self-judgment and criticism, what could you have done differently to feel better? What could you do now to adjust that pattern and repair your cells?

Listen to the noise. Accept it and release it. Then, hear the pure signal of what you truly need to become better, clearer, healthier.

# BURY YOUR GHOSTS AND MOVE ON

No matter at what point in my personal growth, and regardless of the country where I've met them in my travels, everyone I have met knew something I didn't. Not every time did I discover that gem, but each time, regardless of my failings, I've learned from them, even when we parted ways for the rest of our lives.

My teacher in University once used the words of Socrates to frame the class on the philosophy of relationships: "The secret of an enduring life of healthy relationships is to focus all of our energy not on fighting the old who want no growth together, but on building the new and the abiding who crave it."

When a relationship breaks, we ought to do everything possible to fix it, if both parties want repair. But if one leaves, if one chooses to end the relationship with you without reconciliation, then rather than struggling to compromise your ideals to fit a definition of your identity to their expectations, stay true to your integrity, and celebrate the relationships that hold you up and those who thrive in relations with you.

I lost a woman in my life long ago. She chose the arms of another man, and called to tell me of her infidelity. It crushed my spirit for the trust I had in the relationship. My first question I asked was what I had done wrong. How was I not enough?

And in the subsequent months, I changed my behavior to hopefully make the relationship work. But for her, it was already over.

She hadn't done the damage to me. She did the damage to the relationship.

I had compromised myself for her expectations, and in doing so, I damaged myself. It took a very long time to rebuild the erosion I wrought to myself during that compromise of my personhood.

A very wise friend, in the midst of my repair, advised me to "stop trying to fix ghosts." He said, "Ghosts are not broken. They're just gone."

I had been trying to fit myself into an image for which I wasn't created; chasing a phantom of a memory, living in the purgatory of a prior experience.

When I healed, and resumed being true to myself, the right people came flooding into my life, beyond my comprehension. Now, I can honestly say that although some people still pass through a revolving door in their process across my path, the right people always remain … and I cherish them so.

People in our lives come and go. … Some leave heavy, muddy boot prints; others a lingering fragrant nostalgia.

But I've found the hard way that despite some people having such great potential in our lives, this is true:

*"Don't chase people. Be yourself. Do your own thing and work hard. The right people — the ones who really belong in your life — will come to you and stay,"* as Will Smith so elegantly, confidently imparts.

# JOURNAL YOUR ASSETS, TO REINFORCE THEM

One of my early teachers had me change my journal writing. Whereas I had previously used my daily journals much as an accountant would list the debits and credits of the day's events, my professor suggested that I write not of details, but perceptions.

In reviewing my journals, he said he could see the level of my awareness and my attitude by what I chose to recall and how I elected to frame the events I experienced and people I encountered.

What he told me next, changed me forever:

"Mr. Sonnon, how you write weakens, balances or strengthens your mind. Writing is like your martial art: Practice having better technique every day. When your technique is weak, find balance. When you find balance, grow stronger. This applies to our attitude toward life and your awareness of the lessons it holds."

Scouring back through my journals, I began to review them from the point of view of how my mind related to the events and people within the pages. The perception I held for each experience could be "rated" by a weak, balanced or strong mind that day or moment.

When my attitude and awareness weakened, I only saw problems, and stalled at the helpless injustice of my plight. When my attitude and awareness balanced, I saw the challenges, and rose to them, or fell and rose again. But when my attitude and awareness strengthened, I began to cast away the illusion of obstacles to see the opportunity they each presented, to reframe each problem for the potential it unearthed.

My professor's exercise became a coaching tool, and as I read an email, listen to a conversation or reflect upon my own thoughts, I monitor the level of perception being used, and suggest to others and to myself where that level could be more balanced or could be strengthened. Sometimes we can only reflect upon the weak mind's chatter, and let it run its frenetic course, so when it fatigues, a new course may be charted.

You can see this insight run throughout the words of truly great teachers, and the guidance within their indelibly archived wisdom…

When Ralph Marston wrote, *"There are plenty of obstacles in your path; make sure you're not one of them,"* he really meant to say: don't allow your mind to weaken.

When Thomas Paine said, *"The harder the struggle, the more glorious the triumph,"* he spoke to the need to embrace an attitude of challenge.

When Winston Churchill remarked, *"A pessimist sees the difficulty in every opportunity; an optimist sees the opportunity in every difficulty,"* he conveyed that the strongest attitude remains a positive one, for only within that awareness do the potential opportunities manifest.

A blind wrestler who befriended me in university would teach me his skills in exchange for reading him his homework and texts. One casual night we chatted, and I remarked that I could not imagine anything worse than losing my eyesight. He laughed and said, "I could. Losing my vision of who I am and what I have been born to do in this world. The drama sighted people must see every day doesn't blind me to my purpose."

He had a very strong mind, and being near him strengthened my own.

In life, when we encounter people or events, we experience many attitudes with differing levels of awareness: Some use us, some test us, some help us, but all teach us, and by adopting this strongest attitude of the highest awareness, every person and event allows us to bring out our greatest self.

When you sit to take count of your day's events, or your project's development, write with your mental assets, not mental liabilities; for not only our performance in life, but our fulfillment of it, depends upon the quality of our attitude and awareness. End each day with a positive account of what you've learned, and every day, you begin again with a stronger mind because of the pre-framed attitude, and the expanded awareness of your higher vision.

Now, go carpe the hell out of this diem!

# ONLY ACTIONS CAN SPEAK LOUDLY

My first book, "The Process of Extension," published in 1991, was an abysmal failure, colored with purple prose; befouled by an opulent perfume that concealed any fragrance that my passion could have communicated.

I grasped tenaciously at Aikido's philosophy of confluence, of blending with the forces of hostility, defusing and converting them to maximum benefit of all involved, even would-be aggressors. But I lacked the physical skill refinement and aplomb resiliency to allow it to happen in actual combative encounters.

After he asked my intentions in publishing, I explained to my teacher that I felt the need to share my philosophy.

He replied quite candidly: "The message needs clarity because the messenger doesn't own it. As Epictetus advised, "Do not explain your philosophy. Embody it."

At that point, I knew that I needed to reevaluate my approach to training, to prepare, pressurize and prove to myself that I was embodying what I teach and teaching only that which I embodied.

Over the years, though I've written more and more, I've actually been explaining less and less. For now I see the excellence in the advice of my professor. You can only provide the method, not the mentality.

We are much like our children: Say all you want, but if you aren't consistently practicing what you preach, your words will eventually fall on deaf ears. Focus on your daily practice offers a greater explanation than any library could speak about.

# FIND THE FLOW IN EACH MOMENT

"Please teach me mindfulness," I would implore.

"Focus on today's class, and don't be distracted," Dr. Winter would always reply.

One of the greatest teachers faced my incessant requests. When the semester ended for Summer break, he finally conceded, and offered to let me stay with him for three months at his farm. Each day, I anxiously waited to learn his insight, and each day he'd hand me a shovel and a broom to clean the horse stables. He would shovel and sweep next to me, but seemed so pleased with himself to have me cutting the task in half for him. He'd say, "WAKE UP, Mr. Sonnon! You're missing all this crap!" And then he'd laugh to himself.

After each entire day of indentured servitude — tired, hungry and fatigued — I would shower, eat and attempt to keep my head from collapsing into my bowl, awaiting a glimmer of wisdom from the frustratingly vibrant old professor.

Days and weeks passed with the same routine. Finally, out of the deafening silence, I exploded while shoveling manure out of the horse stalls.

"All I've been doing is shoveling CRAP for months, and I haven't yet learned a thing about flow!"

He shook his head at me smiled, and said, "You're absolutely correct, Mr. Sonnon." He walked away saying, "Put your heart, mind, intellect and soul even to your smallest acts. The secret lies inside the 'crap' in your life."

In class the next semester, my professor told us, "Before Enlightenment, you shovel crap and clean stalls; after Enlightenment, shovel crap and clean stalls."

What's the difference?

The tasks are the same. Though the practical necessity remains, your attitude differs.

Be the Flow not the Friction!

Reflecting upon his lesson of missing the flow within each moment, of loving being here now even in the most mundane activity, I only wish I could express my gratitude to him. Growing up on a farm, I still find it nostalgic when I encounter a teacher who values simple, hard work. But it took that one teacher to make me realize hard work was a gift in itself.

If it's one thing I've learned, personal accountability solves most riddles. No one to blame. Not my family's financial situation. Not the socio-economic recession of the 1970s. Not even my genetics. They're just contexts for choices. I could have believed my teachers and doctors (and family) that I was never going to amount to anything. I could have believed the horrible things I was called when released from the children's psychiatric hospital. I could have identified WHO I am AS the friction causing those contexts, rather than identifying with the flow, which envelops around them.

If you want something, certainly a teacher can guide you to see the specific challenges you must face and even encourage you to believe that when you jump across that fog-filled chasm, you will be safe and successful.

But you alone must take that leap. No one can hold your hand. If they've already leaped across, you can't even see them there.

Confidence only comes after you've taken a leap of faith and earn evidence that your courage paid off. You get only courage and faith to do it before you have the confidence of having done it. Sometimes you even lose faith, and have nothing left but to suck it up, know that it's going to probably hurt, and do it anyway.

As my grandfather told me once when I was very young, "Be courageous when you have nothing but fear, because it's up to you alone sometimes."

You have to believe that you're exactly what you need right now. If you want flow in your life, you have to just accept that you're already everything needed, even if you have to fake it until you believe it.

I pretended to myself that I was all that I needed to make it through for much of my life (because I did not see at the time the divine hands guiding and protecting me). Many times I had no clue what I was doing. I only knew that I had to do it, because no one would do it for me. Many times I fell flat on my face. But two out of ten times, I was totally competent. I just had to go through eights to get to my twos.

Even if you think you're incompetent, if you see something that needs to be fixed, it's because you're ABSOLUTELY THE BEST PERSON to do something about it. Only you can be the flow you want to see in your life.

Last night, I took my son out for guys' night: Muay Thai, Sashimi and a movie. During the movie, in the warm room, in the dark, I dozed off. My son elbowed me in the ribs, "DAD! Wake up, you're missing guy's night!" Laughing, and recalling my manure-shoveling lesson from Dr. Winter, I sat up straight at my little man's chiding.

When you do anything, stay awake. What frame of mind do you bring to your work? Do you approach it as if it were a nuisance? Do you remove your awareness from it so that you fill with regret, resentment or worry?

What "ordinary moments" are you missing in your lack of mindfulness? What would you need to do to be more fully present?

Practice mindfulness in even the most insignificant things, as my professor and my son taught me. It does little good to attain clarity of mind in martial arts competition, if you lose it as soon as you leave the mat. Pay attention to the interrupting emotions and distracting thoughts that enter your mind when you do ANY task. See if you can let them go and just focus on where you are RIGHT NOW.

The only discernible difference between enlightened teachers with whom I've studied, and myself, is they do the exact same task as me, but "lighter."

Be lighter. Life is much too serious to be taken seriously.

# MY MOST IMPORTANT LOSS

This was my first world championships, the 1993 World Games gold medal match vs. their team captain, USSR Judo Champion, Georgian Greco-Roman Champion, Master of Sport in Sambo, Zurab Bekochvili.

I had two years of Sambo training at this point, not yet a black belt. So to face such a seasoned veteran, who had been a Soviet Judo champion since 1982, was itself an honor.

My arm broke at 2:04 into the fight.

At a world championship level, you lose more team points by submission than by losing on points. So, stupidly, I didn't tap and concede the match. I figured that I only had to survive the match without being thrown in total victory (ippon) to avoid the loss by submission.

It hurt a lot, and I took the two-minute injury timeout. The ref tried to call the match, tested my arms after the break, but I convinced him that I could continue.

I had lost all grip strength at that point, and basically tried to defend myself for the rest of the match. My attacks were pretty feeble as a result, though Zurab was clearly the superior of the match regardless.

A loss on points, and not by submission or total victory (Ippon) was a great achievement for fighting such a vet. I was only 23 (Zurab was 30), so it was a solid learning experience for me. He wasn't necessarily more athletic, but a better technician. His throws were very clean. I had a lot to learn. At the top of my discipline in the West, I saw the gap between our skill level and those in the former USSR. It was time for me to study there.

It was because of this painful loss that I went on to become the first outsider to train in Russia and learn their training methods. Thanks to Zurab, I earned the passion to go through all the politics, drama and financial sacrifice to become the first to train over there. Without him, I don't know if I would have been so inspired to study at the feet of the founders of the art. ... and I would not have come back, nearly 20 years later, at 40 years old, to win the 2010 World Games in sport Jiujitsu, submission grappling and mixed martial arts against athletes half my age and 100 pounds heavier. I owe this in part to my opponent, Zurab.

In addition, I didn't have health insurance at the time, so my scaphoid suffered avascular necrosis (bone death). The joint mobility and fascial strengthening systems I've developed as a result have shaped the course of my life and future.

Without this pivotal piece of personal history, I would not have had the passionate drive to push through all of the politics necessary to study in Russia. The Internet was very new back then. There were only two very basic sites on Russian martial art. I used contacts that I made during the 1993–1995 world championship events, and started an email campaign. In 1996, I received two invitations, from the All-Russian Federation of Russian Martial Art, and from the SAMBO-70 Academy.

I chose the former, since, although I love the sport, it was the training practices behind it that I wanted to understand — the complete art. And the chance to train with the Spetsnaz legends was too incredible to turn down.

This choice opened me to a world of hate from the American vanguards of sambo because they felt that training with the Russians was unpatriotic. The international president, an American, literally slapped me across the face at the 1996 national championships for accepting the invitation, despite the fact that I had brought the largest team from a single school to nationals in US history (32 athletes).

As my team of over thirty junior competitors looked on, the auditorium went silent.

I stayed my hand out of respect for the impact my retributive strike would have had upon my young athletes.

Instead, I thanked him, "For proving to me that the best course of action would be to reconsider all of our training methods, and compare them against pragmatic superiority of the former CIS national teams against us on the mat. No coach of any worth would ever need to resort to physical intimidation. You've proven that to everyone here," as I gestured to the hundreds now onlooking at the exchange.

I appreciate the historic significance, since this was just post-Perestroika, but without the genius of my coach, Alexander Retuinskih, I believe that the Russian training systems may have been lost as the funding disappeared in their country.

Now we see hundreds of Russian styles appearing in the West. None of these would have had that opportunity without my coach's courage to breach the "Cold War" culture and train an American in the former USSR.

Thank you to Zurab. It was an honor to fight you, my friend. What a great memory. And thank you to my coach, Alexander Retuinskih, for directing me through the years of training to follow … you changed my life, Sir.

How harshly we judge failures in the present, only to realize later the blessed gift they had been.

# DON'T GET EVEN, GET BETTER

My arm had shattered. I had won the silver medal for USA at world games, but the cost was far greater than I expected.

Approaching my gold-class opponent to congratulate him, I asked him bluntly, how did he manage to defeat me and how could I improve. He replied simply, "Need to train better."

Better, I thought? How could I train "better"?

Soren Kierkegaard wrote, *"There are two ways to be fooled: to believe what isn't true, and to refuse to accept what is."*

As a professional, my time was maxed out, and always maximally practiced. If I couldn't practice harder or longer, then only one choice appeared to be available: accept that HOW I practice was ineffective, and change it.

Walking back to my coach, he saw me shaking my head dejected, flummoxed by my loss. I was the best my country had created, but I wasn't on the same level as the Russian victor. My coach said candidly, "Don't get even. Get even better."

Right. I knew that practicing harder wouldn't make me better. Practicing longer wouldn't make me better. Only practicing even better would make me better.

Flying back to my country after world games, I petitioned to become an intern in the USSR sports machine. I aimed to learn everything about my opponent's practice, and emulate his approach. No one told me what a storm this would cause.

The entire USA coaching staff became furious with me, calling me a "traitor," for intending to study with the Russians. The president of the US federation slapped me in the face for seditiously daring to go to the "enemy."

I couldn't understand their vehement resistance. My staff said we should defeat our opponents with American ingenuity.

Nodding in agreement, I added that in order to be ingenious we needed to accurately know what we were encountering, and study their way of practicing. If we knew nothing of how they practiced, how could we improve upon it? They refused, saying that we just needed to work harder.

Wayne Dyer once advised, "The ultimate ignorance is the rejection of something you know nothing about but refuse to investigate." I became the black sheep for my blasphemous acceptance of the invitation to become the first foreigner to intern in the former Soviet Union, studying their sport science approach for combat performance.

No one in the USA coaching staff would even return my calls when I arrived home after my program in Russia, excited to share what I had learned.

All of my team treated me as if I had been shunned.

So, I began to practice not harder, not longer, but better. My practice actually got easier and shorter, because I focused on these improvements every day, and on implementing them throughout my movement, and my life.

Sharing these discoveries with my own students, they too improved their practice, and became champions themselves. This daily practice many years later allowed me to return to the mat, and win once again against opponents half my age and 100 pounds heavier.

You are what you do every day, because life is the true practice. If you refuse to admit the truth, and reject the option to investigate a more effective alternative, ignorance will prevent you from ever improving. If you practice being better every day, admitting what needs changed, being bold enough to investigate options, then little by little becomes a lot; and suddenly, you will find yourself far from your starting point.

You cannot change darkness with more darkness; you can only chase it away with light. Cast your illumination upon the things which you do not know, and because of your courage to implement the changes you to which you have brought light, every day will become a better practice.

# 'YOU MUST LEAVE THIS UNIVERSITY'

In searching for a particular photo of Nikolay Travkin, my business partner, where he was featured on the cover of a Russian newspaper due to our work together, I stumbled upon my lost box of University journals and term papers. THIS particular paper holds significance in my life … as a milestone, and a story I'll recount to my great grandchildren.

It was the day that the dean of my department, Philosophy, suggested that I leave the University system. … And it was because of this very paper that I had written. I'm going to share the paper with you, but I warn you. It's denser than molasses, and just as sticky.

I had gone "mad" at University. It had taken me 10 years to recover from being institutionalized at a mental hospital as a child, because no one — not teachers, parents or doctors — understood how to help me with my learning disabilities as a young boy. The hospital taught me one important lesson, a lesson that they weren't aware they were imparting: Whatever you do, learn what the doctors want to hear in the way they want to hear it, and you'll learn how to pass the exam.

That's all that I wanted: to pass the exams they required to qualify me as "normal" so that they could reintroduce me to general population. I did. And it worsened, because the gap between who I was inside my thoughts, and the exterior facade that doctors, therapists and teachers insisted was normalcy, grew wider because of the hyper-consciousness of its distinction.

At University, to cool my over-heating prefrontal lobes, I wrought epic debauchery … though many of us did back then: girls, booze, fighting. All were pale substitutes for a lack of "flow," and to give me a respite of stupor from the hyper-awareness of the disparity between my self, and my Self. I hurt a lot of good people with my inconsiderate recklessness. I'm very, very sorry for that; if you're reading, you know who you are.

But my teachers equipped me to turn on the lights in the basement of my brain and begin to clean house, especially Dr. Jonathon Ellsworth Winter, former Guest

Professor of Philosophy, at the University of Vienna, Austria, who returned to Millersville, Pennsylvania — his birthplace — to take over as Dean of the Department of Philosophy, Millersville University of Pennsylvania … a humble State teaching college turned liberal arts university.

I had been at an all time high in the Spring of 1993, as I prepared to compete in the Universiade, the Olympic Games for Universities, in my sport, Sambo — its first time in the Games … and my first time representing the USA on a national team.

My training had provided me with the physical platform to exhume the mental corpses I had buried a decade earlier. For me, unearthing the sediment felt depolarizing, like my world shifted. Only my training kept me stable to the degree I appeared, which as I alluded earlier with my debauched tales, wasn't too even-keeled.

So, when I submitted the paper to Dr. Winter, he initially bloodied it with inked comments. When I retrieved it from his office secretary, he called me into his back office to speak with me, and shut and locked the door behind me as I walked to sit behind his behemoth desk in the dusty leathered labyrinth of stacked tomes. I sat and he boomed from behind me, "Reading your report, Mr. Sonnon, I am compelled to ask, from whence did you plagiarize this paper?"

I met his gaze and replied, "You think I plagiarized it?! That means you think it's GOOD!"

Dr. Winter was renowned for never giving a complement, and for giving only three people an A+ grade. For me to receive a complement and an A+ was … well, unusual to say the least.

He immediately softened, which he had never done before, and referred to me for the first time ever, and the first time I had ever heard him use anyone's first name, and said, "Scott, do you mean to tell me that you actually wrote this yourself? Honestly?"

My smile caused him to sigh audibly, drop heavily into his chair and peer over his ageless eyeglasses. He continued, "Well, then, I only have one suggestion for you. You must leave University."

Huh? Whuzzat he said?

"You must leave University," he reiterated, "and you must go out and do something with yourself. If you remain here, at best you will only regurgitate the works of others, who at this time have much greater contributions to the world than you."

But, I told him, I'd be honored to stay. It'd be a dream to become a professor and teach as he does.

He continued shaking his head no, "First one lives, Mr. Sonnon. Then one philosophizes. Scott, I have rarely seen work this sophisticated before, and certainly not here. But big things happen in small places. It's the friction, like coal compressing to diamonds.

"But you're still rough. You need life to squeeze you. You need experiences. Real, life experiences, not some fantastical escapism among these words of dead men."

I was speechless. My mentor, my idol, my dean, just told me to leave what had essentially rescued me from the hardened carnage of my youth. Because of his teaching, I had kicked open the doors on my childhood madness, shone sunlight into the darkness of my buried neurosis, and cleaned out the debris. What the hell was I supposed to do OUTSIDE of the University?

As if clairvoyant, he responded to that thought by saying, "You will find your path and do original work. Just follow your gut, Scott. Remain a true skeptic as I've taught you: be willing to test everything on yourself first, and doubt all of the results until you've confirmed the data multiple times."

I left. At the 1993 World University Games, I lost the gold medal to my Russian team counterpart.

And I knew what I had to do. I had to be the first American to formally intern in Russia …

The rest is history you're probably already familiar with.

But philosophically, I've been refining the discovery that I made 18 years ago … that the ego's awareness of itself causes an unsettling which if left unresolved leads to suffering. How to resolve that disparity between the ego and its awareness of itself became my lifelong quest … to find flow.

# ONLY EXPERIENCE CAN ANIMATE IDEAS

My mentor pounded on my desk, "You need to leave this University, Mr. Sonnon. Your ideas are grandiose, but first one LIVES, then one philosophizes. Without experience, these aren't insights. They're only ideas. Go out and live! The study of wisdom comes after."

Soon after, I left the university system to travel the world, studying, training, and eventually sharing what I had discovered. But it wasn't the journey I had thought it would be, as it had been essentially one of disappointment. Only after its pungent dissatisfaction of expecting the world to fill me, did I travel back home, and discover that it was not the destinations, but the journey itself that had been my mentor's advice.

I kept expecting to find some sort of levitating grandmaster with ancient scrolls, whose secret powers would foster within me a vital, healthy body, a quiet, focused mind and a tranquil, expanded heart. Of course, I did find great teachers in the countries I visited, but not the infallible legends written about in books. Instead, I encountered other striving people, through their own cultural lenses seeking truth, failing themselves, concocting new strategies, and rising from the ashes to try yet again ... but wiser.

I had sought to be filled with their wisdom, heal the torment of my past, and be at peace with my present. But I was full of mere knowledge, and merely ambitious for an anxious future. As Plutarch wrote, "A mind is not a vessel to be filled but a fire to be kindled." Wisdom comes from experience, from living errors, surprises and downfalls. That discovery only revealed itself when I touched back down in the United States.

Standing in Pennsylvania at my bus stop on arriving from airport, surrounded by pastures to the far horizon, the land in which I had been raised, I reflected upon a boy in Russia who had run up to me excited to meet his first American. He shook my hand without releasing it and pulled me in the direction of his farm yelling, "I have ONE COW! Let me show. Do you have one cow? You have many, yes?!"

I shook my head, "No, none." He stopped pulling, furrowing his brow, asking, "But how you take care of your family? Supermarkets? I don't like supermarkets. Only real food safe and best." Looking around my homeland, I realized that I had learned this very lesson in my youth from my grandparents' farms, but had run away from it, seeking the ivory wisdom of philosophers. They taught me volumes of knowledge, but only by sharing their own tormented, restless minds.

My grandparents, like this boy, had strong bodies, quiet minds and big hearts. What REALLY had I been seeking? What was it that I actually needed out in the world?

George Edward Moore observed that, "A person travels the world in search of what they need, and returns home to find it." Wisdom isn't an elusive virtue bestowed upon a privileged, erudite few. It's the pleasant, comfortable character of normal people making ordinary mistakes and deciding to non-judgmentally get up the next day and do it again, but better.

When you stop trying to fill yourself with others' knowledge, and allow your experiences — your failures and foibles, your triumphs and travails — to stoke the fire of your inner trust in simple wisdom, you discover teachers everywhere in everything at every moment.

There's nothing out there to collect. Without experience, others words' aren't insights. They're only ideas. Maybe they're even good ideas; until you apply them, they're inert and cumbersome. Go DO something with them. Don't die with your floating notions. LIVE with zeal and make them real. You're all the answer you've ever needed. Listen to and trust yourself, and act upon that simple, ordinary wisdom within.

# GIVE THE GIFT OF ENCOURAGEMENT

My coach spoke to our team before a tournament, explaining that there may be long hours between our matches. Advising us not to leave the tournament area, he said that any one of us competing would need the others' support, even if the competitor couldn't tell that his teammates were there. Even if we didn't do anything other than sit at the edge of the mat and watch the match, our teammate would grow in confidence because of our presence.

He told us a story…

"Several wrestling teams from around the world were training in a wrestling camp in Asia. While spending the day hiking, two of the wrestlers fell into a deep pit. The other wrestlers gathered around the pit to see what could be done to help their comrades. When they saw how deep the pit was, the dismayed teams agreed that it was hopeless and told the two wrestlers in the pit they were as good as dead.

Unwilling to accept this fate, the two began to climb with all of their might. Some sorrowfully shouted that they should save their energy and give up, since it was hopeless. Yet the two continued climbing as hard as they could, and after several hours of desperate effort, wearied. Finally, one took heed to the calls of his fellows. Spent and disheartened, he quietly resolved himself to his fate, lay down at the bottom of the pit, and died as the others looked on in helpless grief.

The other continued to claw and climb with every ounce of energy he had, although his body was racked with pain and he was completely exhausted. His comrades began anew, yelling for him to accept his fate, stop the pain and just die.

Instead, he climbed harder and harder, and finally clawed his way high enough that he reached the hands of the other wrestlers atop the pit.

Amazed, the teams celebrated his miraculous freedom and gathered around to ask, "Why did you continue climbing when we told you it was impossible?"

Reading their lips, the astonished wrestler explained to them that he was deaf, and that when he saw their gestures and shouting, he thought they were cheering him on. What he had perceived as encouragement inspired him to try harder and to succeed against all odds."

Encouraging words can lift someone up and help them make it through the day. Destructive words can cause deep wounds, and become weapons that destroy someone's desire to continue trying, or even to continue living.

This very situation happened to me.

I recall standing in the middle of my University surrounded by these impressive buildings, which would enable my change. Three o'clock in the morning, before my first day of freshman year, tears flooded my face at the sheer possibility. No one had ever believed I would be standing there. Some told me to give up.

And a few dark nights in my childhood, I tried to end it all.

But my wrestling coach taught me a dire lesson: if we have the ability to encourage others, if we have the opportunity to provide support, even if we don't realize the impact we are making, we could make the difference between someone giving up and giving it all.

When facing a significant challenge, it can demand courage to overcome all of the terrible evidence to the contrary …

You may feel alone. But we all walk alone… together. We all fall into pits at some point and in some aspect of our lives. If it were not for a few pivotal people and circumstances in my history, I doubt I would have had the courage to overcome my challenges, and use them as opportunities to discover within myself the capacity to survive and thrive.

Together, we can help others empower themselves to overcome the challenges in their lives.

# PAINFUL CHOICES MAY BE OUR MOST VITAL

My neck had broken. Somehow the wrestler for the US Marine Corps Team had angled behind me, ducked under, body-locked and hipped-through into full explosive arch. Suplexed, I landed on the top of my head with a shotgun firing down my spine, and the sound of crackling like stomping on bubble-wrap.

Glued to the mat, I watched my opponent stand. As the suplex caused him to touch the ground with me, he didn't win a total victory (like an Ippon in Judo). But through the searing hot pain in my neck, I couldn't move; only watch him tower over me as he stood, mouthing the voiceless words in slow motion, "Are You Okay?"

The official called a 2 minute injury clock; the paramedic and my coach joined me on the mat. As my hearing returned, the paramedic asked me questions on my name and date while checking my eye dilation with a light. Slightly twisting my neck to the side, suddenly all movement awareness RUSHED back to my fingers and toes. I sat up like a Christmas tree switched on. I felt fine. Well, I felt like I had just been pile-driven by a Marine, but I felt functional.

Sixty seconds remaining, the paramedic looked at the coach saying, "He seems okay. It's your call, Coach."

Looking at me, my coach cautioned, "Scott, gold isn't important. You may have had a serious injury, but there's no way to know for sure. Rather than take a big risk, we ought to forfeit the match and try again next year." As this was the AAU Grand National Championship, the biggest amateur event in our country at the time, I couldn't imagine wasting State and Regional qualifiers, and invest yet another year training to qualify for World Championships.

"No," I muttered. "I may only get one chance at this, I have to earn it."

Standing, the official yelled, "15 seconds! What's the decision, Coach?"

"I'm fighting," I said to the official who retorted, "That's not your decision,

Athlete. Coach!?" My coach nodded to affirm my decision, grabbed the pen held in front of him and signed the paramedic's waiver releasing the event of liability for my continuance.

Back to our blocks on the center of the mat, we shook hands, and I said, "Full on, brother. To the bell." He smiled in that way so many Marine friends of mine have smiled, when they see something that sucks, and keep going anyway. I had at least, earned his respect.

Ninety seconds remained in the match. I was ahead by only one point, after his big throw. I needed to hang on. Playing defensive, I sprawled on his shots, and hipped in on his throws, stepped out of his guard pulls. The official blew the whistle calling me passive for stiff arming; first warning. Feinting foot sweeps to avoid a second passivity call and losing a point, my opponent doubled his ferocity. We both crashed to the mat, but twisting to my hands and knees, I avoided points scored against me.

The pain was like a hot poker shoved in the base of my skull. Grabbing his wrists, I arched and sat out of the wrestler's position par terre. This was my last chance.

I had run out of money. I had no more school loans I could borrow. I couldn't afford an apartment, food and tuition the next year. If I didn't win, I wouldn't qualify for the US Team, and in those early years of the internet's infancy when you needed to meet people face-to-face in order to make anything happen, I would never make it to Russia and become the first Westerner to formally intern in their methods. As a result, I would never learn their healing methods, their joint mobility approach, their compensation injury recovery, their biomechanics for skill mastery, their psycho-physiology of resilience and toughness, much of which has become my career focus as a teacher today. I'd lose everything of the future study I had dreams for years.

Out of hundreds of Americans, would I even be chosen by them; was I even the best choice to represent our country, and the cultural liaise between the two post-Cold war truced enemies? Even if I risked it all, there'd be no guarantee and little likelihood someone with my "poor" genetics and financial vacuum would be selected.

Clawing my hands up my own thighs, in the creeping mechanical molasses only those who've herniated cervical discs understand, I stood trying to get the weight of my skull on top of my shoulders. No matter what happened, I absolutely needed to stand and continue. And as I wobbled on my feet, I crouched watching my opponent coiled to shoot in again.

BUZZZZ! The match ended. Turning at my waist to avoid twisting my neck, I desperately looked at the board. One point. I had hung on by that single, delicate point; and won grand national championships with an — unknown to me — broken neck.

My cervical vertebrae mended poorly with fissures. It would be twelve years of ever-maddening anguish before I finally resolved the damage in my neck.

But I had won my place on the US Team, earned my right to compete at World Championships, and gained the opportunity to meet the Russian leaders of the discipline to submit my petition to intern with their trainers.

Today as a father, husband and business partner to a company providing financial support to not only my family but other families, I doubt I would make the same decision. Twenty years ago, single, desperate, perceiving myself with no prospects but those far-fetched aspirations to learn fields of study unknown to the West, I made what seems like an ego-based decision to risk my health and life by "sticking out my neck," literally.

Ironically, without health insurance, ONLY the healing methods I learned in Russia set me on the path to eventually recovering from my injury. If I had not stood, if I had not taken that risk, I would have been without any solution to my injured spine. That single choice, that one moment of unreasonable effort, reinvested my life in a higher cause with the tools to share through my writing, speaking and coaching.

Life gives us seemingly impossible choices, which in retrospect we might not choose again, but without the courage and conviction of your past decisions, this incomprehensibly intricate tapestry of events would not have unfolded with the elegance they now manifest.

True strength often arises at our weakest moments, but in those impossible decisions, our courage awakens, and we become active agents in a destiny beyond the comprehension of our imagination.

# PAIN CAN HAVE A HIGHER PURPOSE

The bones in my neck pulverized, like bubbles popping. My championship a Pyrrhic victory, even the tiny weight of the medal around my neck caused extreme discomfort.

I drove the 15-hour trip back home in a terrifying wildfire of pain spreading down my arm. It passed eventually, and I thought it had healed. But the unresolved sins of our youth return to visit us in later life.

The pain resumed 12 years later on a cross-country flight. Merely twisting my head, I felt a guitar-string twang. The next day, I was immobilized in a straight jacket of agony, unable to move without searing hot pain firing throughout my body. My wife cancelled my public speaking appearance, and helped the host to find replacement speakers.

Agonizing tears irrigated my face as I squirmed under the discomfort of any position. Nothing abated the searing hot scalpel cutting down my neck, shoulder and arm. I could take no more narcotics to numb it, as I had begun to build a tolerance that already required double the dosage for the same duration of slight relief. I had to find a way to heal.

If you really want to understand your pain, you'll find a way to compassionately reconnect to it. No matter how compelling, you cannot flee it in self-pity. If fear, frustration or anger get the best of you, you'll find an excuse to keep suffering. There IS a higher purpose for your current pain! Your body is smarter than you, if you're willing to shift your perspective from punishment to purpose. You live up or down to your expectations of your quality of life, so if you believe pain is a punishment, you'll suffer; but if you view pain as a signal to your conscious mind, you can find enough gratitude to manage it, recognizing the purpose it serves. Every pain secretly serves our deeper growth, greater development or further discovery.

As Eric Hoffer wrote, *"The hardest arithmetic to master is counting your blessings."*

Pain is a gift we reluctantly receive, so to accept it without suffering, begin with a smile. A smile cracks enough light for us to enter a crowbar into the mental anguish. And then we can find an opportunity to laugh. We cannot laugh and suffer simultaneously.

This is NOT easy. Believe me, I know. At times, my corrosive mood could dampen even my children's glee. That's when I realized that I was infecting my family with my suffering. I couldn't "grin and bear it." I had to reexamine and redefine my pain. WHY was it happening?

One day, my hand behind my head, elbow high to shut down the nerve pain slightly, tears streaming, I felt a man next to me touch my shoulder. Tracing my eyes up the length of his arm, I saw it was entirely covered by burn scars. All of the visible skin on his arm, neck and face had been blackened with burns. As he sat there in unimaginable pain, he smiled sympathetically at me, a knowing light in his eyes. He didn't speak English, but he didn't need to. His understanding of pain spoke to me.

What can we do to lessen our suffering? This man had found the answer. Lesson others' suffering.

I had found a method to heal. The pain had completed its message. I had a purpose. Like the man who gave me perspective, selflessly willing to muster a smile of sympathy despite the blanket of agony draping him, I realized my pain called me to others' suffering.

Serving others isn't a pretty little badge we wear. Truly being of service to others means remembering how suffering severs our connection to quality of life. It cuts through our ability to appreciate what blessings we do have. How can we help others lessen their suffering? Give them an opportunity to discover their own blessings to LIVE.

Oscar Wilde once said, *"To live is the rarest thing in the world. Most people exist. That is all."* Bring life back to those around you. Share a touch, a smile, a hug if you can. Understand. We may not be able to offer a purpose for the pain, but perhaps our care will be enough leverage for them to insert a crowbar with our smile, and let loose the healing of laughter.

Laughing heals, my friends. Let us do more of it, and bring it to those who could so desperately use its salve.

# REWRITE THE STORY THAT PAIN IS TELLING

I tried to think my way out of pain, crafting elaborate theories as to the origin and purpose of agonizing experiences. For many years, I researched every text from neuroscience and biochemistry to manual and cognitive therapies; nothing brought relief or escape.

While rehearsing a presentation on the philosophy of pain at university, my mentor stopped me in mid-sentence and asked, "Mr. Sonnon, though I appreciate the well-researched perspective, how do you know that pain is not one of the greatest gifts bequeathed to us? That 'pain is a problem' appears to be the foundational premise upon which all of your research has been organized. What would happen if you questioned that fundamental belief?"

Pain can cause you to feel disconnected from your body, cheated by it, even violated. If pain has caused you to mistrust your body, then begin by imagining how your painful situation secretly serves you. Just pretend it is a possibility, and (re)write a story of how it could be. When you reframe your perspective to possible benefit, you transform obstacles into opportunities.

Perhaps you'll not immediately heal, but at least you will manage more gracefully by doing so. Nothing actually may change at all, except for your attitude. But if it does, it will make all the difference. … For with that reconnected presumption of trust, the power to heal returns.

As Nietzsche wrote, *"There is more wisdom in your body than in your deepest philosophy."* Regain trust in your experience of life. Assume this silently conspires to your growth and benefit. Fight off the despair. And protect the boundaries of your mind from disconnecting again. It may not be apparent instantly, but if you hold on to hope that a purpose will be revealed, the solutions unfold.

Had my back not broken, I would have signed a contract to fight in Japan for three years as part of the UWFI Shootfighting organization. Though I was not doing it for the money, in 1995, having just left my undergraduate studies, $65,000 a year was indeed a lot of money, especially when I didn't have any property owned, only my student loans to repay.

For everything lost, we gain something else. We can either regret or rejoice life's conservation of balance. At the time of this tragedy of a broken back, I could only lament my misfortune. Had I known what was awaiting me, I would have welcomed the injury.

I spent a year of recovery researching alternative health and fitness methods, and eventually was drawn to the unique methods developed in the former Soviet Union. Petitioning to study there, I received a response from their Special Forces trainers, inviting me to become the first Westerner to intern behind the "Iron Curtain" and learn their methods of mobility, recovery and injury-prevention.

Had I not broken my back, I may not have had been interested in this knowledge. I would have been committed to my professional fighting career in Asia.

When you live with an appreciation of the coincidences and their meanings, you reconnect to what William James described as the *"underlying field of infinite possibilities."* Without six years of training with Russian national coaches and research scientists, I may not have had the opportunity to create the innovative health and fitness methods that have become a major part of my vocation.

Though I continued for another 15 years as an amateur fighter on the USA Team, and won my dream of a world championship, I was never meant for a professional fighting career. Something much bigger and better awaited me, once I could no longer define myself by it.

We must be willing to LET GO of the life we had planned, so as to allow the potential of we have waiting for us. For each tragedy, a great possibility awaits; for each hardship, more than a lesson — a legacy. Certainly, it can feel impossible to rejoice when these obstacles appear, but at the very least, we can nod in acknowledgement, and trust in the divinely conscious process, that something BETTER comes. As my teacher elegantly stated, "If you commit your will, if you time it well, and you allow grace in your heart, you will achieve your dreams, or allow even bigger ones."

# FIND THE COURAGE TO PERSEVERE

I was returning an international champ in one of the most dangerous sports in the world in 1994. But the damage I had sustained to my neck caused such pain I couldn't carry my own bags over my shoulder.

"Well, it was worth it. I am finally a real champion," I thought to myself. "Things are finally going to start going my way."

I looked down at the gold medal around my neck, which I hadn't taken off since beginning our return.

After dropping me off at my apartment, my teammates honked in joy and celebration as they pulled away. But my heart immediately filled with dread, as I looked down at my doorstep, and the pile of amassed mail: The first letter, from my university bursar's office, advised me that I qualified for no more student loans. The second letter from the University stated that my position as a resident assistant would be given to another student better meeting their criteria, as my grades had dropped. The third letter, from my landlord, advised me that I was late two consecutive months' rent, and if I didn't pay immediately, I'd be evicted.

Spirit crushed, I fell onto the dilapidated couch that I used as a bed.

The universe felt capriciously hostile to me back then. I had no confidence, no evidence that anything happened for a reason; I only perceived a world of random tragedies and personal disappointments amid scarce resources. It seemed to my underdeveloped spirit that to succeed in one aspect of my life, I'd sacrifice another, and face an even more severe downfall for my incomparably tiny victories.

I couldn't tell my mother. She had supported me through six years of college by working two jobs and overtime, as I was the first of my blue-collar family to make it to university education. She would only work harder, and I knew her body couldn't handle it.

No more options appeared to me. Even the gold-plated medal around my pained neck couldn't be pawned. So I sat in tears; a hollow champion who had let everyone down, especially myself.

Reading a lot of poetry back then, I looked down at my floor and picked up a book, thumbing through the pages. Rumi pierced through my tears with his words, *"Why do you stay in prison, when the door is wide open?"*

My soul anguished, and I screamed, "WHERE?"

I saw no exit. The prison bars were invisible.

There was no escape. I did get evicted, and I couldn't return to the university. There were very dark weeks ahead, couch-surfing from friend to friend, sleeping in a park when I could not find shelter, Dumpster diving for food scraps behind restaurants. I lived a lie, incapable of asking for help from the intense shame of the situation I had created.

As quickly as I could, I started three jobs, as a security officer, a waiter and personal trainer. An owner of what became a boy's halfway home allowed me to stay in his attic until I could afford to pay rent. My girlfriend put food in my fridge when I wasn't at home; an angel who had limited resources of her own (I've never thanked you sufficiently, B).

I don't know how or even why I kept pushing forward. Overwhelmed, desperate, pained ... I kept pushing. A Thomas Monson book, given to me by a friend for enduring my challenging times, read, "Stick to a task 'til it sticks to you, for beginners are many and finishers few." I kept going.

Meeting with my coach, I apprised him that I wouldn't be able to compete on the US Team the following year. My life had become a mess, and I couldn't eat medals, nor make a future on an amateur sport. He placed his hand on my shoulder and said words I will never forget, "It may look bleak now, but victory in one part of your life shows you how to be a champion in any, for how you do one thing is how you do anything. You have proven to yourself how to be a champion on the mat. Now, go be one in life."

No, it didn't happen overnight. It took another year of multiple jobs before I met my current-day business partner, who would so believe in me that he convinced me to start writing and filming my training.

And even then, it took many more years of struggling, one tiny step after another. But each minuscule triumph felt like an intramural club championship, a city, a state, a regional. ... My courage to move forward became confidence that I just might succeed.

I now look back gratefully upon the universe's elegant timing of my pitfalls — in this case waiting to drop several bombs until AFTER I had won my little gold medal, and had learned self-confidence in one aspect of my life. I just hadn't realized at that time that lessons are universally applicable.

Like an EKG flatline, if there are no ups and downs in your life, it means you're dead. We receive grand challenges, not as punishments, but as opportunities for much greater growth, faith, happiness and abundance in our lives. We only need to keep going.

It may be a fight at first, combating self-doubt, desperation and hopelessness. If you're like me, you can't even feel faith at certain times, because it can seem so overwhelming. But even when you lack faith, you can still be courageous.

You never know how brave you can be, until bravery is the only choice. Take another frustratingly, seemingly insignificant step. And another.

And your courage grows into confidence, into faith.

The bars to the prison may be invisible, but you'll never find your way out by submitting and giving up. Like Will Rogers said, "Even if you're on the right track, you'll get run over if you just sit there." You get up and get going.

Eventually, we discover the prison bars are illusions created by our lack of faith. But often faith only comes after the time that you need it.

Sometimes, you just need to do the next thing, even though it feels like it won't matter.

Because it does. Sometimes, your courage is the only thing that matters. Keep strong. Keep going. You may not be where you want, but through your bravery, you're one step closer.

# BELIEVE SINCERELY IN YOUR VALUE

I was penniless and homeless, and had to pay my way through university, so I took on multiple jobs, including retail. I hated it, because I couldn't sell successfully. Finally, I decided that I'd start my own business, and offer canoe instruction, a small but enjoyable activity. Instantly, this tiny niche grew into an eight-canoe trailer pulled by a company van. How could I fail so quickly to sell something that was readily available, but rapidly succeed to sell something marginally interesting to the general public?

We hear it so often, "Sell yourself. Don't sell your product."

But what if you're not confident in your ability? What if this is the first time that you're about to tackle a new circumstance, event or project in which you believe? You may not feel confident. Is it because you doubt yourself?

When others tell us to sell ourselves and not the product, we feel disconnected.

My teacher said, "When you can't believe in yourself, believe in what impassions you." You're selling the infectiousness of your passion. If you don't believe in what you're offering, then you probably shouldn't be trying to convince another person to pay for it, because you either will succeed and unethically manipulate money out of someone, which hurts you and them, or else you will hopefully fail to compromise your integrity.

We feel like we need confidence, but confidence only comes after the time that you need it (because confidence requires evidence). Courage — acting in spite of the lack of evidence — you can have immediately. Not because you have evidence, but because you don't, and you're willing to do it anyway.

Believe in what you're doing and the positive infection spreads, jumping from host to host. If you don't feel confident because you lack evidence, then be courageous and share that infectious belief. The more courageous you are in being transparent and authentic, the more successful you will be.

# AVOIDANCE MAY BRING THE GREATER RISK

No one knew. I was too embarrassed. Too proud to ask for help. Too scared of the consequences to admit the situation. Too aware of the alternatives if I quit moving forward each day.

I was homeless, broke and had borrowed $55,000 in educational loans to go to a university where I could no longer afford the meal plan or the housing cost. From one couch to the next, one building after another, crashing on the floor, in the library, in the dorms. Friends would bring home an extra sandwich from the cafeteria, leave an extra slice of pizza or a box of cereal. … My "diet" was whatever I could find… and some shame-filled nights found me Dumpster diving at the local restaurant.

So, I picked up odd-jobs when I could, but with poor sleep and diet, and heavy studies, with borrowed books, I struggled through three semesters without any consistent lodging or meal plan.

When your family is struggling, and you're the first one to go to university, failure isn't acceptable. I couldn't go home and tell my mother that I had to quit because it was too hard.

She was the first female steelworker in Pennsylvania, having to do twice the job as a man in order to be given half the wages and benefits. She fought on picket lines next to her coworkers, and was laid off for months of welfare and food-stamp cold nights. A single mom, with four kids, and two full time jobs.

There was no way that I could tell her that by myself, I couldn't make it through college.

It seemed very risky at the time, since you could be ejected for lying about residence (since that meant to be on campus and not a commuter — which was more expensive). But there was no alternative.

Risks may seem overwhelming, but sometimes, playing it safe, and avoiding the risks, is the most dangerous action you can take, if you intend to achieve your goals.

Now 20 years later, running one of the most successful fitness organizations in the world, with 21 countries boasting our facilities, a line of patented equipment, hundreds of books and videos, including award-winners, I remember those humble beginnings. And when things do get overwhelming, it causes me to smile, because even though growing up as an organization may seem risky sometimes, remaining safely immature now seems much more hazardous by comparison.

# WHEN YOU FIND BOTTOM, STAND UP

Bottom. It feels like you could not fall any farther. "Bad" can't be imagined as any "good" until you hit "worse." And I had fallen through the bottom of the well even deeper into the catacombs of my depression.

All of my attempts to start a business had failed miserably. The money I had saved for my bills, I had squandered on my idea. Borrowing my way out of this one wouldn't happen, as my friends and family had already maxed out their capacity.

Holocaust concentration camp survivor Dr. Viktor Frankl had had a deeper appreciation than mine for the catalyzing nature of decisive circumstances, writing, *"When you are no longer able to change your situation, we are challenged to change ourselves."*

At that moment, I realized none of my ideas had failed, but all of my approaches had; it was not the concepts I wanted to express that were flawed, but the manner in which I had expressed them.

On those particularly cataclysmic days, I would remind myself that I had a track record of 100 percent for enduring bad days, so even though I had no solutions, the next day would indeed come, and bring its opportunity for self-change..

After the humiliation of being evicted and moving back in with my mother, I took odd jobs to pay off my debts and rebuild my savings. Setting off once more in pursuit of my dreams, I thanked my mother for her help … yet again. "If you want milk, don't sit on a stool in the middle of a field in the hopes a cow will back up to you. Go get it. But make sure you don't rush, sit down under a bull and start pulling," my mother had cautioned.

Taking her advice, I developed a training shoe designed to protect feet from the veritable garden of fungi, viruses and bacteria that can be found on any grappling mat. Trying to sell my idea to major shoe corporations had failed. So, I stopped trying to bring it to them, and just started using them.

At seminars, during workshops, while training, I'd wear my own shoe design. Many asked about them, after noticing how they not only didn't impede my performance, but enhanced it, all while protecting me from potentially toe-breaking movements, as well as the biohazard of martial art mat infections.

People began to request individual orders, but I had warned them that they'd be expensive to order as single units. They hadn't cared. So, piece by piece, I ordered and fulfilled on demand. We made nearly zero profit, because we continually took the meager gains and used them to create extra samples, which we gave out to pivotal people who expressed interest in them at my seminars.

It was too expensive to buy stock in so many different sizes. In my past, I would have tried to borrow my way to it, taking on significant risk. But this time, I had learned to "milk the cow, not the bull."

Looking on my past, I could now see that the speculative hopes of going into greater debt would prove again disastrous, like trying to pull the bricks from my foundation to build my house higher.

Instead, I doubled my work, taking extra private sessions, contracts, and low-paying but consistent second jobs in security, bouncing and protection. We took the small savings and bought a container of stock of the three best-selling sizes. That bulk order allowed us to lower the price per unit, so then came our first school order for the entire student body. Then, another, and another, until the profit allowed us to stock all sizes.

The success of the "Ultimate Grappling Shoes" (or UGS) exploded, and it has become the "most used grappling mat shoe" in the country.

There are definitely others who borrow their way to success, but that path hadn't worked for me. For me, there was no way to succeed without going slowly and investing more effort than just coming up with an idea and hoping someone would buy it.

There are other ways to succeed: fast-tracked ones sponsored by angel investors. But even if you don't get a "big break" like those, if you commit your heart, focus your mind and dirty your hands, you can break free all on your own.

# THERE IS A WAY PAST 'CAN'T'

Lying frozen in bed, suffocating in a corset of agony, my very breath caused spasms of terrifying pain. A broken back, discs slipped and fissures inflaming tissue, I could not budge. Tears irrigated the sides of my face, too frightened to move. My breath braced as hopelessness slowly pulled over my eyes like a shroud.

My wife had called to cancel my speaking event in Atlanta: the first time I had ever missed work since starting my first company. She had found replacement speakers for me, wiped the crust of salt from my cheeks, and told me that I would get through this, like I always do.

I asked, "What if I can't? What will happen to our family if I can't work? The company is too new. No one will understand. Everyone will think me a fraud, if I claim to teach fitness, yet here I am like a broken porcelain doll, invalid."

She smiled, and told me to, "Have faith in the purpose of this. This is all for a bigger reason."

As she left the bedroom, I recalled a story my grandfather once had told us.

A frog was hopping around a farmyard, when it decided to investigate the barn. Being somewhat careless, and maybe a little too curious, he ended up falling into a pail half-filled with fresh milk. As he swam about attempting to reach the top of the pail, he found that the sides of the pail were too high and steep to reach. He tried to stretch his back legs to push off the bottom of the pail but found it too deep. But this frog was determined not to give up, and he continued to struggle.

He kicked and squirmed and kicked and squirmed, until at last, all his churning about in the milk had turned the milk into a big hunk of butter. The butter became solid enough for him to climb onto, so he jumped out of the pail.

As I lay there in bed, whenever I would try to turn my head or torso, the pain felt like a sledgehammer to my spine and would crush me back onto the bed with aftershock tremors of excruciating consequences. I couldn't get up. I couldn't get out.

I began to circle my fingers and toes to stay as far away from the spasms of my lower back and neck as possible, as both parts of my spine had herniated simultaneously. Since the body is one muscle, and all the connective fascia is a contiguous web, the finger and toe circles started to help my spasm to abate slightly.

Over hours, I finally began to circle my wrists and ankles, and the spasms diminished more. A day later, I circled my knees and elbows. I'd go too far, too fast, and trigger the spasms again, regressing back to fingers and toes to start over. But the blessing was that I couldn't do anything else, there were no distractions by books or television or music. The pain was too cacophonous. So, tiny micro-motions, healing the spasms from the outside-in, I kept moving. And without distractions, I could feel precisely what helped and what hindered my recovery.

Two days later, I arrived at shoulder and hip circles, while lying in bed. And I knew it was time. Exhaling and telling my tissues that they had done their job protecting me, that it was time to heal now, and that they now needed to relax so we could continue our healing, I began to circle my mid back down into the bed, gently. ... No spasm. I increased the circle, lifting my chest off the mattress, and pressing it down; then circled it fully clockwise and counter. No spasm.

Directing my attention to my pelvis and my neck, I alternated circling them, slowly shaving off the tension. I wasn't twanging pain, so I began with slow twists. One knee over the other, twisting my waist, and one ear to the mattress twisting my neck. No spasm.

Eventually I slid both legs off of the bed, and brought my elbow under my ribs. One hand holding my head, the other pressing, I ... Sat ... Up. Creeping my hands up my thighs, I leaned forward and, one inch at a time, ascended to stand. I breathed for a moment unmoving, reintroducing myself to gravity after four days in bed. Performing the entire mobility routine again, I thanked my tissue for protecting me from harm, and advised it to not be scared as I began to walk down the stairs. And we did.

That mobility routine became the biggest selling program I had ever created, called "Intu-Flow" — meaning the flow of your intuition used to guide your healing and communication with the architecture of your tissue. That experience not only became the genesis of one of my greatest contributions to my industry, but it allowed me to have the empathic appreciation of the gradual recovery process.

We so often feel victim to our injuries and illnesses. Like the frog, like me, we can't get up and out. But if we don't quit, if we clear our mind of "can'ts," all of our efforts, no matter how feeble, will become the bedrock upon which we stand.

It doesn't matter if it's not physical. It could be emotional pain, psychological torture, financial panic, or occupational dread. Whatever the circumstance, it has a purpose beyond our comprehension. There is a reason. And you will become better, bigger, and more helpful to others because you didn't give up; because your struggle kept churning the milk.

Often in life we forget the things we should remember, and remember the things we should forget. Forget the times that you couldn't. Remember the times that you did. Clear your mind of "Can't." And you will get off your Can. You will get up. Keep going. Keep faith. Keep striving.

# THE DOOR IS OPEN: WILL YOU WALK THROUGH?

Sitting at a shack of a cafe on the Black Sea, my coach said to me, "If you want me to teach you what I know, the door is open. If you don't want me to teach you what I know, the door is open. Just don't block the doorway. Take a step: inside or outside. Distrust your steps, and even in the safest place, your fear will keep you prisoner. Trust your steps, and no matter how dangerous everything may appear, you will remain safe. Either way, you will take a step by choice or by circumstance. Sometimes, God closes doors because it's time to move; because He knows you won't move unless circumstances force you to. So, will you take a step inside or outside, by choice or by circumstance?"

As if on cue, we heard a large diesel vehicle approaching. When it stopped, our coach — a military general himself — told us to quickly get up, calmly walk out the back door of the cafe, to avoid the road, and run down the beach to our barracks. Hastily, we looked back to see a personnel carrier unloading soldiers into the cafe. We ran a bit faster once clear of the lights.

At our room, we waited until our coach finally knocked and advised us we'd be leaving in two hours, at 0400, on our way back to Krasnodar. We packed our duffels, set our watches, and pretended to sleep. Our driver and a translator were waiting for us — car running — when we got downstairs at 0350. We departed in silence. Winding through the pitch-black Caucasian mountains, my teammate and I passed out from a combination of lack of calories, overtraining and adrenal fatigue from the dramatic departure.

We awoke to the sound of horns blazing. Behind a military carrier, our driver was nailing the horn at the uphill-creeping truck. Agitated, he pulled into the oncoming lane and began bumping the truck off the road. My teammate and I sat white-knuckled. Finally, sweat beading, we outpaced the truck, and continued for another three, silent hours.

Were these inside or outside steps? Had I made this choice or was this circumstance thrust upon me? I certainly didn't feel like I trusted what was happening, so it must be the latter.

Flying from Krasnodar to Moscow, we were met by an associate who had loaned his apartment to "keep" us until our return flight to the USA three days later. At last, they revealed the mystery behind our sudden loss of welcome — that our passport stamps were no longer valid, and the soldiers had come to look for "the Americans." I asked why, since the stamps were supposed to be valid for another two months.

We received only, "Politics," shrugged as an answer.

Puzzle pieces fell into place. This had been the post-Perestroika 1990s, and the temporary Prime Minister was up for election as the new President of Russia ... competing with other nominees from parties old and new. The Prime Minister intended to ally himself to the publicly favorable West by establishing programs to bring Russian culture to the world. Our coach had been the primary electoral representative in Saint Petersburg for the Prime Minister. The Russian Olympic Committee had selected us as the two Americans to represent our country as ambassadors to the Russian cultural martial traditions when we returned to the States after our internship.

Our presence in Russia, however, had become an undesirably high-profile program, which, if failing, would have reflected poorly on the Prime Minister's bid for presidency. If we embarrassed the program, or if we had somehow been disgraced (such as being arrested for traveling illegally), those who did not want the Prime Minister in power would have used it as leverage against him. I felt like a trapped outsider; helpless and without resources or options. How could I trust in an invisible game of such a magnitude? I panicked, and then made an unwise choice. ...

There was nothing in the apartment but some stale bread, a half jar of jam, and a bottle of vodka. Instead of being smart and following directions, we convinced our translator to take us out to the grocery store to get some provisions. We didn't make it a block before a police car screeched to a halt on seeing our very obvious American clothing. The driver rounded the car, demanding our papers. The passenger leveled a Kalashnikov muzzle on me, trigger finger trembling with excitement. He wasn't much more than a teenager dreaming of potential promotion for arresting two Americans.

Though our entry stamps had suspiciously expired by sudden policy changes DURING our stay, our translator handed the police our "special license" from the Olympic committee, as well as a hefty bribe. Smiling at the cash, the two officers took down our apartment address and pocketed our passports. He said that we had to report to police headquarters by midnight to retrieve our documents or we'd be prevented from boarding our plane.

The translator suggested that we should head off straight away to "pay" for new stamps. As the policemen departed, we walked to the headquarters. On arrival, we were escorted into a holding cell and a female lieutenant entered the room. Our translator surprised us both when instead of shaking her hand, they both looked around quickly, leaned in, and kissed.

Trust sparked within me, but did not light.

She told us there wasn't much time and we had to move fast. Taking us to another desk, she barked orders to a clerk to mark our documents with the updated stamp. He hesitated, and she barked louder. Finally with a "thunk, thunk," we retrieved our newly revised papers and passports and hustled out of the department.

Belief in the process ignited again, and I began to dare hope that we would get out of this safely.

Returning to our apartment after a silently rapid march, we were introduced to the lieutenant: Oxsana, a master of sport in Sambo, a student of my coach, the head instructor for hand-to-hand combat at the police academy, and a past *amoureux* of our translator.

In the pre-cellphone era, we had no idea how she had been forewarned of our predicament, other than our guess at the level of awareness that our presence had elicited as pawns in this very overwhelming political maneuvering.

The windfall reignited my trust in the steps we had been taking.

Two tense days crept by with no distractions, and we remained locked in the apartment. Oxsana and Yuri (our translator) had left on their own, to rekindle their relationship, presumably.

So my teammate and I sat there waiting for the door to be kicked in by OMON after the inevitable discovery of our spuriously updated stamps. Time clicked by, one painfully imprisoned minute after another.

The door opened two days later, and Yuri and Oxsana drove us to the airport in silence. I don't think I exhaled the entire way. Feeling nerve bare passing the border patrol, I tried not to look nervous. Oxsana called over the supervisor and took us through the "green lane." The supervising captain smiled and whispered, "Alexander Ivanovich is the best. Yes?"

We are protected, I thought. Despite all of the ominous danger of pursuit and arrest, even though we potentially could be used as pawns in a large plot beyond our comprehension, we remain safe. Could I truly believe in this process without any doubts?

Not until the plane was in the air, did I relax. And only when we saw those waving Stars and Stripes did I fully appreciate the magnitude of this grand chess game; within close proximity to players WAY above our normal field of view. We were nothing; just fighters, mere athletes, and neither bright, nor aware.

But I began to discover that no matter how overwhelmed, I could keep faith in the process and trust the steps. I had escaped paralyzing fear jeopardizing our discovery by trusting in the journey.

As we landed in USA, I knelt and kissed JFK ground (much to the disgust of NYC frequenters). My coach's words still echoed in my ears: I remained safe because I trusted in the process, but in the moments I did not, in the time that I collapsed upon myself with fear, even in the safe places, I felt imprisoned.

The truly fearless are not those who don't feel fear, I realized. The fearless are those who let the natural, real dangers alert them, and heighten their readiness without paralyzing them. Fear is a gift of awareness, but faith is freedom from imprisonment by fear.

Robert F. Kennedy cautioned, *"Fear not the path of Truth for the lack of People walking on it."* If you dare to keep your courage, and by choice, take steps forward, you will be safe. Even if your fear turns into panic, and you forfeit your choice to act, circumstances will be thrust upon you to give greater opportunity to believe in your journey, and restore your faith in the process. As Max Lucado suggested, *"Meet your fears with faith."*

# WHAT ARE YOU WILLING TO RISK?

My Russian coach asked me to walk with him to the Black Sea shore. As we walked, he asked, "WHY do you fight? For what?"

A swarming wraith of childhood adversities still chasing me in the darkness, I could not yet articulate, or even admit some of the trauma I had experienced. All I could utter in my simple Russian was, "To win."

He called the translator over and continued, "When I watch you spar, I see you try to win. But sparring isn't to try to win or try not to lose. That is competing. Competing, you do the few moves that you have trained most, that you KNOW will work. Sparring, you should do the moves you have developed the least, which you KNOW will not work if you don't practice them. You're improving very slowly because you want to win and you want to not lose, when you should be focused on improving."

We walked a little more, and then he went on in Russian, "When you compete, what do you win?"

At least I could answer this question, "A medal," I replied.

He continued, "Is that what you hope to win? That is why you lost the gold at World Games, because all you wanted was the gold. Why? Because you think you should."

Shaking his head, he looked away for a moment considering, and then resumed, "When you compete, you fight for a gift. When we compete, we fight for our jobs. If we lose, we lose our house, our car, our food, everything. That is what it means to fight for something. We fight for our families, and our community impacted by our jobs. To be a warrior doesn't merely involve what you fight with, but rather what you fight for. If you compete again at World Games, make sure if you lose, it's all gone. Then, you will focus on IMPROVING every day so that you CAN do your very best when EVERYTHING is at stake."

It took nearly 15 years before I could accept the challenge he dared on that pivotal day.

But coming out of retirement in 2010 to compete at World Games, against the best fighters of their nations, half my age and twice as heavy, in front of the live television feed, his words came flooding back. Looking up into the bleachers at my beautiful wife, and my students from around the country who had come to cheer me on, I thought, "Here it is. This is it. Everything is on the line: my reputation, my team, my company, my livelihood. If I lose this, most everyone will figure me a fraud, and I will lose everything."

My coach's wisdom infused that moment in time, and though awarded the gold, I had won something much more precious to my growth. I won a hard-earned understanding of priorities. As my teacher told me back on the beaches of the Black Sea, repeating the Cossack cadet code, "Your life is not yours alone; it belongs to your family, community, and to the world."

Not what you fight with, but what you fight for...

When I realized how many lives would be impacted by my loss, I recognized the need to shift my priorities to focus on their betterment, rather than my own. My coach's reframe empowered me to shift my paradigm from self-interest to family, community, national and global service. That gold was FOR them, and now because my reputation grew, my influence expanded, and more families can be reached with the work.

I can help more people because of that one moment, where I shifted from my own lack-luster fool's gold, to the pure preciousness of living for something bigger than another medal. Though I remain vigilant of the ego, that like a skulking ninja surreptitiously seeks to reacquire control, when I stopped living for my own selfish desires, with the realization of how truly weak attachments are, I began to reach outward.

Another teacher, on my new path of service, advised, "When you find yourself getting discouraged, encourage others, and their courage will inspire you." Within aiding, supporting and truly loving others lies the true gold mine of our lives.

# MASTERY IS BUILT ON PREPARATION

For two years, I did not pass my instructor exams in Russia to become the first Westerner certified in their system. They were harder on me than anyone else, because the political spotlight was upon me. An American teaching their system had to be flawless.

The joke about me throughout their country was, "Wherever Scott goes, the wood gets softer," referring to how often I would get the technique "wrong" and crash into their unmatted wood floors, over and over again.

Though some chided me, saying it was impossible for an American to ever pass the Russian exams, though I felt overwhelmed and frustrated by the inequity, I restarted, re-strategized, and prepared every element patiently, meticulously and diligently. I made it a goal to be so good that they could NOT fail me. Instead of quitting and trying to get even with those who "unfairly" made things harder on me, I aligned myself with getting even better ... and not allowing there to be any option but to succeed.

I passed, despite the "impossible" difficulty of the exams, and I became an ambassador to their system. When I did, and started teaching, others claimed that I only passed because my teacher had favored me, because they wanted a "paper American," because they had to make a political point of me, not because I deserved to be passed. When I heard these petty comments, I had to smile. They had no idea how hard my teachers had been upon me, and the wood that I softened by my years of repeated failures.

Prepare dutifully. Focus on perfecting form a little bit better each day than the day prior. And little by little becomes a lot.

Mastery of the basics comes only through preparation. Don't do it for anyone else, because people will always look for a reason to criticize what they don't believe they can do. Do it for your own path of personal development. And be so good that others cannot deny it.

# FIND AND FEED THE REAL NEED

Walking through Russian border control, a woman and her daughter began screaming in distress. Turning back, I saw that my colleague's wife and child were being held as more guards arrived.

I overheard that his family had "incorrect" stamps as Kazakhstani citizens and, regardless of their American husband/father, were being denied leave from Russia and being deported back to Kazakhstan.

Approaching I calmly but sharply said in Russian, "Excuse me."

Handing the special license which the Russian government had given me, tucked with 5,000 rubles inside, I motioned to the mother and her girl, "They are small problem." Then, nodding to my license, "This. This is big problem. Let's make small problem go [away]."

The lieutenant visibly considered the consequences of both actions and pushed back my license, emptied of the rubles, and waved the family through the border crossing.

On the plane, my colleague huddled around his still terrified family in disbelief that they were free. Eyes glassy and full, he mouthed a thank you and returned to their embrace. It was one of the best moments of my years in Russia.

My teacher used to say: Learn the difference between what your opponent immediately desires and what he truly wants most; then, when he wants the former very badly, offer him the latter. Most of the time, he'll take it immediately, forgetting his plan, and with that receive a sudden psychological disadvantage.

At 2010 World Games, I shook hands with a young, fast fighter from the UK Team, and as the match began he launched out, over and over, with the stamina that youth and training give. After my many fights that day, even in good shape, I knew I needed to conserve my energy to last through the final fights still to come for the remainder of that day and win gold.

Grabbing his collar, I drove him away, stiff-arming him from my body. I felt him considering how locked my arm was, and knew he wanted to set up his flying arm bar. So, I kept it there, offering it to him. Waiting. When you're a young fighter, it can feel overpowering — an obvious opening — but I have been too often trapped by attempting to exploit what I would later discover to be a snare cast by my opponent's greater experience.

As soon as he shifted his weight to the opposite foot, I began moving in. The instant I felt him weightless, as he jumped up for the arm bar, I spun to encircle his leg. We landed together on the ground. Rolling, I finished the knee bar and won the match.

I learned to apply this approach in even my own nutrition. When I craved fast burning sweets, I knew that I actually needed slow burning protein. So instead of caving to the craving, I fed my real need and the impulse evaporated; my body developing a gratitude for the protein that eventually outgrew any interest in sweets.

When I felt weak and drained in my training, instead of just pushing harder, I looked for what was holding me back: some tension or locked movement. And by releasing it, the nerve force surged back in … producing a profound appreciation for removing the brakes from my potential.

Developing this sneaky strategy to building willpower helped me in more than just fighting. It allowed me to quit tobacco in the 1990s, improve my test scores in University, and even navigated me through the nightmare of dating.

Discernment of your TRUE needs will win critical victories over immediate desires. Don't cave to the crave. Feed what you truly need.

# 'EXPERTS' MAY NOT BE SO SMART

Asked this question about twice in a week, I thought it interesting to write a response: "From your years training with the Spetsnaz trainers, throughout Russia, what do you think of the no-touch knock-down / knock-out tactics of psychic energy taught in Russia?"

During one of our camps in Moscow, the city's leading Systema instructor came to give the special forces trainers a demonstration. Of course, being the first American to train in Russia, they asked me if I would like to volunteer to experience the demo.

Being the brash, naive young man I was, I said, "Please, let's do it."

The instructor began swinging toward my head with a strike. I waited for the impact, which never came. He had stopped.

He swung again. I waited. He had stopped. He shook his head, "No," and jutted his chin at the slowly and obviously inbound strike coming toward my head. Not understanding what he wanted me to do, I jutted my chin at the strike too, assuming that was part of the demo. I stood there waiting for the psychic energy to knock me down or knock me out.

The instructor got frustrated, motioned for me to strike him, and as I launched my strike at the speed he requested (slow and obvious), he flinched, and ducked out of the way covering his head. He then said, "Now. You." Confused, and completely missing his point, as he began to swing again, I stood there waiting for his strike to make me flinch, dodge and cover. It didn't.

"What was I doing wrong?" I thought.

He then tried a tackle, a kick, a knife slash and a stick attack. I stood there waiting for each. Nothing happened. He would stop the attack half way, and restart with a different angle or weapon. Finally, exasperated, he grabbed his assistant, started the same attacks, and with each one, the student fell over, and sometimes even went unconscious. The instructor looked up at me each time and said, "See? Understand. This! And this. And this. You understand?"

Nodding, I said, "I think so." He started to attack me again. I stood there waiting for my body to go limp like his student. As the attack came in, I looked down at my body waiting to see a knee buckle, or a leg collapse, or maybe my spine go numb, something, anything. But nothing happened. I looked at the instructor with an innocent apology on my face, and said, "I'm really sorry! I must be doing something wrong."

Incensed, he yelled at me in Russian. Not understanding, I looked over at my friends in the special forces, who were stifling chuckles, which I assumed was because I was getting the drill wrong. I looked to the translator for help, and she said, "Master says because you're a sport fighter, you're not smart enough to move away from the strikes. Normal people move because they don't know the pain they will get, so they jump away, and also pass unconscious from stress of fear. He says, you have trained here in Russia, so already too know pain from Sambo and do not fear pain.

"So, he say you have lost the ability of psychic energy. If you believed that you would be seriously hurt, you'd be knocked down or knocked out by master's psychic attack, he says." She smiled serenely.

Flummoxed, I asked the instructor how long it took him to master the skill. "For me, 18 years." I then asked, how long would it take a sport fighter to become "stupid like me" and lose touch with psychic energy. He replied, "Within 1–2 years, you would lose effect," the translator relayed.

So, completely innocently, I asked, "Is it wrong to just spend a couple years playing and enjoying sports rather than a couple decades trying to learn a skill which only affects people who have no training at all? In my country, even the bad guys have significant training; often more than us, since they have the luxury of time in prison with no job or family, and plenty of people to fight. So, would learning the skill of psychic energy even help us in my country?"

Enraged, he raised his voice, yelling, to which the translator remarked, "The master says you do not know real violence, so nothing can help you."

He stormed out of the demonstration hall. At that point, my special forces friends could not contain themselves from laughing at me. One pretended to strike the other in the face, and when the other got hit, he raised his hands and said, *"Shto? Nye ponimayu."* Their act sent raucous laughter throughout the crowd. I had still not gotten that they had this all set up as a prank on me.

They had wanted to test me and see how "suggestible" I was, which my good friend later disclosed, "In our country, we do not surrender our judgment because someone tells us something will work. We doubt it until it can be done on us over and over — until the evidence cannot be denied. You seemed very willing to do whatever painful drill we asked you to do. We wanted to make sure that you had not left your common sense back in USA when you came to Russia."

He smiled, hugged me and said, "Let's get back to our 'stupid' sports."

Don't believe everything an "authority" claims. Even if you know little to nothing about the subject matter, believe in your naivety to learn or to filter hogwash. Maybe you'll learn something otherworldly! Maybe not. I've experienced strange things, so I'm open to any possibility, even if it's outside the scope of my experience.

But just because I'm open-minded to what is beyond my experience, doesn't mean I'm so open-minded that my brain falls out at the mere claim of something transcending my experience.

# ENJOY THE GAME; THE BOX WILL WAIT

One of my Russian martial art coaches loved chess; which may be even more of a Russian national sport than Sambo. Often he'd see me worried about the size, strength or speed of my opponents, and he'd recount an old proverb, "After the game, the king and the pawn go into the same box."

He had once continued, "You have anxiety because you are getting sucked down into the mere game. Look from the top. Imagine you are pieces on a chessboard. Your pawn only weakens because you feel small next to his front, and so you feel anxiety about your lack of potential. But now view it from the top, see your pawn in its full strength, what it represents to your opponent, and realize it is the most important piece on the board."

He taught me that my pawn could have the greatest courage and cause the entire opposition to rattle. If I remained brave enough to approach the opponent's rear line, even a pawn could transform into the most powerful piece on the board: a queen. "Even the humble, unexpected pawn can change the course of a game," he'd insist.

So what are you going to do in this game? If all you are doing is going back into the box, if you can't take it with you, then HOW you play the game remains the only point to this all. Your true powers exceed the movements you may feel restricted to execute. Your importance lies not in your potential powers, but by your very courage. So, how you choose to stand, how you decide you will act while you are on the board, is the entire point of our game.

Even the humble, unexpected pawn can change the course of the game through bravery.

None of us is getting out of here alive, so let us enjoy the game, but more importantly, let us not be deluded into collecting pieces or wins. Let us focus our goals upon the courage to follow our values even against overwhelming odds, even with those who have become blind to the point of the game, and the inevitability that we will all go back in the box.

# DOES YOUR REAL FOE LIVE INSIDE?

Staring across the mat, I was certain my opponent would defeat me. He was younger, stronger, with a better pedigree: a better version of myself.

My coach grabbed my chin and pulled my face toward his, "Don't look at him like that. You're more experienced, aware, and longer trained. He can't do anything you haven't already done, can't launch anything without you detecting it, and can't predict anything that you'll do, even if he's trained in it. You've already won this. Or lost it if you keep looking at him like that, and not yourself."

Repeatedly placed within this stressful position of facing an opponent who means to do me physical harm, and yet carrying the child I once was within me, I have never felt "confident" stepping on the mat. But I always stood to the challenge. When I, despite fear and frustration, faced those foes, not one has been as dangerous as the opponent my imagination had created. I had made nearly every challenge I faced so much harder than the reality I encountered, and continually underestimated my own resources and abilities by my outward focus away from myself.

Many of the obstacles you imagine are not even there; as Sun Tzu wrote, "Most battles are won or lost before they're fought." They're lost because we imagine our victory or our defeat, and by the strength of imagining, make it true even in the most minute decisions. Steel your focus on your goal while making those seemingly insignificant choices, so that those small steps carry you in the right direction. As you do, the phantoms of obstacle and opposition evaporate.

Eventually life will leave you. It does for everyone. And as you approach the end, all you're going to have is the ability to look back at the choices you made and reflect upon them: did I make the best choice I could with the level of understanding and awareness I held at the time?

Jack London's unwritten credo declared, *"I would rather be ashes than dust! I would rather that my spark should burn out in a brilliant blaze than it should be stifled by dry-rot. I would rather be a superb meteor, every atom of me in magnificent glow, than a sleepy and permanent planet. The function of man is to live, not to exist. I shall not waste my days trying to prolong them. I shall use my time."*

Use it. Make the decision. Harbor, within your psyche, no allies to your obstacles. Lend those forces to yourself. Imagine you.

# IF CHANGE MUST BE RADICAL, SO BE IT

My coach first assessed my fighting skill and said, "The good news is that you only need to change everything."

Dumbfounded, I gasped, "How is THAT a GOOD thing?" He replied, "Sometimes, it's easier to start over and make a complete overhaul, than to change one or two things deeply embedded in your lifestyle."

In my case, this also involved my nutrition; changing what I ate, when I ate it, and in which combination of foods. I had to increase the quality, the quantity, and the frequency of my meals. And I also, indeed, had to displace all of the unhealthy substances to which my body had become addicted.

Doing so, I faced tenacious gremlins whispering their powerful hold over me: sugar, dairy, wheat, pasta, pastry, bread, soda, alcohol and coffee. I had to wipe the slate completely clean and start over, with dramatic lifestyle changes, in order to get clean and clear.

Slight modifications or exclusion of one or two failed because they remained inextricably intertwined in the lifestyle behaviors I had habitually woven. I had to tear apart the fabric and begin completely over.

Family and friends who did not want to change their situation observed my radical shift and laughed, offering no support for my challenges. Some were toxic individuals who are no longer around me, and some observed the health improvements that my overhaul made, and implemented changes themselves.

No proper education could be found because nutrition had been such an inaccessible and biased discipline at the time of my decision to change. And even if the education had been available, nutrition is so highly individualized that I still would have had to make the choices to investigate and experiment with what specifically worked for me and what did not.

In some changes, I could prepare meal plans, grocery lists and schedule my cooking. But most of the real hurdles only presented themselves once I realized when these plans went awry, I had to improvise without compromise. In many situations, despite lack of preparation, sometimes I had to still do it anyway.

The addictions DID need to be addressed and healed, but those few legitimate dragons could ONLY be faced when I accepted that, phantom or real, I WOULD face them. The decision to confront and overcome them all was simpler and more feasible than attempting to face only one.

Mark Twain wryly joked, "I've lived through some terrible things in my life, some of which actually happened." We all have chemical wraiths in the belfry of our minds; imagined phantoms, which we allow to immobilize us into indecision. We rationalize why we cannot change a harmful or suboptimal situation ... excuses that just aren't real. Oh, there are a few legitimate dragons we must slay, too; but they aren't everywhere, and they aren't omnipotent.

It takes great courage to be who we really are, because we're hidden on the other side of those invented horrors, and revealed only by facing our few, real demons. Who you first meet in a person is what they had eaten, and when they had eaten it. Whom others meet in you is the same.

The question my teacher posed to me still echoes in every emotional outburst I feel, "Who is acting right now: you, or what you ate and when?"

You can and should get support, educated and prepared. But only one person will ever be able to make the choice to change the situation; and because of your personal power, even if you have no support, education or preparation, you can STILL do it.

As Calvin Coolidge said, *"Only persistence and determination are omnipotent."* Regardless of the legitimate excuses why you cannot, despite how hard it appears, and how difficult some issues will indeed be ... if you want to make changes to improve your health, still do it.

# TRICKS AND SHORTCUTS ARE FALSE PROMISES

Asking my martial arts teacher to share the "tricks of the trade," he laughed, "Clever little short-cuts won't help you. Stop trying to learn tricks, and just practice your trade. Tricks are the trade done very well."

I secretly ignored him. Only after training with masters in different counties, did I realize the wisdom in his guidance: Though their styles differed, the process was identical.

Then, I saw this lesson repeating in fitness, yoga, writing, producing, organizational management and even in community development and family life. You can't replicate flow from someone else. You can only quietly practice every day, and slowly unlock your own flow.

So here's a list of the 10 most critical discoveries I have made. When I adhere to this in a new discipline, endeavor or venture, all flows smoothly; when I try to shortcut the process by being clever, flotsam stagnates the current.

1.  Master the basics of your craft. There are no advanced techniques; only refined basics performed with elegant virtuosity. When frustrated, practice more. When that does not work, be patient and keep practicing.

2.  Refine communication: Speak with your true voice, but FOR the audience, not "at" them. Then, be silent in your head as well as with your mouth, and HEAR what they actually respond even without their words. The dialogue you create plugs you into the heartbeat of actual growth and success.

3.  Seek what YOU are to be learning from every experience, especially when you're teaching and providing a service or product. Don't be afraid to say, "no," to every idea others offer, but validate that you value their contribution. Then, provide rationale for the strategies you've successful applied. You may just find their ideas reinforce and improve your own.

4.  Be yourself but respectful; seriously committed but not emotionally attached. Just because you think you would do it differently, doesn't mean

you can or that others should. Consider the context, and improvise an appropriate application that suits all of the needs of those involved.

5. When you're confused, wrong, surprised, and all eyes are upon you (and this will happen a lot), PAUSE. Exhale, smile, reorient and resume. Be accountable for the energy you bring into people's lives with your visible course corrections. How you handle recovery weighs more than what you do when you recover.

6. Be excited when you're wrong; and be forthright with gratitude when others point it out. Inside the labyrinth of choices, you can't always see the upcoming dead-ends; allow others to lend you their angle of sight.

7. Practice transparency and authenticity. Being strong isn't being invulnerable. No one buys it (for too long before suspecting BS). Share with conviction your truth, but acknowledge your hard-won failures.

8. Give a little more than you get until you can give for nothing. People silently distrust transactional behavior. So, if you do something for someone, try to minimize having to ask for something in return, until you can do it without needing anything in return at all.

9. Be willing to do everything alone, but delegate to those who continually offer to help. When things fall through and a person neglects their stake in the project, don't begrudge their absence; gracefully recalculate and expediently continue.

10. Don't expect others to rise to your expectations. Surpass your own. If you truly want to elicit participation or advocacy, then lead by example with energy, enthusiasm and excellence. Others will observe this repeating pattern, and through exposure, start doing the same, and then you will feel their energy accelerate your collective efforts.

When people attempt to subvert your intentions to make a difference, to cast predictions of your impending failure, to criticize your character and abilities as inherently flawed, exhale and detach from an emotional reaction to their venom.

They're only telling their own story; not yours.

A teacher's lesson from an entirely different direction crystallized this realization. I had been repeatedly thrown by my opponent, hoisted off my feet and pounded into the mat like a tent stake. Taking out my legs again and again, I'd contort in the air attempting to land at least on my knees, rather than flat on my back. But I was figuring it out. His technique only worked because I didn't know how he was launching it (ignorance), and because my bracing to resist it (fear) I gave him the platform to enter.

Between rounds, my coach whispered, "Sink down. The lower you drop your center, the harder it will be to be thrown. Get your feet under you to launch YOUR strategy." So, I exhaled and relaxed. Instead of dreading the moment he entered, I went straight toward my goal.

He could no longer launch his technique, and as a result could no longer throw me. Now, I took HIM down. He grew more and more worried about my entries from multiple angles; and the more frustrated he became, the easier it was to enter at will.

I didn't win, but I had not been beaten. After the fight, my opponent came smiling with his hand outstretched, saying, "I don't know how you recovered, because I was sure I had defeated you. One of the best matches I've ever had, bro."

We can lose, but not be beaten by our fear and ignorance. And on the mat together, we steel our will and hold our emotional control, as our partner exposes where our attention has weakened. By pressing on that vulnerability, our partner shows us where we can become stronger.

Similarly, when one close to you, in fear and ignorance, presses against you, exhale to prevent the emotional tailspin.

Only their fear and ignorance of their own worth causes them to project their perceived inadequacies upon you. Keep going. Accept that in your goals, you may even lose, but that you will not be beaten. As Vince Lombardi said, "In great attempts, it is glorious even to fail." But you shall not be defeated.

You will be surprised by the illumination it brings to your life... And even those who fearfully, ignorantly, project their own darkness upon you, will be brightened.

# PRACTICE IS FOR LEARNING, NOT WINNING

"How can I tap you every class, but at competitions you're always taking the gold from fighters I know that I could not beat," I asked flummoxed by my first coach's unusual teaching style.

He replied, "I'm here to learn and practice, not compete and fight. You should be, too."

I foolishly retorted, "If that were true, then I would be doing better at competitions like you."

Smiling, he asked, "Have you been learning to win, or losing to learn? Most people get stuck with the latter — trying to not look like they're losing — so they only ever learn FROM losing. To avoid making the process take so much longer, take risks practicing your new skills. If you want to reach new levels, you have to practice in new ways; don't keep repeating what's safe. Then, you really lose. Then, you only ever learn how to lose, because that's all you're practicing. Practice to win by allowing yourself to make higher quality mistakes."

I laughed then, because I had always been in the slow learner category of life ... and it took me many more years to realize I needed to consciously practice the necessary failures (improving tools, skills and ideas), rather than unconsciously repeating unnecessary failures (misusing, misunderstanding or misapplying tools, skills and ideas). I had worked very hard repeating my low quality mistakes.

Henry David Thoreau cautioned, *"A man may be very industrious, and yet spend his time poorly. There's no more fatal a blunder."*

I had been stuck in the mindset that if I stopped my coach from beating me, I would absorb his experience, skill and attitude. Instead, I discovered that I needed to invest all of my effort into learning the drills, not defeating them. Put effort into the technique, not effort into the activity, as I eventually came to learn in exercise as well.

So, placing myself in each uncomfortable and unexpected vulnerability my teachers could find, I began to allow myself to fail while attempting to improve. I stopped trying to avoid losing.

The longer I am alive, the more I watch the oldest practitioners of any discipline who still seem to be learning. They've stopped trying to not lose. They've perfected the art of learning.

Practice failure rather than failing at practice; the former involves the necessary mistakes you experience when you improve, but the latter — the unnecessary, fatal blunderings of true failure.

# FIND THE TEACHER WHO INSPIRES YOU

My teacher screamed, "Just shoot in and take him down!" He then had me repeat it sloppily over and over until I vomited from exhaustion, after which he would exclaim, "NOW, practice has begun." Training would continue until we would submit, after which he would berate us for surrendering to the intensity of the drills.

"Get tough," he'd yell!

"How," we wondered, as there was never any way to know if we had since we always failed to last until he ended our training.

Another teacher explained to me that if I created an angle and changed the level of my stance, I'd be able to penetrate far enough to perform my takedown. He advised that I listen for my opponent's exhale and move so that I would enter on his inhale. My timing would always be just slightly off, as I was forever one step behind the execution of his explanations. Why could I not apply these exemplary descriptions? What was I missing?

Yet another teacher drew me a diagram of the angles and levels, and then demonstrated each one over and over with elegance and power. He'd place us in solo movement drills and then partner us to apply the movements together. He'd show us how, if we practiced the movement and felt the partner, we'd know exactly how to time the angles and levels. We did, and we excelled. I share this method with my own teams now with equally excellent results.

But my greatest teacher caused me to reflect upon all of my skills, the poor and the precise, and inspired me to apply and refine my abilities for a higher purpose. In the past, my teachers had led me to expertise in acquiring, refining and applying my skills against resistant opponents, but I had failed to expand my practice into a lifestyle. My understanding had been limited to the mat. Therefore, I could only ever defeat my opponents, lacking the ability to create anything greater than victory. How could I transcend competition, and to what?

My greatest teacher inspired me to look at what I had learned through the discoveries in my training, and apply it throughout my life; for how you practice one thing is how you master anything. From her inspiration, and seeing the lives she impacted through her transcendence, I wondered if my training could hold the same transformative effect. Victory had become insufficient motivation. I needed something more than defeating opponents and achieving victory. Team, and the support community it fostered, evolved into my central focus; HOW we trained together, became more important than "what" we trained.

Because of her, I had finally become a true beginner again, and repeatedly enter this beginner's mind each morning as I awaken to the new opportunity to decipher the tasks of the day, and help others to do the same. For each of us, to become a team, a community transcending our drills and skills, to become something beyond the striving itself.

William Arthur Ward said, *"The mediocre teacher tells. The good teacher explains. The superior teacher demonstrates. The great teacher inspires."*

I honor all of my teachers for their influence upon my life, and their sacrifices in bringing me to greater illumination of purpose and vision. You inspire me.

# NEVER EASIER – BUT ALWAYS BETTER

My first University wrestling coach, a US Olympic Greco-Roman wrestling team alternate, destroyed us daily in practice, in medieval Dan Gable "puke-or-die" fashion.

Unlike the others on my team, though, I couldn't quit. If I did, it only meant backsliding into illness and pain. Quitting is only an alternative if you find the absence of the present discomfort more favorable. For me, the discomfort of today could not compare to the anguish of yesterday, so I refused to stop. I'd slow, falter, fall, get back up, flail desperately, but I couldn't ever quit.

Coach constantly changed the exercises, drills and techniques, never allowing us to anticipate what we would be doing or practicing, training or drilling: a constant confusing, crushing chaos.

One day, out of frustration, I approached him and said, "Coach, may I have a moment?" He nodded so I continued, "I'll never give up, but can I just ask when this is going to get any easier. I feel like I can't absorb everything you're teaching at this intensity."

He looked me in the eyes in that far-away glare only a coach who's ruminated over every fact and figure for years can do, and said, "Sonnon, it ain't gettin' easy ever," slamming his meaty paw into the desk. "You don't need to remember what you're learning. It's in your nerves and in your bones and in your muscles and in your sinew. That's where I'm training you: in your body, not your mind. I can't train your mind. That's your job. If you don't quit, then you did your job. Now, let me do mine."

"Yes, Sir," I said walking out of his office.

He appeared right behind me and yelled, "Sonnon! Get in the center" (of the mat).

"Damn," I thought. Now comes the pain, as coach was notorious for crushing us personally when we needed attitude adjustments. He wasn't some enlightened grandmaster; just a crusty old Olympian still able take any two of us at once with relative ease.

He called out techniques and told me to hit them.

"Faster," he yelled.

Then he called out variations we hadn't ever worked on. I paused, and he barked, "Now!" So, I did. Effortlessly. (Not as fluidly as him, but definitely not as if I had never worked on them.) Over and over for 30 minutes.

At the end, he stopped me, looked at the rest of the team, wagging his fist at us. "Now, do any of you have any doubts that you've been working on more difficult skills?" Not a peep was heard from us.

He went on, "Just because it ain't gettin' easier dudn't mean you ain't gettin' any better. It means y'ar. Now stop looking for pats on the back like little prima donnas. You ain't gettin' 'em. You earn those at the tournaments. They're gold, but they belong to your team anyway so better get over waiting for applause. Go play football if you want cheerleaders. Nobody gives a rat's ass about grapplers."

My coach wasn't the nicest guy. I would never let him coach my kids, since I know now as a national team coach that there are highly superior methods of conveying the same message with positive, generative methods. But even someone with his degree of problems and with his poor manner of communicating them, can still offer insights.

In this case, I learned it will never get any easier if you're growing, because as soon as one skill becomes easy, you're already at the next challenge.

My grandfather used to say, "Be careful what you wish for. You may just get it." That applies to challenges. If you want to be more prepared than the challenges you face, that means that only greater challenges await you, because you're never thrown anything that isn't just outside your comfort zone … just close enough for you to exceed your expectations and rise to the occasion… or else quit. That also means you've been building and building the springboard to jump off … and that "ain't never goin' to get any easier." But you ARE getting better.

# ACCEPT WHAT THE MOMENT OFFERS

The Dalai Lama shared, *"This is my simple religion. There is no need for complicated philosophies. Our own brain, our own heart is our temple. My philosophy is compassion."*

Once at Capital Games in Washington, DC, a fighter was attempting to place an ankle lock on me, and didn't realize that in an international Sambo championship, you're prohibited from making verbal noise (since the athlete might may be crying out in pain for the match to stop, so any noise is taken to mean submission).

He called to the referee that my foot was trapped in his jacket, and the referee blew the whistle ending the match. Incredibly angry, he screamed at the ref as to the injustice of his loss.

I intervened; asking the official if we could continue as my opponent hadn't understood international rules. The referee conceded, and called to restart us in the same position.

My opponent — stunned that I would sacrifice a cheap win — redoubled his effort in hopes of securing the win. He desperately switched from one lock to the next; but flailing placed his own leg in knee bar position. I captured his heel and held it close, as he submitted himself, and tapped.

After the match, he shook my hand telling me he respected me for not accepting a dishonorable victory. He admitted his excitement at the chance to win after nearly losing, caused him to use too much force and become "blind" to the danger he placed his own legs in.

I've lost from the same desperation on and off the mat; in my business, in my fitness and nutrition, in my relationships, in parenting… It's a lesson I have had to repeatedly re-learn.

Most of what my teachers have taught me remains inaccessible to me when I try to force things. Only when I open my senses, when I do not hold regrets of the past, or anxiety toward the future, can I respond to what actually unfolds in the present.

When we impose our plans upon life, when we force our intentions, we either respond too late and ineffectually, or we instantly feel the push back of life's reactions to our force. However, when we respond to the forces acting against us without emotional reaction to them, force cannot escalate because it has no fulcrum to leverage upon; in fact, it even defuses like trying to punch a lake, flowing around the strike.

*"Empty your mind. Be formless. Shapeless. Be like water, my friend,"* advised Bruce Lee.

Good things come to those who are patient. Better things come to those who refuse to give up.

But the best things come to those who compassionately respond to the forces they experience in life. When in doubt, wait. When you regain your courage, keep going. And when you hold your faith, let go and flow.

# WIN WITH DIGNITY

"Get the hell out of my way, Kid," yawped a meathead from across the room, as he shoved one of the junior athletes out of the way. He ran on to the mat, to stand across from me.

I asked, "Was that really necessary? He's only a kid. Be a role model."

My competitor scowled at me, "You have no idea who you're talking to, do you?"

No. I didn't. The ref called us in to shake hands, so I extended mine. My opponent slapped it away and laughed, "It's only going to take one takedown. Don't blink, Cupcake."

"Whoa. This guy's really full of himself," I thought. And then the whistle blew.

He was strong, explosive and aggressive. But he was so tense in grabbing my jacket that I could feel when he intended to shoot in before he did. Nothing mystical. Not really even an advanced level of sensitivity. It's just that ego walks through the door long before your body can react, because the tension telegraphs your intentions.

He'd shoot in, pushing me hard, trying to take me down to ground. He seemed too powerful and athletic for me to waste precious energy, in a long day of tournament fighting, to wrestle with him for ground submissions. So, whenever he shot in, I would marry his attack, pull him in even faster to over-commit, spin and wheel him across my legs. Over. And over. And over again.

He wasn't changing his tactic. So, even though I wasn't getting massive points for the throws, I kept whittling away at the scoreboard.

Frustrated, he grabbed both of my lapels and shook me, snarling. I laughed out loud at myself as my head shook like a bobble toy, because he was so strong. He snarled in anger, instead assuming that I was laughing at him, and seethed, "You're done punk."

With that he tried to lunge in even harder, more explosively and aggressively. But this only made my counter work more effectively, as I really wasn't using my own effort to throw him. It was all his.

Feet over head he went, landing on the ground once again as the ref blew the whistle, ending the match. Standing he threw his hands up at the referee yelling, "What the hell was that call ref?"

The referee pointed at the scoreboard: 12–0. Technical superiority: achieving 12 points greater than your opponent ends the match. My opponent again slapped my hand away yelling all of my, "P***y foot tripping isn't real wrestling. Real wrestlers dominate the ground."

He stormed off the mat, as the referee lifted my arm.

My coach walked over to me, and held his hand out in congratulations while looking around. He casually leaned in, saying, "You just beat an Olympic alternate from US Wrestling."

To be honest, if I had known who I was wrestling, I would have been very intimidated. I had been a terrible wrestler in school before I went to college. The match probably would have gone a COMPLETELY different direction if I had known I was facing one of the best wrestlers in the country, if not the world. But I didn't know anything, as he made sure to tell me.

Ironically, my ignorance allowed me to see his character, rather than his pedigree. As a result, I fought the man, not his record.

My coach was fond of saying, "Better to have a quiet victory, than a loud defeat." This event anchored that, for all of the times that I've been so clamorous in my own ambitions.

"Work hard quietly," he'd say, "and let your victories blow the trumpets for you."

# IF IT FEELS WRONG, IT IS WRONG

My Dozen Dating Rules (any future boy will need to know before dating my daughter) that I learned the hard way...

Avoiding trouble is difficult and getting into trouble is easy, when you're open to it. As a young man, having lost dramatic weight, and having earned a spot on the US National Team, I behaved like a reckless kid.

Once a few us snuck out into the city after lights-out, and found — as young kids do — a party. One of the girls from the team asked if I'd dance with her. We spent the entire night dancing, since neither of us were drinking, so with the noise, I didn't learn much about her. She finally pulled me aside and asked if I would walk her back to the dorms as it was nearly dawn, and her father would be waking soon.

"Father? Who's your father?" I stammered.

"Our coach," she smiled walking ahead pulling me by my hand. My feet felt the compulsion to run.

All thoughts evaporated when I realized my predicament. This was an amateur sport. I raised the money to travel with the team, working a third job on weekends. My mother had sacrificed an enormous amount of time and effort to help me get to regional, national and finally world championships.

And I go and throw it all away by sneaking out after curfew, and jeopardize everything by fraternizing with the girl's team; moreover, the coach's daughter. What had I done!?? Her father was going to kick me off the team before I had the chance to compete!

He had never gone to sleep. Instead he had gone to the police, who — since we were foreigners — had been scouring the streets to find us. So, he was rightly furious, when he saw me holding his daughter's hand.

The US Coach — the man who was for all intents and purposes in control of my destiny in the sport — pulled me inside and had "The Talk" with me. I remember each word, like crackling electricity on my ear drums.

"You," pointing at his daughter, "go to our room, and go to bed. I will deal with you later."

"Sonnon, sit down. I've got a dozen things to say to you."

1. If it feels like what you're about to do is wrong, don't do it. Listen to your morals. They're your navigator. You get lost without them.

2. When you're asked to do something you feel is wrong, speak up and say EXACTLY what you mean, in as few words possible, as clearly as you can.

3. Don't try to be a people pleaser or a herd follower. Leaders stand alone and are often NOT adored, because they speak up.

4. Trust your instincts. If it smells like crap, you don't need to taste it and rub it all over yourself, in order to avoid taking a step in it.

5. Never speak badly about yourself. So, never do those things that you'll regret and cause you to have negative things to say about yourself.

6. Never give up on your dreams, especially by making foolish decisions which will sabotage them. Is that clear enough?

7. Don't be afraid to say, "No," to things that you know will get you into trouble, even if everyone is doing it. You'll earn, not lose, respect by doing so.

8. Don't hesitate to say, "Yes," to the voice inside you asking you to stay focused on your dreams, even if no one else is.

9. Be kind to yourself; not nice. "Nice" means telling pretty little lies to make yourself feel better about the trouble you've caused. "Kind" means

you're speaking the candid truth to yourself even though it may be very uncomfortable to hear.

10. Let go of what you can't control. If you must break the rules which are enabling you to follow your dreams, in order to go do something foolish, then — let go of it. Foolishness is a distraction testing to see if you REALLY want your dreams, or if they're only fanciful wishes you don't deserve.

11. Stay away from drama. You're smart, sensible and aware. Knowing what will cause you drama is easy; getting into trouble is an avalanche. You can't out maneuver it once you're in it. So, just avoid or end it immediately.

12. Respect yourself and others enough to do the right thing, even when no one will ever know that you did. And don't do the wrong thing, even if no one will ever catch you doing it.

"Now, I don't want to see you speaking to my daughter again, until the championship is over, we are back at home, and you are calling her at our house to come over and meet her parents before a formal date. Until then, prove that you're man enough to deserve taking her out."

Years later, when I became US Coach, responsible for the tangled herd of mischievous puppies (which I once was), I recounted the same with them.

Now, looking at my beautiful blossom of a daughter at her recital, and hearing of their advance teams traveling to other countries for dance competitions, I think of my coach, and wonder if I would have had the same magnanimity, had I discovered someone with my daughter.

To honor my coach, and respect my daughter, I reflect upon this advice which has become such a plank holder in my morality as a man, coach and a father.

# DISRESPECT IS A SIGN OF WEAKNESS

"I'm not grappling a freaking cripple," the fighter said to me, looking at his opponent who was walking onto the mat with an unseen deformation of his right arm hidden in his jacket, and amputation of his right leg visible above the knee.

His opponent overheard him and, smiling, said to me, "Don't worry. I'll go easy on him."

As this was a weight classed sport, the missing mass of arm and leg allowed him to hold much more muscle mass in his body. Despite the missing limbs, he cast a shadow over his fully limbed opponent.

The coach of the smaller grappler ran over to me, complaining that it was an embarrassment to let a disabled grappler fight in the championship, especially against last year's champion (his athlete).

I told the coach to leave the mat or his fighter would be disqualified, since as an international official, I knew that there was nothing in the championship rulebook that would prohibit an amputee from competing.

I told both fighters to go to their blocks and shake hands. The bigger grappler held out his empty sleeve saying, "Sorry, can you give me a hand?" Reflexively, the other fighter reached out to help him before he realized the joke. I tried not to laugh, since as the official, I had to remain indifferent.

When I blew the whistle, the bigger grappler grabbed the jacket of his "fully abled" opponent, and snapped him powerfully down to the ground, as if he'd been wrestling a child. Though his opponent initially fell to his knees, losing no points, the big fighter spun around to his opponent's back, and back-mounting him, instantly rolled him over into an arm bar. All of this happened in 13 seconds, the fastest win by submission of the championship.

You don't have to disrespect others to justify your own position. It only shows the shakiness of your position. If you felt certain and confident in your position, no insults would be necessary.

My experience demonstrates that the body is incapable of lying. Somewhere, it screams the truth, no matter what the lips utter.

Others disrespect you because they silently want to share a vulnerability; because they secretly want you to provide a solution to their self-perceived weakness. If anything, the larger grappler, missing one arm, was the one who "gave a hand" to his opponent with the humbling experience that followed.

This is a matter of health for our body. As Loretta Lanphier, NP, CN, wrote, "The cells in your body react to everything your mind says. Negativity suppresses your immune system."

When someone insults and disrespects someone, even themselves, they begin to damage their own health. Therefore, we subconsciously seek out those people who will provide us with a positive alternative to our negative perspective ... especially if we are attacking them.

Like the larger fighter in my story, try not to take things personally, as what people say about you reflects upon them, not upon you. So you can tell more about people by what they say about others, rather than what others say about them.

Take pity and be merciful as you hold your space and keep your truth, but like the big grappler, humorous confidence in your own validity and competence may be precisely the solution to help even a would-be belligerent aggressor from their negative perspective.

# SHINE THE LIGHT ON YOUR IGNORANCE

I had never tapped before to a choke, but against my British Jiujitsu counter-part at the 2010 world games, his triangle had locked in, and I became lost in the wilderness, forced to submit.

The words of my yoga teacher, Amma, pass through my mind as I review my performance: *"Fixing the mind in each external action should proceed with attention; for without external alertness, internal alertness is not possible. Nothing should happen without your knowledge. Not even a single thought should go by without you being aware of it."*

So, therein the imperative: If something does happen without my awareness, go into that ignorance and illuminate it.

At the private dojo in his home, I approached Professor Scott Devine, the first American black belt in Brazilian Jiujitsu under Relson Gracie, with my ignorance.

"I feel like I cannot see it coming. The choke just appears. How can I counter it?"

He laughed and said, "If he sets it up, you can't counter it really, so don't let it happen."

Joking aside, he went on to explain all of the nuances that build into the structure of the choke.

"At first, everything in a dark basement seems dangerous, so you're all tense: move here, and you step into something, move there, and you step into something else. But little by little, you learn your way around, and you know what is coming before you step in it."

Henry Ford advised to not find fault, but a remedy. And like so many other ignorant areas in my past, I needed to remedy my lack of proper attention. When you're paying attention to the wrong thing, or too many things, the important ones literally disappear (this phenomenon is called "inattentive blindness" in coaching psychology).

I was blind to the set-up of the choke at the world games, because everything had seemed dangerous in the Brazilian Jiujitsu guard position. It seemed like one big mess in which I hadn't been able to differentiate the minutia as I could in other positions. When my opponent distracted my attention by going for one thing, he opened up another; his actual intention had remained invisible, until it was too late.

At first, it seems like one fighter is lying across the other, magically pinning him to the ground. Then, as you train, you learn that this "cross-mount" position has specific pressures to cage your opponent, all of which must be managed. After extended training, you become aware of the subtle weight transfers that expose freedom to reverse or sweep.

Once mastering the fundamentals, even minute nuances can be used to distract the opponent, causing him to believe he's in danger in one direction, and to become "blind" to the vulnerability in another, intended attack, until it's too late ... as my British counter-part had done at world games.

When you begin anything, the big things look ominous, and you can feel blindsided by surprises as distraction happens often. This can occur when you start a new nutrition plan, new exercise program, new entrepreneurial initiative, or even a new relationship. It happens even in activities you've been doing for awhile when you start going into a "deeper" connection with the activity. We all make mistakes, get blindsided and distracted by unimportant things.

But if we continue to practice, if we shift our attention to our ignorance, we start to see so much more hidden inside our blind spots. You weren't ignorant. You didn't have poor attention. You were attending in a different direction. Ask yourself what could have become invisible from focusing in another direction? Go find that.

When you get blind-sided, smile. You just found something remarkable. You've been given the chance to make the invisible known.

# HARNESS THE STRENGTH OF YOUR LEGION

The toughest grappler I ever fought was blind; fingers like impossible vices, senses superhuman, heightened by the removal of vision. He knew where you intended to move before you began, by interpreting even the slightest muscular anticipation.

I couldn't imagine how he could be so successful. Allowing me to tutor him by reading him his textbooks in exchange for teaching me more of his grappling, I asked him how he accomplished such a feat. He replied, "Because my opponents want to win, but I MUST win. For them, it's a sport. For me, it's my scholarship. When I step on the mat, I only have to face them and their doubts and fears. When they step on the mat, they must face ALL of my family's support and love and sacrifices to get me here with what little money they could contribute. It's simply a numbers game, and they're outnumbered by our necessity for me to earn my degree."

This left its mark upon me, and taught me why HOW I fought was as important to me as succeeding. Victory wasn't good enough. I needed betterment. I had to leave my fears and doubts at the edge of the mat, and be BETTER than I've ever been. That meant having faith in the long lineage of my coaches, and honoring them by giving something better than I had ever given before, something worth remembering.

Before I stepped on the world games mat against some of the best national champions from each of their respective countries, I repeated my mantra…

Though I step on this mat alone, you are outnumbered, for within me lies a Legion.

The strength of my global family gives me the courage to step into larger, more complex, and more chaotic challenges … to harness each more ominous resistance, and create confluence where there had been none.

Where I had once thought the battle was in defeating a perceived opponent, I now realize that it was in harvesting the love of a family within … for even the fears and doubts of my would-be opponents flee from that hearth of calm certainty.

As Abraham Lincoln said, *"Now, I destroy my enemies when I make them my friends."* As I share this discovery, and support the legion within each of us, resistance evaporates. No opponents. Only betterment.

# BODY, EMOTIONS INTERTWINE IN LANGUAGE

After many serious injuries, like having my neck and back broken, a common phenomenon appeared: a linguistic component to each injury.

With nearly every injury and illness, there was a story. And when I started coaching others, though I remained firmly in physical, non-therapeutic, training modality, I couldn't help but notice these self-organizing tendencies to have a verbal analogy to physical experiences.

Even changes in posture held this powerful language: Feeling someone is a pain in the neck, feeling a burden on your shoulders, being all choked up, stabbed in the back, unable to grasp the answer, like your heart is heavy, knots in your stomach, punched in the gut, kicked in the groin, unable to stand on your own two feet, buckling at the knees, backpedaling, tripping over your tongue — each of these common emotional expressions correlates to a physiological change.

I found it odd, curious and worthy of study. Though Western rationalism guides all my investigation of a topic, the dismissal of this phenomenon by clinical medicine compelled me to seek explanations in other cultural approaches.

In my travels, I have experienced many different traditions and disciplines that attempt to define it: *Ayurvedic* (Indian medicine) discusses the points called *Chakra; Zhong Yi* (Chinese Medicine) relates the meridian flow of *Qi;* Zdorovye (Slavic folk medicine) addresses the energies of Triglav, to name a few…

Returning to the USA, I found rational healing modalities such as osteopathy, cranial-sacral therapy, neuromuscular therapy, Rolfing, Somatics, applied kinesiology, and many others had developed rational explanations for this phenomenon.

I am not a healer. I am not a doctor. I am simply a coach who listens and learns. When I listen, the person tells me a story with very strong verbal cues of how their movement has become dominated by an issue. As long as they don't have an issue needing referral to a health care professional, I aid them in restoring the lost movement beneath that stored emotional event.

When we address the physical, we often begin to re-experience the type and strength of the emotions they describe, in an area of bound movement. Having overcome my childhood obesity, abuse for my learning disabilities and trauma from violent encounters, and working with many like me, I prepare for the body's reactions before they happen. And I listen when it erupts into language.

Physical injuries and traumas, illnesses and diseases, as well as emotional, psychological and spiritual issues, come at a cost to movement. If we believe in a holistic approach to wellness, we cannot deny the interconnectedness of movement, language and emotions with healing and recovery. When you restore lost movement, correct poor posture, overwrite ineffective breathing patterns, remember to give yourself extra time to untangle hidden events that may be layered into an immobility. Now, I am not saying that everyone needs a therapist. On many issues, if we just listen to ourselves and learn from what it teaches us, we can work it all out on our own. But sometimes we could use a little support (and other times, a lot).

Talk to someone about it. You're not crazy. You don't need to be paralyzed by it either, because it seems that sometimes, simply talking through it expedites its resolution. Male culture often doesn't allow us to discuss such topics for being too "touchy-feely," just like female culture often can feel the need to protect against violation of trust.

If we are given a safe space in confidence, it can give us a chance to disclose. If you can't start with a therapist or find an appropriate doctor, then ask a trusted colleague or confidant their opinion of the right professional to whom they can refer you.

And keep moving, daily. Most of this works itself out through gentle mobility, intense exercise and compensatory stretching. Drink extra water. Eat clean, simple meals of whole, organic, fresh, rare and raw food. Sleep well. Skip the alcohol, painkillers, sugar, dairy and grains. And you may discover that 85 percent of the issues resolve themselves.

# TAKE 3 STEPS TOWARD RECOVERY

When I contracted a flesh-eating bacteria named MRSA from a grappling mat, my very active immune system attacked it, and covered it with a waxy, protective coating. Unfortunately, the bacteria began to leech out into my system, causing dangerously high fevers, excruciating pain and toxic shock.

By the time we had discovered that the boil on my back was MRSA, we were in a medical Emergency Room, having it extracted by scalpel with no time for even any anesthesia. Despite the explosive eruption which resulted for the three following days, creating a biohazard of my strictly quarantined room, the severe adverse side effects of decolonizing the superbug by using sulfa antibiotics destroyed me. Anorexia and perpetual nausea evacuated 36 pounds in three months.

How I recovered, regained that lean muscle loss, and transformed from the riddled symptoms and fallout, must begin by answering the question:

WHAT IS RECOVERY?

Recovery emerged from the expertise of health care professionals, involving the elimination of negative symptoms, restoration of lost function and re-establishment of healthy vitality. Many of us have expertise and lived experience with injury, illness, pain and disease, including that from disuse, overuse and misuse of our bodies. So, in order to define recovery, we must begin by acknowledging the WIDE array of mental, emotional and spiritual effects before, during and after we recuperate from our immediate circumstances.

Recovery, then, must consider and accommodate the deeply personal and individually unique process of changing attitudes, values, feelings, behaviors, plans, back-up plans and back-up-back-up skills throughout our lifestyle. It includes a way of living a flexible but fulfilled, optimistic but truthful life of service and contribution to society, even while within the limitations of our injuries, illnesses, pains and diseases.

## Recovery Step #1: Develop a Positive Identity

Our first step in recovery must incorporate a positive identity outside of our injury, illness, pain or disease. What elements hold vital importance to you? It will change from person to person, and from one period of life to the next. Deciding how to prioritize your focus will help you establish the appropriate rhythm of your recovery. One person's condition will have a different rhythm than the next person; and one condition will have a different rhythm than another of the same person's conditions.

I set my focus upon service to others. By focusing on service to others, I regained the ability to increase my own consistency of performing my recovery methods, compassion for my long-term recovery process, and confidence in my attitude toward all of the fumbles and foibles along the way. For you, it could be the same, or about family, about God, or about your inner will and spirit. But you must set it upon the highest purpose in your life.

If you make your goal only to mitigate and endure the injury, illness, pain or disease, you can be derailed by any of the seemingly endless obstacles, setbacks and pitfalls that appear on the road to recovery. Set it high, and keep aiming there; the journey will make sense when you have a direction.

## Recovery Step #2: Framing the Condition

The second step involves establishing a clear, positive meaning to frame the experience of your injury, illness, pain or condition. This includes making sense of the experience so that it can be held in a digestible box: framed as part of who we are, but not defining all of us as a whole person. It may have nothing to do with a professional diagnosis, and could be a spiritual or existential crisis which we are overcoming; or it could be as simple as recognizing the formal name of our condition.

For example, MRSA taught me humility so that I could better respect and appreciate the complexities of our wellness. I had good sleep, rest, nutrition (and hydration), active recovery, intense exercise and stress management skills. With all of those attributes combined, I shouldn't be able to get sick or injured, ill or be in pain, I had thought. MRSA taught me to realize that these are only contributors to our future recovery. They're not necessarily prevention, though they can be.

Some health challenges will come. When they do, having our recovery methods available, reclaiming them when they're not, and coordinating them when we are missing elements, all factor into our total process. Without having had MRSA bring me so close to death, I would have never been able to reframe my view on the diversity of lifestyle wellness, and appreciate the complexities of life.

Sometimes we can compartmentalize our condition without any psychological or emotional seepage, and remain unaffected, simply going through the recovery process unimpeded. When we can, that is great. But in some cases, like that of myself and MRSA, we need to create some positive attitudinal framework — whether others believe in our assignment of meaning to it holds objective validity or not; it helps us appreciate the purpose of our recovery, and the value it will bring others through our self-development.

**Recovery Step #3: Self-Developing from the Condition**
Framing our injury, illness, pain or disease provides a context in which it becomes one of life's opportunities to self-develop from our condition. Some professionals call this post-habilitative self-care. But it extends far beyond the conclusion of our physician's rehabilitation.

We are much more than a physical body. Your body isn't considering these words, but your beautiful mind is. What do you imagine could result from your recovery? What could you do? Are you willing to address ALL of your process, including the psychological components?

Your body isn't experiencing these ideas, but your sophisticated architecture of emotions certainly is. How does it make you feel to recover from your condition? How would it? What would it feel like to shift from disempowerment to empowerment?

Your body isn't willing you to apply these principles, but your pulsating, energizing spirit is. How powerful is your will to recover? What could you do if you restored your willpower completely? How powerful would you be then? What life could you bring to others who are suffering, because of your courageous will to recover?

I don't suggest that you must do everything on your own. But understanding your own physical self-care, and your mental, emotional and spiritual self-care begins with you. If you truly orient your compass to offer your contributions to society, to serve others, your community, your family and God, believe in and build up yourself. We not only want you to be well, but we need you to be. Get going.

When I was recovering from MRSA, I felt embarrassed, humiliated and ashamed that I would expose my family to an agonizing and potentially mortal risk. My willpower drained as I fell into pity, self-loathing and lethargy. My very existence had become a threat to my own children! But then I initiated the 3 Steps:

1. I developed a positive identity about my recovery and realized that although I may not have known it at the time, there had been a purpose that could help me better serve others.

2. I framed my disease as an opportunity to expand my understanding of wellness and recovery, and to establish steps which could improve my condition and keep others from falling prey to the same situation.

3. I took care of myself and used the opportunity to improve as a whole person: not merely my body, but to improve my awareness, to lift up my attitude to create an environment conducive to healing and wholeness, and to spiritually energize all of my activities so that my recovery process became infused with gratitude and love for life and those around me.

I healed. I fully recovered, and am now stronger than ever in my life. But I have to tell you something. If you don't follow the above steps, NO recovery methods will ever help (whether you think they're working or not). You must first have the positive identification, framework and care. If you trust me, then allow me the privilege of sharing with you the methods my teachers shared with me.

Best wishes on your path, and if you ever get lost, confused, or exhausted, remember the three steps above ... and you'll find your way again. I believe in you, even if you do not.

# BALANCE THE WARRIOR AND THE YOGI

Perhaps you're more enlightened than I am. But in the event that this can help you as it has me, I'd like to share a lesson I learned from my teacher, Sri Mata Amritanandamayi Devi (or "Amma"), who gave me the honor of my Sanskrit name (accepting me as a formal student) over these 10 years of studying devotional yoga with her.

For years, I've wanted to ask Amma a very important question (to me) during the open forum Q&A sessions at our annual retreats. But with hundreds and thousands of other people there suffering deep emotional and physical torment, I held my tongue in order to not disturb their healing process. The shaved head, the tattoos, the fighter's build … I already stand out among these gentler folk.

This year, my question was answered:

What is a righteous fight?

I've invested 20 years in my formal martial art education, 30 years in combat sports.

I didn't do this for glory. Initially, it was just so I could keep myself from the daily harm and humiliation I endured. Imperceptibly, my training evolved into a form of personal development, to continue my transformation — physically, but also mentally, emotionally, even spiritually.

Without any reservation, I can say that martial art has done more than save my life, it has given me Quality of Life … and continues to increase that Quality with each day of deepening practice.

The more I mastered my movement, the less force I required to keep myself from harm, until I started to realize that the responsibility of mastery also meant minimizing harm to my opponents. How little harm was required to cease their aggression? It was easy to see in sport: I wasn't in better "condition" than my opponents, I just used much less energy than they did to accomplish much more than they intended. This "minimum harm — maximum benefit" maxim eventually leeched out into altercations, confrontations, even verbal arguments.

I've always been a spiritual person, but when frightened for safety, it never crossed my mind to try to help an aggressor. I just wanted to get away. But I am "away" now.

I am practically invisible to violence, even with the marginal areas and high speed groups that I train. So, over the past 7–8 years, I've found my spiritual awareness increasing … or should I say, an increased awareness of my spiritual under-development.

I've come to the point that I'll do anything, everything, possible to prevent harm to others, including placing myself in harm's way, because, frankly, I know I can absorb significantly greater force (with little to no damage) than others can, thanks to my teachers and my daily practice.

I remember very clearly June of 1995, training an MMA fighter for his next event (back then called "NHB"). He would thrash and twist, and I tried to calm him down, explaining that while rolling he needed to relax and minimize his energy output.

As I was holding him in a heel hook, but not applying any force, he started to flail back and forth. He rolled us onto our sides, and quickly darted the opposite direction. Because my arm was pinned on the floor, I couldn't release the hold in time. He snapped ligaments in his knee, shredding them audibly like a balloon exploding. He had four kids, worked as a carpenter as his livelihood, and was now hobbled for life. I didn't compete for two years after that, because I kept hearing the echo of that POP every time I touched a leg.

# ENTER THE YOGI

For the past decade, I've formally practiced Hatha yoga, even though I had been practicing a Russian variant for years before that. During that time, my inner experience of movement continued to refine, like a microscope changing lenses to see ever deeper into the tiny obscurities of my structure, my breath and my motions.

I found myself wanting to prevent the possibility of doing anyone harm. I just couldn't fathom causing the emotional and physical turmoil that I faced. Had I become what had terrorized my childhood? Perhaps, you as my reader would think this silly even to consider, but you need to have experienced what I had as a kid to appreciate the contempt with which I hold violence.

I hope you can appreciate my need to know from my yoga teacher: Was my fighter aspect now in conflict with my spiritual development, and if so, what should I do?

Teaching others, am I perpetuating the hazing?

Of course, martial art is not about fighting; fighting is the medium to learning how to fight less — the better you become, the less you actually fight. But is there a point in personal mastery where you must relinquish the path altogether?

Honestly, I was nearing the bile-lifting point, teaching others how to be prepared for a fight (the tactical / functional conditioning), as well as teaching security, counter-terrorism and law enforcement personnel the actual skills. Wasn't this an offense to my aspirations for peace? Now, perhaps you're a more enlightened person than I was, and immediately see through this dilemma. But for me, it was a process unfolding …

The more gentle folk immediately had conflict resolution advice for me … and yet when observing them in confrontations, they folded like tissue into whimpering victims. Living truth requires courage, I had learned. Soft words are only powerful when you have a hard hand to back it up.

The more aggressive folk had a more Earth-locked pragmatism, believing that exclusively a more heavily armed and armored society ensured peace. But too often, I saw these individuals tyrannically imposing their will upon others with an ad baculum "might makes right" position that turned my stomach. It wasn't peace they created, but a quiet war upon those who differed from their perspective.

I felt patronized by the gentle folk for my fighter nature, and ridiculed by the aggressors for my spiritual aspirations.

And then … my teacher.

Any time I think that I had a rough childhood with my physical and learning disabilities, with my impoverishment and abuse, Amma's story comes to me: facing rape, public beatings, giving away the meager food she did have in her village home … and having physically embraced and counseled over 26 million people.

Dr. Jane Goodall, while presenting Amma with the 2002 Gandhi-King Award for Non-Violence, said, *"She stands here in front of us. God's love in a human body."*

At this retreat, my teacher gave the following Three Steps for Addressing Violence:

Physically remove yourself from the spot. Run, move, shut the door or hang up the phone. Just leave until the emotional heat dissipates (if ever). Okay, no problem. I can run faster, farther than most people, even while carrying my kids. I've learned to remove myself from the escalation before its tipping point (and can continue to improve there).

If you can't leave and they persist, then speak your truth and try to reach the heart of divinity which is within every person. Appeal to their divine nature. I've studied conflict resolution techniques such as "Verbal Judo" among others, but this was something deeper. You actually have to give a shit, and reach across the void — through the fog of your frustration or fear — and call to the greatness within an individual who has temporarily "lost it."

If they follow you, insisting on your persecution, get angry. Anger is healthier than sadness, because it takes corrective action. The gentle folk laughed uncomfortably at this guidance, but my mouth was hanging open, as if suddenly I had a place in this peaceful society. If a deer comes and eats your garden, you can't reason with it; you pick up a stick and threaten it. Though … for me, this begged the question, what if the deer calls your bluff. (Okay, so maybe not a deer, but you know what I mean.)

Then, came the answer. Though addressing the massive crowd of students, she looked over at me, as if she knew how this problem vexed me in particular. She offered the story of Krishna appearing to Arjuna on the battlefield …. written in the Mahabharata.

Arjuna, a fighter and leader, on the very day his people were facing annihilation by an invading army, decided to become a monk to avoid violence. Lord Krishna appeared to Arjuna, not because he was spiritually developed enough to deserve it, but strictly from compassion for the impending massacre of Arjuna's people. Krishna told Arjuna that his duty to protect the innocent overrides any offense to his spiritual aspirations, "Remember the divinity within each of us and fight!"

My mouth dropped.

You see, it was this part that had plagued me. Was it more enlightened to visit violence upon those who persisted in persecuting the innocent, or in removing yourself completely from the violence altogether?

Again, perhaps you're more enlightened than I was. But for me, in this wisdom, my fighter and my yogi were finally wed: If persecutors do not cease hostilities even when threatened, your duty to protect the innocent from harm overrides any spiritual aspirations of personal non-violence.

I'm not suggesting this imperative applies to you. I am a fighter, trained by some of the brightest and best coaches in the world. If I've exhausted all other options of peace, and imminent jeopardy looms upon innocents, then even if harming others repulses me, I'm morally obligated to do so (until such a time that those hostiles cease their aggressive advance).

I must be courageous enough to face the specters that may come from causing harm to others, if urgent necessity demands. But better that I do this than the gentle folk who don't have my training and aptitude, and better that I do this than the aggressive folk who lack the restraint and mastery to use the most minimal force necessary.

Keeping God in my heart, compassion for even those lost in the fog and friction of violence, I've learned my duty to fight when circumstances leave no option. And I can do so knowing that I can look in my teacher's eyes without guilt. Certainly not pride, but definitely not guilt.

My duty as a fighter found a place of ease living next to my nature as a yogi. … Perhaps, it took me 40 years to grasp this realization, but I do own it now. And hopefully, this wisdom will be of use to you as well.

# REFRAME SUFFERING WITH EMPATHY

My teacher sat at the front of a line of thousands. I watched her for hours, as each student and each of their families would receive a sympathetic, adoring hug from her, and she effortlessly refreshed between each audience she gave. Hours turned to days, and I would pass out from fatigue, only to awaken with her still as fresh as the morning, continuing to sit, talk and hug the endless line of people needing her help and support.

How did she do it? I was a world champion athlete with perfect nutritional mapping, at the height of my endurance, and yet my stamina paled in comparison.

Each of her departing students would walk by me carrying the swirling intoxication of roses. Fascinated, I paid closer attention, and surely, with each tear-filled face, and every beaming blissed-out smile, came the hint of rose pedal.

Finally entering the line myself, I looked forward to asking my teacher the question I had been harboring for too long: the searing pain of my broken neck, causing lightning pain to continually shoot down my arm, unable to sit, incapable of moving, devoid of power. Did she have a recommendation on a doctor for healing it?

Person by person the line diminished between us, and the aroma wafted across the hall. And finally my moment arrived ... and passed. My agonizing question disappeared as I sat with her. With only a handful of minutes to speak with her personally each year, amongst the millions of her students worldwide, I could only manage to sit in my silence, and receive my embrace. She said to me, "You can be in pain, but need not suffer," and she touched my neck.

She continued, "Pain is a part of your job and your life, but you can be free of suffering from it."

As I left her, a cloud surrounded me, but not my eyes, not my mere emotions. How could I not suffer this constant pain? Her fragrance abided though, infused by her hug. Walking back to my children, I gave them a hug, and they dashed away.

Returning to my position running the protection team, I went about my work happily, not realizing that I had been relieved of suffering my painful neck.

Later, my children ran back to where I stood post, and grabbed my pant legs asking me to come eat with them. As I knelt to explain that I couldn't leave my position quite yet, I noticed the smell of roses. Then I realized as Gandhi once said, *"The fragrance remains in the hand that gives the rose."*

We are, each of us, facing a death sentence. The greatest gift of my unsafe childhood came from the ubiquitous awareness of that impending conclusion. The blinking rapidity of a hundred years is too soon to die, and most of us do not have that long. For much of our lives, we will endure physical pain, but emotionally and psychologically, we need not suffer it.

There is a difference between pain and suffering: The former exists, but the latter only reflects upon the former.

We commit such atrocities to ourselves and to others in our suffering. It clouds our vision and numbs our awareness to the harm we plod trampling delicacies. Realizing this creates intense and enduring empathy for our common plight. We all face the same ignorance. We each endure the same pain. To my own, my teacher had given me an answer: When discouraged, encourage others; when empty, fill with love for helping another's plight.

As another day clicks by, one less — one gone, have I wasted it on my own suffering or have I invested it in lessening the suffering of those I touch? As Albert Pike advised, *"What we have done for ourselves alone dies with us; what we have done for others and the world remains and is immortal."* What we do for our own avoidance of pain and desire for pleasures evaporates with our fleeting, fickle thoughts; but what we do for others, abides, lingering like a rose from hand to hand.

> *"Beginning today, treat everyone you meet as if they were going to be dead by midnight. Extend them all the care, kindness and understanding you can muster. Your life will never be the same again."* ~ Og Mandino

# MY MOUNTAIN TO CARRY

"Stand like a mountain," advised the woman who has physically touched more people than anyone in the history of humankind.

For many years I had remained on the exterior of the humanitarian community led by Sri Mata Amritanandamayi Devi, whom her students call "Amma." But through her example, embracing tens of thousands of people in front of my eyes, without seeming to fatigue, with a glitter of recognition in each hug she gave the endless stream of people coming to see her, I began to be pulled to service, first working on her personal security team, and eventually as the lead security coordinator.

Her advice appeared to run opposite of my life's experience. If anything my life until that point could have been summed up as, "flow like a river," not stand like a mountain!

As a child, I had rolled with the pounding of ceaseless beatings. As a young adult, I had absorbed the troubles challenging my goals to transcend my impoverished, learning "disabled" circumstances. As a father and husband, I have cultivated the surrender of my egoic desires for those delicate, beautiful souls who depend upon my lifting us from economic squalor into financial stability. My very career had been built upon pioneering this niche discipline of "flow fitness."

Standing like a mountain seemed to erode my strength, as the crushing tidal waves of resistance bashed into my shores. When she advised me that I needed to compassionately but courageously hold my space, I felt unqualified.

Why she asked this of me, and how it manifested, changed my life.

Amma had given me the spiritual name, "Kailash" after several years as her student, and talked about the origin. Mount Kailash, found in a lotus shaped mountain range within Tibet, was the home of Hindu's Shiva in Indian mythology.

Having received my spiritual name by a truly enlightened teacher, who many call a saint for her exhaustive humanitarian efforts, I felt greatly obligated to study its implications. The name Kailash could be understood as "vessel of pure consciousness." Named so, I had been advised by the Swamis that my essence represented the strength to hold a calling higher than worldly life — IF I could remove my ego from congesting this vessel.

That was a BIG "if"!

My ego had spent a lifetime buffeted inside that vessel. Thrown by the trauma of events, I had learned to go with the flow to avoid harm in my life. And when I had tried to stand against that tide, I had always failed to hold my ground.

*"You must resist the flow in life, if you encounter an injustice or a danger to others or yourself,"* Amma advised at one of the lectures.

She had provided me with an opportunity to transcend my prior failures when she placed me in charge of her security. Accepting the position thinking it was another "bodyguard" job, very few violent encounters had needed to be resolved. I only later discovered that she had been the one guarding me by bringing me close to her and giving me a position where I could learn compassion.

I stood on stage with her while a crowd of sleep-deprived, under-nourished students — after days of round-the-clock events — pushed the steps to get one final glance from her before she returned to India. Whenever the rare emotionally challenged individual stormed the stage, we escorted them off so that their impulsivity did not threaten the peace of the event. So my team lined the stage to catch these stragglers and help them to the exterior rooms.

That's when I saw her: An elderly woman in the middle of the crowd had not been able to stand up, right before the audience would be exiting. In the traffic of hundreds she would be trampled, and appeared incapable of escaping the impending threat. Radioing my team to fill my position, I jumped off the stage and wove through the masses until I could get to her, but it was too late. The massive crowd began to surge directly toward us.

Standing, I turned and outstretched my arms to create a shield over the fallen woman ... And they came. Unable to realize the import of their actions, most of the crowd pushed into us, and I struggled to hold space over her body. These were not violent people, quite the opposite: They were loving admirers of a woman who has physically embraced more people than anyone in the history of the world. Their immense grief at her departure mixed with their intense physical challenges caused some of them to be ignorant of the danger they posed to this fallen member of their community.

Isn't this a metaphor for life? Most of the harm we bring to others is not in wanton apathy, but in ignorance created through our unaware state. I could argue that violence originates from ignorance of our own potential, our innate divinity.

I could have used more aggressive skills to keep her protected, but it would be antithetical to the compassionate awareness of our impact upon others and ourselves. So, I did my best to part the flow around the woman's body. Suddenly, there was a break in the crowd, and I radioed two of my team, who jumped down and scooped up her body. While I kept parting the flow, they helped her to safety.

Afterward, I reflected upon that event, the nature of the community ethically restricting my actions, compelling me to use higher application of skills to not harm those ignorant of the threat their lack of awareness posed to others, and — standing my ground — compel them to flow around me to avoid unwittingly trampling a victim in their lack of awareness.

Finally I had realized what it meant to stand like a mountain, resisting the flow of ignorance and lack of awareness to protect innocents from hazards, in myself.

I strive to work on this nearly every day. Each new circumstance in which I'm placed, I find myself being given an opportunity to keep silent and just go with the flow of some injustice. But I've been given a chance to voice my disagreement with these events, even if it makes me unpopular.

We are all called to a higher purpose. When we hear that calling, we gain the responsibility to act. I had been conditioned during my early life to just go with the flow. But I've come to discover sometimes ... To be authentically aligned to our values, we must resist it.

# PREPARE FOR THE DECISIVE MOMENT

Pulling my baseball cap over my eyes, I snuck away to train, as I usually do. Without my morning and evening workouts, I often suffer pain, fatigue, memory loss and diminished capacity to perform my responsibilities.

But, perhaps counter-logically, if I do these two workouts, I feel zero pain, have great endurance and stamina, clear focus and rapid cognitive function even on 18-hour days (an incredible feat for me, if you know my background).

Despite being in the corner of the gym, I was noticed by one of the tour staff of the event I was working.

"Aren't you, Kailash, the bodyguard? I remember you from last year when you saved that old lady."

My teacher had given me the name "Kailash" as her student. She believes that I can live up to it, which I continually doubt, but strive to execute. It was explained to me that it means, "the mountain on earth which holds sight of God." My teacher said, as a result, I have spent my life and would spend my life attempting to hold my values against the pressures of the world to lower standards.

As head of her security team, one year, my teacher ominously foretold that I would learn what it means to be "Kailash."

Two days later, I had to dive into a massive crowd that had begun trampling an elderly woman. Despite being a professional fighter and fitness athlete, the weight of hundreds of bodies threatened to crush us both as I wedged over the woman until the crowd passed. Protecting the poor woman, who was unable to move or stand, felt impossible, until the danger passed.

I learned that day what my teacher meant when she told me, "Be Kailash."

The young man at the gym asked me, "How do you train to prepare for those kind of situations?"

I replied, "Constantly."

It's a principle that some on both sides of the spectrum often misunderstand.

Si vis pacem, para bellum is a Latin adage translated as, "If you want peace, prepare for war." It is usually interpreted as meaning, "if you want to have peace, you must be appear so strong that enemies will avoid attacking you."

But it is often mutated into, si vis pacem, fac bellum — "for peace, wage war."

On the other side of the spectrum, many of my pacifist friends believe si vis pacem, para pactum — "if you want peace, agree to peace."

Unfortunately, agreeing to peace does not help when ignorant of the harm we bring to others, like the crowd into which I dove to protect the fallen elderly woman. Not everyone agrees, as well. I've had to remove knives and guns from people who had not made the agreement to peace. Sometimes, you have to be prepared, even if you'd prefer peace.

Pacifism may work for some, but not for me. However, neither does warmongering. I prefer understanding and responsiveness over the binary twins of war and peace, which are linguistically incapable of existing without each other. If I understand the other, or seek to truly understand the other, I can better respond to what has caused their ignorant aggressions. Similarly, if I seek to understand others, I must bring awareness to the blind ignorance I still suffer, and illuminate them with my attention and discipline to remain awake.

Sometimes, you must act to stop violence, even if such action offends your spiritual sensibilities, as it does mine.

At the gym, the young man said to me, "Wow, what you do seems so cool. I'm just an artist."

I said to him that my daughter wants to be a performance artist when she grows up, and I shared with him the words of Thomas Jefferson, "We are fighters, so our children may be farmers, so theirs may be artists." I told him how I couldn't imagine a world without my daughter's art. It would be as broken and battered as I am.

When I find myself where I could wait for others stronger than myself to face a difficult situation, or when I find myself where I could reduce myself into ignorance as well, I imagine all of those who could come after me who might benefit from the one choice to stand like a mountain. I imagine my daughter and my son, and theirs.

It is HOW we fight which defines us, which distinguishes whether we can stand like a mountain and hold up our virtues to the skies of divinity, or whether we slip into the abyss of our petty toxicities. If you want to hold your peacefulness, some must be prepared for the force of ignorant hostility. However, everyone will be challenged emotionally to reduce to rage, to walk down the mountain of virtue, and swim in the very ignorance we seek to overcome.

To be the mountain, you must stand-under. Only through understanding can you truly respond to hostile encounters and keep your peace inside. It will never, ever be easy, I've learned. However, every time that you resist reducing yourself, and each time that you courageously place yourself in the face of that force, you will grow stronger. You will be capable of holding your peace against tougher forces, for longer, and against more complex conditions.

If you find that you can fight for an important cause in protecting others, including yourself, be the mountain and keep your sight on God.

# EMBRACE PRESSURE TO DEFUSE IT

I hadn't quite understood why Amma made me the lead of her security team, until I felt the tidal pressure of the crowd.

They were just people, not with malicious intent, but with distracted attention, unaware of the dangerous implications of their pressure to the young, or the infirm among them.

I discussed with my people how we could create institutional change within the event by our attitude, presence and demeanor. We could change the entire experience of the audience by how we embraced the pressure of the crowd.

When you feel pushed over — pull.

It's a simple principle taught to us from day one in martial art. If you attempt to drive back, after pressure hits you, the transition often places you on your heels, pushing you over. Even if we could keep your feet grounded, the counter-pressure would escalate the crowd's energy and transform them from distracted attention to focused aggression.

However, when you feel the pressure, if you embrace it into your center, the force redirects around you. Absorb the force into yourself, and you turn it around.

When you act as a team, those with you help to maintain a positive attitude toward the pressure. By doing so, you not only prevent emotional escalation, you often defuse and deescalate it, by calling the crowd's awareness back into the consequence of having lacked attention. It becomes a teachable moment for us all when our attention meets each other in that brief moment.

That engagement, that very fleeting event of connecting awareness, has become my practice. I train to hold neither weight nor grudge, neither opponent nor opinion, but rather to hold my practice. All of our nutrition, hydration, exercise, meditation and prayer, all organizes around this practice of connection: to feel the pressures of the world, and have the strength to avoid pushing back, and instead, pull them in.

I try to do this with my writing as well: To connect with you for a moment, so that our conjoined attention can improve our energy, attitude and effect for the rest of our day.

Force only begets force, and escalates quickly out of control. But if you have the courage in the moment of feeling the push, to turn your awareness toward the pressure, and PULL it to you, you can affect your entire experience, and the energy of everyone you touch in that one brief moment of connection.

# SPEAK AGAINST INJUSTICE, EVEN AT YOUR RISK

For over a decade, I have withheld a story of my past, and virtually excised a major figure in my history out of embarrassment.

He had been the national team coach for my sport when I began it. I had spent years traveling with him as one of the US Team athletes and coaches.

His verbal abuse, we accepted as part of a "tough love" campaign common among some wrestling circles, but the torture we'd receive when he became enraged at us abided in our psyche like whipped puppies.

We were young adults ourselves, but there were those quite younger than us on the espoir and cadet teams, which caused us some protective concerns. Something always felt "off" to us, but due to a history of abuse, my tolerance level for this sort of behavior was skewed.

One day, the allegations came forth, launched by the courage of one of the younger teammates living in the coach's house under his guardianship. The sordid story unraveled quickly: The allegations led to a court hearing, and the coach attempted to flee the country. Fortunately, he was caught, pled guilty and was sentenced to prison for his crimes of sexual abuse and child pornography.

My teammate demonstrated courage at great physical risk against a trusted guardian and national team coach. Imagine the period of time between alleged actions and guilty plea, of being a young child facing someone who was supposed to keep you safe, but had abused you beyond comprehension.

Sometimes, speaking your truth does not bring you immediate peace, but severe personal danger. But as I have come to learn as well, the truth does heal you, and sets you free. The courage to speak your truth is victory enough, but when it feels that exposing the truth has not brought instant justice to a misdeed, remember ... eventually Karma says, "I saw that."

Have no fear that Final Judgment will inevitably come, and pity those who commit such misdeeds, for the consequences hold ultimate severity.

Speaking your truth is the real triumph and personal vindication against accepting unjust lies upon your shoulders. Stand up. Speak out. And never be silenced by fear of intimidation, violence or shame.

# UNDERSTAND THE ROLE OF PAIN IN TRAINING

In the 17th century, René Descartes hypothesized that pain transmits from an injury to the mind, like a rope pulled to ring a bell. Severing the mind from the body, Descartes' theories still proliferated as beliefs. Descartes thought, *"I think therefore I am,"* (*cogito ergo sum*). Pain was just a bodily event, while his mind, a disconnected "ghost in the machine."

Those of us who have faced severe injuries know pain overrides the mind. If anything, "I hurt; therefore, I am not" (*morsus ergo non sum*).

Unlike the belief that the nervous system works like a telegraphed wire, your brain controls pain signals via specific "gates." Gate control has proven over 40 years of research that your brain can influence the generation of all pains.

Pain elicits sensory responses, thoughts and emotions, which have an integrated impact upon you. It is individual, even when the stimulus is not. Though we cannot know exactly what someone else feels, our brains mirror what we perceive in the pain of others, which is the neurophysiological basis for our empathy.

After breaking my back and neck in competition, I knew only searing hot painful movement, which dominated almost every waking moment and left me without restful sleep. It makes me well acquainted with what others actually experience when pain competes for performance, so all of my protocols cater to those of us who actually overcome pain.

Unfortunately, most training approaches assume that you have no pain.

One of the most significant milestones in my career came when a major federal law enforcement agency concluded its second academy class using TACFIT as its official physical training system. Tracking all data, we defeated prior PT approaches on EVERY performance-related test.

The potential reason why: In the history of the agency, never before had there been zero training-related injuries during an academy class. Yet our first two (out of two) training classes ended with ZERO training injuries. This has huge implications.

TACFIT also proved greater average improvement across all performance-related tests than the three prior non-TACFIT classes combined:

- An average increase of 1 pushup (without training max pushups).

- Increase of 4 sit-ups (without training sit-ups at all).

- Increase of one-half inch of flexibility.

But here's the biggest, and most exciting: both TACFIT classes averaged improvement over one minute faster in the 1.5 mile run than the prior classes … WITHOUT RUNNING. We do no running in TACFIT. And all of the significant hours we saved from not running were used for increasing practice time with tactical skills.

Anyone who argues that carry-over and transferability doesn't exist, now have become silent. Better, stronger, faster with no injuries. TACFIT.

Thank you to all of the recruits for their tenacity, to all of the instructors for their diligence, all of the supervisors for their guidance, and to all of the chiefs for their foresight. It has been an honor to watch you make such institutional change from within to create a healthier, better federal agent.

If we look at gate control of pain, pain trumps performance. Perhaps TACFIT is so successful NOT because it involves superior exercises, but because RECOVERY has been woven as the primary attribute of fitness.

How do you recover from pain and injury so that you can perform immediately, as well as eventually? How do you organize a training protocol so that it maximizes the clear signal of precision by minimizing pain? Make recovery king.

Be prepared to overcome pain, but make wise, informed decisions regarding when it is worthwhile doing so, and when it is not. Take an active role in your healing process. You are the physician, and doctors, trainers and therapists are merely educated cheerleaders for your healing process.

Hang On Pain Ends.

# EXHALE, AND LET THE HEALING BEGIN

"JUST STOP! I'm f-ing tired of your g-damned stupid fantasies!! They just won't come true, Scott! I don't want to hear about it anymore. I want a normal life, with a normal boyfriend, going to normal parties. When you realize that, maybe you could grow up and forget about all this nonsense," surmised the girl I had been dating at the time in university.

My ideas have always afflicted me. I don't try to create them. For many years, I hadn't wanted them. But they're no less valid than emotions, which sublimate to consciousness without control.

So, when the girl I had trusted, and whose opinion I most valued, had derogated my ideas, I experienced a reflexive clutching in my heart. She had crushed me.

Granted, since I was a child, I had been told that I was "abnormal" — by doctors, by teachers, by peers and family. But, when you let down your guard, and trust someone to take care of your heart, the blade can pierce the deepest.

People can't change your truth, but your truth can change people. I've channeled these crazy ideas of mine into programs, tools, techniques and technologies to help people heal themselves, grow healthily strong, and live their days exuberantly (and unapologetically) with ALIVENESS.

Helping others grows the heart; and although I can still be hurt by those close to me by a heartless word, I now recognize what eventually killed my father. His heart disease, where doctors had claimed it to be congenital, resulted from the slow cannibalization of his spirit, the overwhelming burden of his choices eroding his life.

After not seeing him for many years, he appeared at my school, and his first words to me were ones, yet again, of hurtful intent. As I walked over to shake his hand, he said, "I heard you were in Russia. When I was there during the war, it was so much worse than anything today. You don't know what tough times are. They're not to be trusted, and you should just forget about learning anything useful from those people. This whole teaching thing of yours is useless and evil."

My greatest accomplishment at the time, being accepted as the first Westerner to formally intern behind the "Iron Curtain" and learn their approach to physical training and combative performance, had been smashed under his boot.

On the very year of his death, I created my greatest gift to him ... a system to help those dealing with excessive stress and recover quickly and wholly ... a contribution to the world, through my crazy ideas, which had healed my own heart, in the very way that his needed healing.

His silent psychological pain he had suffered had led to his remarks.

My opportunities had given me the chance to learn the precise methods that could have healed him, and prevented his death.

The tone of the heart so impacts throughout the body that I studied the disciplines, modern and ancient, to use breath for controlling heart rate and blood pressure. When you're able to control your breath, you influence the healing power of your heart, the power of your performance and the longevity of your existence.

Your heart is primary control — the most powerful organ. It breaks, heals and becomes stronger again. Your heart, not your brain, houses all of your power and lives as the most important muscle, affecting all the others. The brain may drive the bus, but the heart empowers it. Where your heart goes, your body follows.

Exhale. Thrive on your passions, and never let someone else's heartache diminish your pulse. They're not evil; merely broken.

So, power up yourself. The larger you grow your heart — the primary muscle we ought to exercise — the greater you can heal yourself, and the more your impassioned living helps others heal and grow as well.

My grandfather provided a positive role model of hard work and independence.

My grandmother's positive attitude planted a seed that still grows within me.

Mom was my staunch defender from my very first moments of life.

Here we are at Chincoteague Island, Virginia, when I was in fifth or sixth grade.

I was honored to have my university mentor, Dr. Jonathon Winter, at my Sambo black belt test in May 1993 with two-time champion Greg Lees at left.

Mom was there for me yet again, at my first black belt test in Sambo, 1993.

In February 1993, I was honored to attend the World University Games, with assistant coach Andy Bachman, at right.

I'm in impressive company here, with, from left, Greg Lees, two-time world champion; Gen. Alexander Ivanovich Retuinskih; Alexandr Krivorotov, the first distinguished coach of Sambo in Russia; and Prince Boris Vasilievich Golitsin of the Russian royal family and the Golitsin defensive style, who taught me bayonet fencing.

My Russian instructor license.

In Moscow's Red Square in 1997.

Prince Golitsin teaches a technique to defeat two abductors at the same time, while Gen. Retuinskih watches, right. Note the composure and balance of Prince Golitsin in applying his technique, and how uncomfortable I look.

A light moment with Gen. Retuinskih in 1996, as we celebrate in a floating café in front of the Hermitage in St. Petersburg, Russia. The general's inhibitions were lowered enough to let me know I had made him proud as my coach.

At the event at the Great Concert Hall Oktyabrsky in Saint Petersburg, celebrating 10 years since Russian martial art was officially resurrected. I became the first American allowed to perform on that stage, where I'm pictured sixth from the right.

Jodie shows her grappling technique in 1995. Her father made her take self-defense before going off to college. He chose my class for her training, and the rest is history.

My visit to Israel in November 2009 included a visit to the sacred Western Wall
in Jerusalem, and a life-changing pilgrimage to the Jordan River.

My training partner and good friend Alberto Gallazzi and I startled other Jordan River
pilgrims when the thin cotton robes that we were issued became transparent in the
water, revealing our tattoos, fight shorts and fighter physiques.

At the time we launched my patented Clubbell training tools in 2002, I weighed just 159 pounds, my slender frame making these 15-pound Clubbells look big. Now our students regularly train with Clubbells up to 45 pounds.

Gen. Retuinskih, my business partner Nikolay Travkin and I in 2002 at our induction into the International Martial Arts Hall of Fame in Orlando, Florida.

The circle is complete: Here I am at Sambo-70 in Spring 2014, when the former student was invited to teach Russians about their own martial art.

Alberto Gallazzi and I compare notes during a training session in Southern California in 2010. Alberto has helped to push TACFIT and Clubbell training to incredible heights, and is our European director.

It's always rewarding to work with Alberto, who is a jiu-jitsu champion and creator of Survival Jiu-Jitsu. It's especially nice in places like Capri, as we are here in 2011.

My expression says it all – my TEDx talk in 2013 about my learning disabilities, where I publicly revealed my institutionalization as a child, was one of the hardest things I have ever done.

Jodie and I share a romantic sunset in 2012. She is truly my best friend, and her happiness brings me joy.

The women in my life in 2014.

Father and son sport hats and dark glasses on a rare sunny day in Bellingham, Washington.

# PART 3

---

# FINDING PEACE

# BATHE IN THE HEALING WATERS

When my father returned from the War, he brought home violence inside him. Because he passed away from heart disease in 2005, I didn't have the chance to hear this story from him. I had to piece it together through a painful, but liberating journey.

A four-year-old cannot comprehend violence, so the image of my father beating my mother caused me to feel I had done something wrong: "If I had only been better behaved, maybe they wouldn't fight."

Walking into my mother's room where she lay crying, holding her swollen face, I could only say, "I'm sorry, Mom. Please don't cry."

Fortunately for her, they divorced the next year, and except for fleeting images of scant, horrific memories, that ended my relationship with my father. He took everything in the marriage: the accounts, the farm and horse ranch, the house and cars. My mother agreed to sign over all assets in exchange for him relinquishing all custody of us kids.

So we moved into a trailer court, and my mother arranged two full-time labor jobs, becoming the first female steelworker in Pennsylvania.

Her hate for my abusive father burned within her. Too young and unaware, I imported that hate within me. Not that she was unjustified for how she felt as a result of the physical and emotional abuse, but I had not had the chance to develop my own independent, adult relationship with him.

We saw him on holidays for a couple of years. One Christmas, he returned from a baptismal pilgrimage to Jerusalem. It was a strange thing for a child to comprehend that he had given up his alcohol and rage and turned to God, becoming a senior member of his Church.

He handed me a wooden camel with a bow on it. Overwhelmed with my own problems — my learning disabilities, joint disease and obesity, the fights and humiliation I faced at school, our impoverishment thrust upon us when they divorced — I felt enraged that with all of his resources, he couldn't give me a computer or something practical. Instead, he handed me a damned wooden camel.

I threw it to the floor, the leg snapping off. My brother scooped up the pieces and later gave them to me glued back together saying, "You may not understand it, but he's trying to share with you a piece of him."

I threw it into my closet, unable to forgive him for hurting Mom, for abandoning us, for leaving me alone to face all of my issues. I eventually forgot about the camel; lost somewhere in many moves.

Thirty years later, I was in Israel to train their special forces. The Israeli lieutenant colonel wanted to give a special gift for the work.

Driving north to the river Jordan, we arrived where Jesus had been baptized by John at Al-Maghtas near Jericho. I didn't know what was expected, so, when we emerged from the changing room covered in tattoos and wearing fight shorts, stunned parents grabbed their children. Embarrassed, we found the appropriate robes, donned them, and returned to the waters.

When I came out from under the water, the full weight of significance struck me: "As soon as Jesus was baptized, he went up out of the water. At that moment Heaven was opened, and he saw the Spirit of God descending like a dove and lighting on him. And a voice from heaven said, 'This is my Son, whom I love.'" (Matthew 3:16–17)

My eyes went first to the sky, then immediately to a small vendor at the river bank. In his cart were wooden camels.

Uncontrollable tears welled my eyes, and the lieutenant colonel asked if the event was overwhelming me.

I nodded and could only manage, "My father was here." The LTC replied, "Yes, all of our Christian friends have a similar response."

I muttered, "You don't understand. My FATHER was here!" I dashed out into the dressing room, changed in solemnity, walked to the vendor, and delicately picked up one of the camels. Paying the carver, I placed it gently in my pack, so afraid that I might snap off its legs.

The weight crushed me when I returned to our room, and I hid in the bathroom, holding the camel. My entire life had evolved into a career of helping to restore the health of soldiers and their families, of helping those who face extreme crises to recover from and prepare for the shock and trauma of violence.

Somehow, I had experienced a private miracle. In my own process of healing by helping others heal, I had journeyed back to the exact spot where my own father came to forgive himself for the damages he had experienced from war, and the cost his family had unfairly borne as a result. I cannot imagine a worse penance than to endure the knowledge that his own son could never forgive him for internal events which must have felt out of his control.

Looking upon this camel, its legs unbroken, standing strong on my desk in front of every word I type, I feel so sorry for the cross he had to bear.

Of course, his violence could not have been permitted or excused, but it can be understood and forgiven. And I ask you, Dad, to forgive me again, for taking so long... You have been here all along, silently steering my life from Heaven.

When it is all finished, you will discover none of this life has been random. It will seem like you must discover things out in the world — skills and tools, concepts and theories — and that your life fumbles along, one coincidence after another.

But, like assembling a puzzle, each piece appears disconnected until close to completion, when your eyes begin to focus on the bigger picture, and each seemingly unrelated segment coalesces into a masterful mosaic.

As Rumi wrote, *"Your task is not to seek for love, but merely to find all of the barriers within yourself that you have built against it."*

Today, alive and bare, I fully remove those barriers to you, Dad. I honor you and our elegant life we had alone, but together. I honor you by keeping down the walls that prevent me from being the best father I can to the tender spirits of your grandchildren.

I love you, Dad. Thank you for this amazing life.

# STRESS – THE SILENT ENEMY

My father was a warrior who, when he returned from the Korean War, was unable to reintegrate into our family due to posttraumatic stress syndrome. I was too young to understand, and only knew that my father was angry, abusive and detached.

I blamed my physical and learning disabilities for his hardships as a parent, for their divorce, and for my estrangement from him.

So, I set about understanding my condition and how to overcome those limitations.

In October of 1995, already a world medalist and national coach of the Russian Sambo martial art, after years of petitioning, I became the first American invited to formally intern behind the post-Perestroika "Iron Curtain" of the former USSR.

The first invite came as a phone call from SAMBO-70, the second largest academy in the world, to dorm at their facility and learn authentic Russian wrestling. The second invite came as an email from the Russian Scientific Consultant Practical Training Center to study with the military's Spetsnaz SOU trainers in stress physiology and combat biomechanics.

Unable to accept both, in a major surprise to my teammates and colleagues, I accepted the latter invitation. The years I spent training with the Russian coaches laid the groundwork for understanding how and why I was able to overcome my own limitations, as well as why my father, as great a warrior he was, was unable to reintegrate into family and society after the war. Though both groups trained in Sambo, the special operations units trained differently than the professional athletes.

Not merely the technical aspects differed from the mat to the field, but also the manner and means remained completely different. The tactical operator needed to train in light of the stress of his service, as he didn't have the luxury of the sport dormitory life.

During those years, I accepted the position as the US Coach of the first American team to compete at the World Police Sambo Championships (1999, Kaunas, Lithuania). Due to the disparate geography of the people I was training, I began developing training protocols that would address the stress physiology of the law enforcement officers on our team, rather than their athletic capabilities alone. They needed to remain operationally ready, pain and injury free regardless of their competitive fighting and training, and they needed to decrease the adverse effects of stress upon them, rather than increase them.

Over the next decade, I continued my research in related disciplines and continued to test and refine my approach.

Compiling a team of professionals from all of the relevant fields — federal law enforcement, special operations groups, fire rescue departments, dignitary protection teams, as well as fitness professionals facing the most diversely related populations to continue to reach out to non-active civilians, we discovered a large interest in our services and approach: outfits that want a system which prepares them physically for the rigors of crisis response, allows them to become and remain pain and injury free while increasing their fitness levels, which decreases their response to stress, helps them to recover faster from stressful encounters, and aids in reducing and eliminating the adverse effects that stress has caused their lives and their families' lives.

Only decades later, on a TACFIT assignment with my training unit, when I found myself in the same baptismal waters where my father made pilgrimage to recover his soul in the River Jordan in Israel, did I finally feel reunited with him … and feel that my path, struggle and work finally accomplished my original mission in my own family.

# IN WORD AND DEED, WE HONOR OUR VETS

Some gave all. All gave some. Honor to our Veterans.

On the eve of Veteran's Day, I felt gratitude for those who have given their support and advocacy over the years.

My career exploded over the past few years, allowing me to train some of the most prestigious special units and agencies here in the United States, and with our allies around the world. More importantly, it gave me the opportunity to spend time with their families and come to make an astounding discovery.

I was not alone.

The violence, fear, shame and guilt I felt as a child was not unique, but a product of a missing father and grandfather, whose military service cannibalized the integrity of my family and ultimately the health of my filial patriarchs. The soldiers, sailors, marines and airmen I've trained, who were generational military like myself, were struggling to find the balance between service and a loving family life; to prevent the atrocities they had stopped from visiting their own homes and hearts.

As a child I did not understand my father or grandfather. They seemed distant and angered. I did not know the disease violence had wrought upon them; worse still, neither did they. They were doing what they thought was their duty to be virtuous, but in the process sacrificed too much; taking too dire of a toll, and robbing them of a life with their families.

I can't say if my grandfather suffered PTSD, as my father obviously had, but the traits were common from the stories I've heard from other family members older than myself.

My entire life unerringly steered toward emancipating the lives of military service personnel and their families from the traumatic stress of violence. The discoveries made along the way now apply to all of us, in managing and recovering from stress, through tactical fitness; in saving us from the number one killer on the planet: stress related disease … and the daily suicide of emotions it erupts.

My father and his, and perhaps theirs, endured an inheritance of mortal stress through their service to their country. On Veteran's Day, my family will take a moment to celebrate their lives, and honor their generational sacrifices. I am more than merely the product of their genes. My family is directly influenced by their invisible hands reaching forward in time to prevent other men, women and children from suffering the incalculable toll that violence incurs upon our bodies, minds and spirits.

Thank you, Dad and Pappy. I love you and miss you both.

I wish I could feel your hands on my shoulders again, telling me as you once did, "Good job, Boy, but keep going. There's still more good to be done."

But I feel you in my heart. And your sacrifices will not be forgotten by us, or lost in the next generation.

# CHOOSE THE GENIUS OF MADNESS

In 1998, the senior CNN health correspondent, Dan Rutz, shook my hand, thanking me for a weekend of training in Zdorovye, the native health system of natural movement I had brought back from my training in Russia.

He said, "When we first met at our office in Atlanta, with your pirate beard and ponytail, I thought you were a bit crazy. Now, I'm convinced you totally are, and I love it. I suspect our audience will feel the same as I do."

I've been ridiculed most of my early life for disappearing to marginal territories, studying with fringe scientists, doctors and coaches. From each one of them, sifting through their more ethereal theories, I discovered a few unique gems of sanity that would have otherwise gone unseen.

You have to be a bit mad to challenge to the status quo. Courage is a kind of insanity: you're consciously choosing to do the difficult, righteous, daring thing despite your fears compelling you to either run away and quit, or never take the chance to begin with.

Marilyn Monroe said, *"Imperfection is beauty. Madness is genius. And it's better to be absolutely ridiculous than absolutely boring."* Proudly wear those scars and blemishes from your mad ideas. Snicker a little at your craziness. Live out loud with outrageous passion for your own way, and I promise you'll never experience one day of boredom.

# BE HAPPY RATHER THAN NORMAL

For many years, I adapted my brain to the current of mainstream thinking so that I could conceal my alternative paths to solutions and appear to be "normal." But through repeated experience, normalcy didn't work for me. More importantly, attempting to meet this illusion of the neuro-typical norm limited me.

In 2007, I had broken a world record on "club swinging" in the most number of "mills" — a type of swing pattern that involves the entire body — in an hour. The prior record had been 1,000 repetitions with a 20-pound club. I managed 1,433 with a 25-pound Clubbell. (http://vimeo.com/m/7741911)

To achieve this record I had to track repetitions per minute, across hand switches right and left. As a result, I had to count time, repetitions achieved in sets between hand switches and total repetitions across hand switches.

I had been able to do this parallel processing due to a math approach in which my mother had had me tutored, called *Chisanbop*, a form of Korean kinesthetic counting which allowed dyscalculiacs to process math through movement.

As Paulo Coelho wrote, *"I prefer to be happy and crazy than normal and bitter."* We are each and every one of us unique. Much as there are as many martial art styles on the planet as there are people in the world, "normal" can only be defined within the individual not between individuals.

Be uniquely you. Imagine how much richer the world will be because you dared to share, because you once again courageously stood alone in your "madness" and expressed your own way.

# THE NEXT BEND IN YOUR JOURNEY AWAITS

I stood at the beginning of a 42-mile course. For several years, I had been rebuilding the strength in my broken back. And now, I thought, I would put my recovery to the test.

Mile after mile passed like a slowly dripping faucet filling a bowl. My mind would falter, and my stride would fall apart; my body would wobble and my thoughts turned to worry that I could not make it, that I needed to discontinue or I would break down into reinjury.

Though we treat it in the opposite manner, our mind is a canvas and our body the brush. We use our body to perform elegant strokes convincing the canvas into a masterpiece of attitudes, ideas and views. I had started to run not to change the limited shape of my body, but to change my mind's limited shape of my potential.

I turned a bend and another six miles stretched out in front of me, my heart sinking and mind waffling. But one step after another, I brought my mind back to my exhale, foot strike, alignment and pump.

"Keep it held in your technique; this is your yoga. Flow through distractions; that is your martial art," I would repeat over and over until my mind would reintegrate with my gait.

And then I would round another bend, and it would fall apart yet again. If we are only as powerful as we imagine, then I had aimed to hold my body's technique so I could stretch the boundaries of my imagination. Recovering from my moments of mental lapse became the focus of the trip, not the duration and distance of the course.

My pace might have been the slowest on it. With no signs of passing others or they passing me, my mind would slip to worries of finishing last, of loss and losing. But I didn't have to be great to finish; I only had to finish the next step to realize my greatness. And then, the step after it ... and so on.

Step after step, holding my mind upon my technique, I would focus my effort not on the speed of my run, but on how rapidly I could recover my focus when my mind would fall from concentrating on the cycle of my gait.

Given from birth a mind, a body and a lifetime to explore it, how we use the first two determines the third. Use one to exercise the other: the mind compels the body toward its purpose; the body expands the mind of its potential.

It's your path and yours alone. Others may walk with you, but no one can walk it for you. Even if no one else supports you, regardless of whether your road appears barren and remote, keep going. Let your body convince your mind of your unlimited potential. Around the next bend, you may forget again, but less long. And again, less long still ...

# VISION GOES BEYOND OUR LINE OF SIGHT

The excessive amount of flying and writing I did last year viciously brought back my eye disease, and I am finding it difficult to see the keyboard again, but I have seen so much and so many of you already that how could one complain?

My frequent flights to Russia several times a year in the 1990s, with inadequate oxygen delivery through my contact lenses, led to corneal deprivation and elicited a rare eye disease, called Thygeson's Punctate Keratitis — an autoimmune response scientists still cannot understand or cure.

When my eyes grow tired, they feel like they're covered with a painful, milky sand, causing extreme burning, tearing, discharge and extreme photosensitivity. It can happen from extended contact lens wear, altitude, long flights or even reading a book or computer screen. The pain isn't often unbearable, but the vision becomes barely functional.

Many people at seminars don't understand why I disappear at the end of events, or don't participate in after-hours social activities. After 14 hours, my eyes, voice and brain become inoperable.

My greatest salvation over the years has been my studies. I'm a voracious researcher, and an obsessive data tracker. Although doctors said that I wouldn't be able to achieve any significant academic goals, some of my books are now used as university textbooks, because of my interdisciplinary studies.

Within books, I found a universe beyond the errors of doctors and teachers. And through my daily messages, I reach tens of thousands of people daily, and sometimes into the millions, sharing the fruits of those studies.

Without my vision, if this degradation would continue, I cannot imagine how my life would change. I have seen so much in my life. I've had the honor of training thousands of incredible athletes, and speaking with many more seeking to improve their health and that of their loved ones.

I have seen my beautiful wife and best friend finally become as truly happy as she has always deserved, my lovely children thrive into confident full young individuals, and my dear friends triumph in their individual quests against odds they thought insurmountable. I have seen my teacher smile with pride at a deed no one could have known I had done and I see her unconditional love in all that I do and am.

I have seen so many terrible and wondrous sights in my life that I could never begrudge my failing sight except for one issue …

I love writing to you. All of "this" began for me on the Internet back when it first started in the early 1990s, when we had dial-up bulletin boards and I created the first martial art website of its kind. Though impossible to find like minds densely populated enough in a geographical area, an expanded search to a global scale cast the net wide, our community evolved and proliferated.

Great abundance has come from my writing and speaking, sufficient enough for me to be able give back on Facebook and my blog. It comes at a cost to my eyes, but I pray that it will be able to continue. We will continue to search for alternative solutions, and I am confident we will find a cure. As I sit here waiting for sunrise in Maui, I wanted to say that it has been a great honor reading your comments and your stories. I am truly grateful for the vast movement we have co-created.

# APPLY A COACH'S PERSPECTIVE TO YOURSELF

Somewhere in my competitive career, my life transitioned. I began unknowingly coaching others, and it held a dramatic impact upon my own performance. Begin coaching, and you can no longer see ANY opponent as an obstacle.

You realize that s/he struggles just as hard as you do to overcome anxieties, fears and doubts. We all face the hazard of excessive stress, on the path of adapting to positive challenges, and coaching makes us sensitive to our common plight.

I told you the story my University wrestling coach shared with me about motivating others, and the power of that support. He also taught me that my own development cannot come at the expense of others.

One late night in the wrestling room, coach watched me attempting to trick my (obviously superior) opponent with sneaky moves. He stopped me to ask if I felt successful.

I replied, "No, I feel like I can't pull off any moves at all. I feel overwhelmed and under-gunned against these stronger, more experienced fighters."

He took out a roll of mat tape, and laid down a line on the mat. He then asked me how I could make the line of tape shorter. So, I tried to tear the tape into smaller pieces, but if you know mat tape, it's impervious enough to survive a nuclear holocaust. As I stood to look for a scissors or box-cutter, in frustration, he stopped me.

Taking another piece of tape, much longer than the first, he laid it next to the original. Then he asked me, "Now, doesn't the first line look shorter?"

I nodded as I began to understand that trying to cut someone else's line doesn't improve our own, and ends up being a frustrating and sticky mess. You can, however, always make your line longer. We all start somewhere.

It's not how far back you start. It's how long you stick with it.

I spent much of my life trying to make my line longer, until championships no longer fulfilled me. At some point, I wanted something bigger, more substantial: I wanted to help others uncover their potential, and reveal the discoveries I had made which expedited my health, performance and well-being. I devoted my life to helping others "make a longer line."

Despite what people may misunderstand from the victories I've had in martial art (or the much more extensive losses I've had as a child), I have never had any intention of being better than my opponents, only in becoming a better version of myself.

Thrusting myself into competitive resistance at the highest levels I could sustain, I intended to produce MY best — as in better than I've ever done to hold my peace, remain calm and clear, smooth and steady, in the most difficult artificial circumstances I could find: martial arts.

Martial art is merely a metaphor — a controlled environment where you are able to pressure test your emotional control and mental focus. I train in the same way for fitness: focusing on how fast I can recover to proper technique while challenging my nervous system with ever-expanding complexity. I practice my yoga in this way: finding my way to exhale into deeper levels of internal resistance. I honor my nutrition this way: eating to increase my emotional control, mental focus and physical capacity. And I use my writing and speaking for the same purpose: If I can become a better version of myself, I can better serve others.

Only when I can expand my martial art, fitness, yoga, nutrition, writing and speaking into a lifestyle, do I truly engage the full capacity of these vehicles as means of self-transformation.

As Hemingway wrote, *"There is nothing noble in being superior to your fellow man; true nobility is being superior to your former self."* Today, be more noble than you were yesterday. Be more you than you've ever previously risked sharing with the world. When you stop trying to find solutions OVER others and start considering how to create solutions FOR others, you realize you're the solution you've been seeking, and we can share that message with everyone we touch.

# TAKE YOUR PATH, AND LET THE PACK FOLLOW

My son and I were working on his math homework on the plane flying home from Costa Rica. He was getting every single answer wrong. So, I asked him to try a trick I had learned to help me with my math challenges (dyscalculia).

I suggested that after each sentence in the word problem, he do four slow exhales, and write out in formula only that sentence before moving to the next.

Looking at me, he asked why it would work. I said his brain automatically knows the answer to every question, but if he goes too fast, they get squished together. The exhale tells his heart to slow down his brain. This lets the answers come out of his hand in the right order.

He got every question answered correctly! I said, "Good job! See, your brain knows every answer, if you give it time to get out of your body!"

He smirked, "Yeah, my brain is pretty awesome." I busted out loud laughing. Then he leaned his head on my arm and said, "You are too, Dad. One day I'm going to know all the answers like you."

"Love you, Son. Hold on, though. Don't tell Mom, but I don't know even close to everything," I cautioned. "Let me tell you a story..."

I once complained to my teacher that each new variation on a technique I had used to win a fight, others would take and name their own with a different label.

My teacher laughed saying, "Success has a thousand fathers. Failure is an orphan. Be a proud parent to your failures because no one else will want them; but they're what give you the experience you need to win. If someone else wants to be another father to your victories, let them. Love your mistakes."

Looking at my son, I told him, "There were two men who discovered the light bulb: Edison and Tesla. Both of them had trouble learning language, like your Dad: they were dyslexic, so they had to figure out ways to learn that were different."

"Edison said: I have not failed. I've just found 10,000 ways that won't work." I cautioned my son that if it looks like I have gotten something correct, it's because of 10,000 times of getting it wrong. And I still am getting things wrong, so I can discover the right way or even a new way for me to do it.

My son hugged my arm again and said, "Don't worry Dad. I won't tell Mom. It'll be our secret that you always make mistakes."

I laughed and said that it was definitely one secret I haven't been able to keep from Mom!

# OBSTACLE OR OPPORTUNITY? YOU CHOOSE

*"Obstacles are things a person sees when he takes his eyes off his goal. Keep your dreams alive. Understand to achieve anything requires faith and belief in yourself, vision, hard work, determination, and dedication. Remember all things are possible for those who believe."* ~ Gail Devers

I was speaking at a University and one of my students mentioned to the audience that I could bend spikes with my hands. After my speech, one of the students asked, "Can we see a spike bend?"

Spike bending can be door-opening: inspiring others to reclaim confidence in themselves as to possibility, when you witness a feat that you previously thought impossible.

A professor passed around a spike so everyone had the opportunity to attempt to bend it. No one could budge the metal because they thought it was impossible (because they try to bend the spoon, for you "Matrix" movie buffs). Most pried it like they were breaking a piece of celery — thumbs pushing away in the middle with no leverage. "Bending" is neither a miracle, nor is it a gag. It is commitment of will to something deeper.

Strength is neurological efficiency, but this runs very deep. Intramuscular recruitment is really a matter of "faith" that you can do what you have not done before, elicited by your conviction to do it and focused by proper visualization on the true purpose for doing so.

Concentrating my anxiety, I imagined how much one of the spectators might need to see the spike bend, how indelibly the event would impact their lives, as it had me when my coach did his spike bending demo and blew open the vault door of the "possible" in my mind.

The spike bent because the need of the audience to witness a previously conceived impossibility broken overcame the resistance of the obstacle to remain unbroken. How many times did we observe this recently in the Olympics in world record-breaking performances falling like dominoes after the first; and then also the reverse with the string of epic mental failures following the psychological impact of public criticisms? What about the police officer, Brian Murphy, shot nine times at the Sikh temple in Wisconsin, who told the medics to help the victims first? THAT was the motivation of morale!

Without proper motivation, "spikes" — the obstacles we perceive as impossible — in our lives remain unbent. Morale bends the spike. Our need to see our spikes bend must be greater than the spike's resistance to being overcome. The energy described by ancient martial arts, yoga, Sufism, strongman feats, qigong, is just a metaphor for the true force: service to others. Like my teacher said to me long ago, "If you want to overcome perceived impossibility, serve others."

Energy is a metaphor for the by-product of the RELATIONSHIP between us: the love we have for serving each other.

Events like bending spikes must be a matter of imagined necessity to serve each other. If you don't think you have much to live for, if you don't love till it hurts, of course you lack energy. If you're feeling low, lost, overwhelmed or underequipped, then put your energy into serving others. From service, you will regain your strength, and overcome the obstacles you face, because WE NEED YOU TO, and that energy will infuse, envelop and empower you.

Is it any wonder that a world champion achieving the impossible, a survivor of a tragedy miraculously enduring, or the hero incredibly overcoming the overwhelming, expresses gratitude?

Like my coach told me, if you want to bend the spikes in your life, love more than you are.

# WHICH WAY DOES YOUR SWORD CUT?

Because my father returned from the Korean War overburdened with psychological turmoil, I never had the opportunity to know him: my family disintegrated into divorce while I was only 4 years of age, and my father died of stress related heart disease before I had the opportunity to reach out to him and create a new relationship.

My career inadvertently became guided toward helping to solve this problem of stress upon our health, to prevent others from suffering its effects, and their families from its collateral damage. Although my primary outreach remains health, fitness and nutrition, I remain at my heart a martial artist, and I maintain a martial artist's view on wellness. Studying the impact of stress upon the body, through psychophysiology in Russia and stress physiology in the USA, I discovered the science underpinning an old martial art:

The sword has a double-edged blade: one that gives life and one that takes it.

In Japanese, there are two expressions:

*Satsujinken* — the sword which takes life.

*Katsujinken* — the sword which gives life.

It is the same sword; the difference is in the person who uses it. Stress (positive stress levels or "eustress") is how our health and our fitness improve. Without stress, we die, as I discovered working with the Russian Cosmonaut researchers, when they taught me methods to slow the rapid aging caused from subsisting in zero gravity.

But too much stress (excessive levels called "distress") cannibalizes us … which is evident by the early mortality rate of tactical first responders, whose average lifespan is only 54 years young — the number one killer being stress-related heart disease, as it was with my father.

Stress is the sword that gives life and takes it. We walk the razor's edge. You will make mistakes whether you take action or you avoid it. But if you avoid it, your health and fitness have no chance of improving. If you do take action, and you do step across the line into distress, focus on your recovery methods — mobility, nutrition, sleep, walking, playing, laughing, stretching, massage, sauna. … These are how you heal the accidental, unavoidable wounds from handling the life-giving sword. Without doing so, you shall surely fall on the life-taking blade of distress, for inaction registers to your body as excessive stress and accelerates aging, disease and death.

It is not easy. It is often not even this simple, because stress blurs our clear thinking. But if you focus on recovery, you'll spin the hilt in your hands, and return to the life-giving blade of eustress.

# STRIP AWAY THE DISTRACTIONS

Due to my childhood fascial condition, coordination became a major challenge for me, which is why "Flow" became a life's passion.

Sports, exercise, martial art, even Hatha yoga with all its health building qualities, left me without the precision to "enter" a skill. I just couldn't access the technique as it was taught. With others seemingly thriving in an indecipherable language, I felt mute and dumb to movement efficacy.

So, I invented my own process to segment movement into digestible components until they were small enough for me to practice, like eating an elephant one forkful at a time.

Several years later I was in Russia being qualified as the first national team coach for our country in an obscure combat sport known as bayonet fencing. My coach said to me, "I can show you the (door) frame, but only you can enter."

He then showed me the four corners of defense and explained, "No attack can exit this frame if you defend just this small frame," as he drew a box in the air with the training bayonet of his fencing carbine. "You move too much not because of lack of control, but because you are trying to defend against everything and anything all the time. Address this tiny box and you gain four times the efficiency at one-quarter the total stress."

This insight reverberated throughout my fighting career, and into my writing, business and spiritual life. If I wanted to address a specific area of concern, I needed to reduce my concentration to the critical components. I sought the "doorframe" in each goal.

Teachers show us how to reduce our unnecessary efforts. Stepping through these doorways becomes the easy part. We feel like we have made such an achievement when we "enter" a goal but we must acknowledge our teachers' influence in pointing to the critical "frames". My greatest respects to my teachers for communicating this to me when I resisted it for so long.

# TO IMPROVE, SEEK OUT YOUR IMPERFECTIONS

Even after overcoming obesity to become a champion fighter and transforming my learning disabilities to become the first university student in my family, I still could not overcome the perceived inadequacies of my self-worth.

In counsel my mentor at university cautioned, "Mr. Sonnon, there is no way to happiness. Happiness is the way. But there are a wondrous myriad of ways to malcontent. How horribly lethal we have mastered those ways. If you want happiness to return to your life, then you must unlearn what stops it."

If you're unhappy with your nutrition, fitness or attitudes, it's not that you must learn to have energy, exertion and excitement. Instead, we must only unlearn the congestion of habits that block them.

As J.E. Purcell notes, *"You must unlearn what you have programmed to believe since birth. That software no longer serves you if you want to live in a world where all things are possible."*

But we rightfully should ask, "How do we rewrite the software?" You cannot delete negative, destructive programs. You can only overwrite them with positive, productive ones.

Why?

We are genetically programmed for error-focus. As hunter/gatherers, our brains evolved to find what doesn't work, to eliminate that behavior, as our mind is the tool that has allowed us to survive as a species over predators better armored and armed than us.

Our mind created tools to persevere against much more ferocious competitors.

So, we can yet again use our mind to create new tools, in this case mental software to overwrite negative, destructive attitudes to errors and mistakes.

Feel encouraged when you find a weakness during exercise, when you feel fatigue barriers of conditioning, or a pain or ache in your movement, because these are the "parking brakes" to your potential. Disengaging these restrictive forces allows your innate driving forces to punch the accelerator. You don't need to become strong so much as to release your inherent potential for power that is tethered by these brakes.

When we find a destructive habit in our nutrition, when someone points out that we have an attachment to a behavior that serves no or little nutritive purpose to our potential, we ought to feel elated and grateful. By practicing changing your mind, you can change your world.

That sounds great, but how do we do it? With practice, you reactivate a circuit, neuro-synaptic efficiency increases, and neural connections become more durable and easier to reactivate. In other words, whenever you do specific tasks over and over again, they take up less of your brainpower.

Initially it will be hard to change your exercise, nutrition and mental behaviors; but not for long, and never forever. It can feel that way, as you push the Sisyphean boulder up the side of the mountain, but it will suddenly summit — ingraining your new program — and roll over the other side into automatic lifestyle behavior.

Embrace error-focus, rather than perfection-orientation. Errors allow us to grow. We just need to reprogram our attitude, adopted since childhood, that errors are bad, and reframe our attitude to be grateful when we discover them.

Fulfillment and gratitude for errors, surprises and failures requires work ethic. Author Shawn Achor frames this rewiring as "The Positive Tetris Effect" in The Happiness Advantage, "It's something that requires our brains to train just like an athlete has to train. We can retrain the brain to scan for the good things in life-to help us see more possibility, to feel more energy, and to succeed at higher levels."

Here are the tools that I used. The process took me years to master (and I still make mistakes and fail to immediately relish all errors). After several months, the process becomes automatic: When new errors, surprises and failures unearth, you no longer will need to reprogram a positive attitude over a negative one, because your positivity will be automatic.

1. When I found a negative program, I asked how the error, surprise or failure was ultimately serving my growth and development. Every event conspires to our success, whether we know or not; and even every bodily pain and anguishing thought serves us somehow. Begin with asking how. You won't know at first. But when you allow yourself to do this drill, your intuition will point you unerringly to the source. You then unveil gratitude.

2. Express your gratitude for your advocates, role models, teachers and influences. Practice grateful expressions for your positive influences. Then, get ready for the hard ones: Practice finding gratitude for those events and people who appear to not overtly act in your best interest. Teachers and doctors who claimed I was genetically "broken" deserve only my compassion for their ignorance. Yet, I have learned gratitude for those painful periods of my life, for without them, I would not have dispelled our collective illusion of self-incompetence. I feel grateful that they allowed me to see how unlimited our potential truly is.

Now, I seek to apply this lesson in all of the challenging and painful episodes in life. And when I cannot, when I feel self-pity for my circumstances, I practice kindness for those who commit those acts against me, and others … for their lot is much worse than mine.

3. Acts of kindness allow me to shift everyone within my sphere of influence, and permit me to step outside my own self-interest. Self-interest is an unfulfilling prison with invisible bars: The longer we seek personal pleasures (and avoidance of pain), the more strongly imprisoned we become. An act of kindness changes your world suddenly, like a rock thrown into a pond rippling outwards, impacting friends and their influences, and so on. By serving something greater, deeper and higher than my individual self, I regain my freedom, and step outside the prison.

But as I practice in one direction, I can allow myself to be vulnerable to negative attachment in other directions (before the practice of framing errors, surprises and failures as positive, productive events becomes an automatic lifestyle behavior). So, when you are focused in one direction, say your nutrition, a negative pattern can stealthily invade.

For example, you have the willpower to change your eating habits, but people keep pressuring you to "live a little" and stop being an "obsessive control freak about dieting." If they'd only leave you alone and realize how much better you've become, maybe they could better themselves! And then you realize you have just adopted a negative attitude toward others. So you immediately reframe their resistance as an opportunity to practice.

Without their pressure, you may not have recognized how your willpower had been eroding, and just succumbed to your own creeping gremlins for cheat days and impulse splurges you rationalize as "earning." Thank God, they provided you with the clue of where to strengthen yourself! And as they see your energy improve with consistency, they begin to ask you how to replicate what you've done.

So, you need to be continually vigilant of the invasion of negative patterns of eating, moving and thinking.

4. Be vigilant for opportunities to expand your practice of positivity. WHEN you find a negative pattern skulking about, be elated! Only the unseen can hurt us. Consciousness equals awareness. Our food, fitness and attitudes are the first shells others meet. Practice here most often. It is a day-long practice, which is incredibly difficult at first. But keep faith. Your brain's natural plasticity will eventually make the effort easier, by making deliberate cerebral changes to enable more efficient energy and excitement.

Each new circumstance, event or challenge, hold the above four in mind:

1. Find the value of the experience;

2. Express gratitude for it;

3.  Apply it throughout you life; and

4.  Remain vigilant for any negativity, for you have then found another glorious blockage to your potential which you can unlock and restore to full empowerment.

# ACT WITHOUT EXPECTATION OF REWARD

My teacher told me, "He who feels he deserves the fruits of his labor, pity him."

I know what she meant by pity: Empathize with his plight, for the one who seeks his own pleasure and jealously covets his own rewards, lives a cold, hollow, lackluster prison sentence.

In my early and teenage years, I sought escape from my unacceptable circumstances, expecting emancipation to bring me happiness. Later, I fixated on achieving fulfillment through accomplishment (my 30s) and found it to be fool's gold, and before that, the much more arrogant pursuit of achieving enlightenment through my studies and training (ah, my 20s), which led only to the suffering of angst at my permanent imperfection.

Today, I realize that no expectation can be fulfilled by my effort to commit or omit an action. But in those too infrequent moments when I act spontaneously with grace to help another, to stop everything and listen to my child's playful banter, to shut down all that I'm doing and hold my wife's hand and hear about her thoughts, to end any professional objective to extend an ear, shoulder or hand to friend or stranger, in those moments that I act without expectation, my world fills. I feel full. No other words describe.

A woman contacted me on Facebook recently. She told me that she had been a student of mine at my martial art school in the early 1990s. She reminded me that she had made an unscheduled visit to meet with me in my office. I was in the middle of an animated phone call with the largest contract of my career at the time, providing security training for an entire airport. She sat and waited while I ended the conversation with a silent pantomimed, "Sorry!"

Seeing that she was in distress, and knowing that the negotiation needed a break, I told the director that we could either talk later after he considered my action plan, or he could find someone he felt would be willing to jeopardize passenger safety in order to keep their status quo. Infuriated, he replied that he would make sure that I'd never get more work in the field ever again.

On hanging up, my student said to me that she was sorry if she had caused me to lose an important job. I told her that the airport director was being an ass, and needed to cool off. Obviously something was troubling her, so I told her she was a very welcomed interruption.

She told me that she had been having a difficult time at school and went on to explain broken relationships, challenging college selection, parental pressure, and more … and asked me what she should do.

I asked her what was her optimal conclusion to the situation. She said, to go as far away as possible to focus on what SHE wanted to study. I said, as long as you're running to, and not from, your dreams, never regret not knowing what life would be like if you had not.

So these many years later, by Facebook message, she told me that she departed on that journey after she graduated from high school. She eventually earned her doctorate and went on to the "most fascinating job" she could imagine.

But what I didn't know, she told me, is that on that day, she had been at the end of her rope, as she had just been raped the night before by someone close to her.

Instead of hanging herself to end her own life, she felt that if I could drop what I was doing for a teenage student, even though I was involved in what could have been a major career development, then she could certainly be strong enough to go after what she believed in, to heal, and no matter how much resistance she encountered from family and friends to conform to their expectations, she would go after her dream.

I was speechless.

Thanking her for being willing to trust me, for her courage to realize her dreams and for the privilege of sharing her story with me, I said she ought to share with others her story. She "LOL'ed" and said she felt that if I and so many others were courageous enough to share our stories in order to inspire others, she was certainly going to do the same.

Thank you for the permission to talk about the conversation. I look forward to reading your story, as you are one of my heroines!

The rest of my life dedicates toward practicing holding that space of action without expectation in my family, work, training, in my community locally and globally. We can never imagine the impact we have in those precious selfless moments when we act without expectation.

I receive a few hundred courageous stories a day by private messages. I try to respond to them all, and regret when I cannot thank and applaud each individual for the bravery of their self-disclosure. I want to encourage all of you to share your story with each other. This community we co-create holds a powerful elixir of strength and transformation. You cannot imagine how many people benefit from sharing your hardships and your bravery to persevere.

And you may also find, as I did, a beautiful catharsis in becoming transparent, and heal yourself by helping others.

As a great teacher once spoke, "Keep the lesson. Discard the drama." The drama belongs to ego: It can hold bombast for our awards and achievements and corrosively begrudge our hardships and shortcomings, but neither hubris nor hopelessness can ever assist our growth, and always hasten our collapse. Yet our lessons! Our lessons belong to our spirit, and from them we uplift ourselves and others, and can only ever grow and soar.

Keep sharing your courage with everyone, as you do with me. And as you help others grow stronger, you may find that you do as well.

Take Risks. If you succeed, you will have grown stronger. If you fail, you will have grown wiser.

# 45 DISCOVERIES I'VE MADE

After the 1999 World Championships in Lithuania, I mapped out how I had hoped to grow as a person in the subsequent decade.

Journaling every day showed me that we can improve our situation if we make ourselves aware by turning on lights in the dark places where our addictions lurk. They can't stay concealed if you journal, for illumination awakens our awareness.

Addictions crawled out of my pages: the usual suspects of sex, caffeine, alcohol, sugars, simple carbs, sleep, but also lesser known felons: procrastination, infatuation, self-righteousness, blame, envy, entitlement, narcissism. I had replaced old destructive addictions with new generative ones; which have the tendency to become just as destructive: dieting, weight loss, fat loss, muscle size, competitiveness, victories, achievements, recognition, fame, even success is an addiction.

I have discovered that only conscious living through deliberate behaviors and intentional attitudes can give me any hope of not mutating a new healthy choice into yet again another pattern of routine attachment.

This year, I'm 45, and in honor of those years of journaling since 2000, here are the 45 discoveries I've made:

1.  Life doesn't appear fair, but those who make the best of what they're given have the greatest quality of life.

2.  When in doubt, just take the next small step. The finish line is wrapped in fog, and most times we stop unknowingly... inches short.

3.  Life is too short to waste time on haters. Keep going, and you'll need new haters because the old ones will start to love you. They secretly are cheering you on, as they want to know it is possible for them as well.

4. Surrender what ego wants to hide and be transparent; thus you become truly free. This is the hardest. Boy, can we be blinded here, because it's the ego looking at itself.

5. Pay off your credit cards every month, not merely financially, but mentally and emotionally as well. Let no debt go unpaid, even if you can only pay it forward to the next person. Invest in yourself by giving to others, rather than going into debt borrowing.

6. Don't try to win every argument. Seek to understand the causes behind the others' motivations. Empathy happens even in the most reluctant, like me.

7. Take the time to recover from the effort you expend. Growth happens only after the work, not during it. So take the time to reflect with gratitude. It's ironic that the drive it takes to tackle a goal can become the challenge in appreciating its realization.

8. It's okay to get angry. Let it out and then let it go. Be kind, but be honest.

9. Imagine who you want to become and adopt the attitude and behavior that future purer version of yourself would do. WWTRYD: What would the REAL you do?

10. When it comes to love, resistance is futile. It is the slowest dripping erosion, but it will create a Grand Canyon where apathy once stood tall.

11. Make peace with your past, so you don't repeat it in the present. Forgiveness sets us free as much as those who are forgiven.

12. Don't compare your life to others. You have no idea what their journey is all about. And if you suddenly had your own life exchanged with the one you so dreamed of living, you would beg for your own problems to be returned.

13. Doubt your superstitions but honor the intuition of your rituals.

14. If a habit has to be a secret, it can only cause you destruction. Live transparently.

15. Everything can change in the blink of an eye. But don't worry. There's a reason for everything, and it's all for your betterment. It will be this or it will be something even better.

16. Take a deep exhale. It calms the mind and clears the goal, even in the greatest fog.

17. Suspend what isn't useful, beautiful or joyous, and we find that everything we are doing is, except the attitudes about them which aren't.

18. Whatever doesn't kill you, really does make you stronger. Unless you don't recover from it, in which case it just takes longer to kill you. Recover. Heal. Grow.

19. It's never too late to have a happy childhood. The second one is up to you and no one else. You weren't responsible for a bad first childhood, but you are the second one.

20. When it comes to going after what you love in life, don't take no for an answer. Others say no to your dreams because they've been repeating no to themselves for so long they believe it.

21. Don't save anything for a special occasion. There are no un-special moments. We don't realize it until our last one.

22. Over prepare, then go with the flow. Unless going with the flow goes against your values. In which case, resist the current, and be the courageous one who changed the flow. Trust yourself to do something you haven't done before. You will be afraid and have doubts because it's the challenge you've been preparing for.

23. Be eccentric now. Your eccentricities are often the surface of your talents and gifts. Love being weird. Weird is awesome.

24. Waste not thy hour. Savor each succulent experience BEFORE it's a memory. How easily we can be distracted from the preciousness of a simple hug, a kind deed or a loving thought.

25. No one is in charge of your happiness but you. There is no way to happiness. Happiness is the way. Don't wait for anyone or anything to bring it to you. No achievement will give it to you. Only your decision to be happy brings happiness.

26. Frame every so-called disaster with these words, "In 10 years, will this matter?"

27. The first one to forgive is the happiest.

28. What other people think of you is none of your business. What you think of them is none of theirs, so keep it to yourself if it's unkind.

29. Time heals almost everything. Give it some more. But help it along with care and attention.

30. However good or bad a situation is, it will change. Don't be attached to either.

31. Don't take yourself so seriously. No one else does. Life's too serious to take seriously.

32. Express gratitude for others while they walk with you. They won't be there for long. Much shorter than we had imagined.

33. Don't audit life. Show up and make the most of it now. Showing up is half of anything. If you feel unskilled and ARRIVE, you're already halfway ahead of everyone else.

34. Growing old beats the alternative — dying young. Relish your scars. Honor your teachers. Celebrate your children.

35. Your children get only one childhood. Realize what you're about to say or do lasts their lifetime. Let them live with that lesson rather than against it.

36. All that truly matters in the end is that you had loved ferociously... Someone, something, and God.

37. Get outside every day. It is the first and best "Playstation." Take your shoes off. Get down on your hands and get back to basics.

38. If we all threw our problems in a pile and saw everyone else's, we'd grab ours back quickly, so when your problems seem ominous remember that you're uniquely designed to surpass the challenge, like no one else could.

39. Envy, hopelessness and dread are a waste of time. You already have all you need. Always.

40. The best is yet to come. Really.

41. No matter how you feel, get up, stand up and show up.

42. Yield. Trust the process. Then, kick ass daily.

43. Everything we now desire is just a substitute for our Higher Purpose. The faster that we dedicate all of our life in that more divine calling, the more we feel alive.

44. We can't find bliss. We can't follow it. We must lead it. And it can only be found in helping others. No matter how shiny the distraction may appear, help others, and the great gold will appear... in your heart.

45. All of the above is probably just blather, and next year I will do a better job of understanding and communicating, because if we do our jobs as humans, the following year we will be different, and we will appreciate the mystery with a bit more clarity and ease than now. The learning process will never end.

# THE PEDANTIC DEFEAT THEMSELVES

"You are NOT a real yoga teacher. True yoga is a spiritual path of Hinduism and if you're not practicing yoga to further that intent, then you're not doing yoga," posted a very angry yoga guru who had been off-centered by a link I shared on silly comments made by yoga teachers.

Although my Indian yoga guru has physically embraced more people than anyone in the history of humankind, although she has made me the lead of her protection team, although she has given me a spiritual name Kailash to represent standing strong like a mountain, I am not Hindu. And I never will be.

So despite her cultural teachings, I merely learn what helps me help others manage pain and endure struggles.

I am a simple man. If something helps me and others heal and grow stronger, I will share it, regardless of origin.

I also have zero problem poking fun at myself and my silliness, or that of others. Because of my dyslexia I've often baffled my classes with cues like, "bush chack into piled," (push back into child), or, "skift your lart to the high," (lift your heart to the sky), and, "thing your thelly to your brighs," (you can figure it out).

My failings as a yoga teacher, and of not being Hindu, do not alter the health and performance benefits of what is being shared and practiced. Though there are many styles and types, yoga means to "unite" — to yoke the mind, body and breath into one unified focus.

This poster said, "Well you're just stretching then. That's not true yoga. You're a fraud and should be forced to stop telling people your books and videos are yoga. They're not valid teachings if they don't obey Hindi tenets. You make it impure by diluting it."

*A rose by any other name would smell just as sweet.* (Romeo and Juliet Act II, Scene II, William Shakespeare.)

We use our exhale to restore relaxed tone and, holding there, direct our mind to surrender the consciously braced excess tonicity.

That's all the "truer" we need to get.

Call it whatever you wish, you'll not be able to "force" your definitions on anyone. The attempt to force religious views on others has led to more bloodshed and atrocities than any other intention in human history. For that reason alone, mindless obedience should be held suspect. As Howard Zinn has wisely cautioned, *"Historically, the most terrible things — war, genocide and slavery — have not resulted from disobedience, but from obedience."*

Stop fearing names. Stop seeking to make others obey, and impose your definitions upon others. Stop judging others with categories of true or untrue, real or unreal, legitimate or fraud, based on your own perspective of a thing.

If a rose smells sweet, and you pick it so that others cannot "make it impure," you haven't protected it; you've killed the flower. Love isn't possession; love is appreciation of beauty, growth and life.

*"The purpose of life is to live it, to taste experience to the utmost, to reach out eagerly and without fear for newer and richer experience,"* illuminated Eleanor Roosevelt.

For those of you who want to practice yoga to help heal your bodies, and hold no religious interests in the cultural origins of the physical discipline — ignore those who would tell you that you're doing it wrong.

If it heals you, if it helps you and if it makes you stronger, if it gives you a richer experience of life, it is right, true, real, valid and legitimate ... and pure.

And if you laugh at my teaching foibles, I'll laugh with you, because healing, growth, beauty and love are much too serious to be taken seriously. And laughter truly is the best medicine.

TO REMAIN ALIVE, YOGA TOO MUST GROW

In some ways, martial artists have evolved more than yogis. It has been many years since I've heard a martial artist say, "That is not true martial art. That is just a fusion of boxing and wrestling, not authentic martial art."

Yet, with the release of Clubbell Yoga, a yogi decided to make the claim it is not "true yoga" and rather is "just strength training done using yogic postures."

Yoga is union, not exclusion. Particular yoga STYLES may mandate prescription of specific variations of asana, but "yoga" does not. Not in the Bhakti or Karma yoga I practice with my teacher, nor the in the variations of Hatha I was taught and share. Not by the words of Jois, Iyengar, Bhayan, Bikram, Satchidananda, or Vishnu Devananda. Each described their presentation as but one approach to yoga. Even Patanjali describes compiling what had "evolved" over time into the sutras.

And these yoga teachers have used wooden clubs, poles, ropes, stone rings, even wooden "barbells" to load the structural alignment. This has been documented even in photography before some of the aforementioned style founders were born.

Yoga is not a noun. It's a verb. To unify. In the lust of spirituality, they make the egoic error of claiming to have cornered the definition of the "true way."

Those who say they know the one true way have lost theirs. The only true way is your way, and there are as many styles as there are people on the planet. A good teacher has no styles, only a mirror to help you discover your own way.

# WHO NEEDS YOUR HELP?

An irate individual posted that people who strive for self-betterment do so only out of anxiety.

Though she has a right to an opinion on the issue, her prejudice toward the good intentions of others blinds her to the benefits that others could bring to her life, and she to theirs. It is totally okay if you don't care about such things, but my page will remain a safe place to discuss how to make one's dreams into realities, and how to help others do the same.

Unless psychology has dramatically changed since I assisted research at a neurobehavioral clinic, no study ever performed proves that striving for your aspirations is merely a product of your anxiety. This medieval pathological attitude was debunked decades ago with the birth of positive psychology, and the vein of it I studied: Flow psychology.

Doctors claimed my childhood learning disabilities could be medicated. I am overwhelmed with gratitude for the levels of challenges in my life, and did not want to let their prescriptions dull my wits, which I now apply to the problems agencies and institutes ask me to unravel, or to slow my outreach services for those who cannot afford professional courses, or to diminish the speed of innovation which has permitted me to redefine my so-called "disability" as "virtually unlimited potential."

An equal amplitude of stressors applied to two different people can produce opposite effects, depending on their approach to preparation: the ones who views themselves as victims get shoved into a downwardly spiraling vortex of anxious despair, and the ones who view themselves as growing and serving others get lifted in an upwardly spiraling zone called "flow-state." The direction you go isn't dictated by the degree of stress, but by your attitude toward it.

My personal aspirations are accomplished. I've done everything with my life that I sought for myself. Though each medal, plaque and diploma did not provide me with contentment, they are important in that by first serving my own recovery,

I gained the ability to serve others. Only self-betterment brought me to where I could stop living for myself and start living for others. Only by achieving my goals did I become of real service to others.

"First, heal thyself. Then, you will discover that when you're discouraged, the greatest solution is encouraging others," my teacher once told me. So, now I am truly free to share unabashedly what I've learned in the process. No, that's not anxiety. It's excitement to serve.

When you look around, truly you see four groups:

1.  People who need help.

2.  People who have lost hope that being helped or helping others is possible.

3.  People who want to help, but don't know how.

4.  People who are helping.

Each group deserves our support in the way that they can accept it at the moment (and sometimes in the way that they cannot). But this is not anxiety. It's a privilege and duty. If you are aware of a problem, you have a responsibility to act upon it, because you are uniquely in a position to do something to help. *"You may not be able to do everything at once, but you can do something at once,"* Calvin Coolidge advised.

That's not anxiety. It's the honor of striving to help others, regardless of how others, even "experts," will claim your pathology. If serving others is a pathology, then we ought to gladly live with that illness and use it to the best welfare of everyone we touch.

# LEARN TO LOSE WITHOUT BEING DEFEATED

Returning from teaching in Singapore, I saw that a man posted on my timeline, "I watched a video of you losing to my master at world championships in 1993. You didnt learn humility to God then and you havent by holding up your genetic flaws with pride. You lost then and your still a loser. You embarrass youre country. There is no honor in flaws. There meant to show you how little you really are but your to blind to see it."

To him I would say this: You watched a video of only one loss but you haven't seen the many hundreds of my losses — on and off the mat — that weren't filmed. However, you're correct: those losses did not teach me how insignificant I am. Instead, what you see as defeats and defects taught me how truly big-hearted each and every one of us CAN be.

Yes, BECAUSE of God's gifts (which you view as flaws and failures), I returned to win world championships several times over; despite that single loss you watched from 20 years ago. But my real victories are not on the mat. They're in my heart. Because I have been so often beaten, and yet chose to get up again and again to learn from the experience, God has taught me how to grow an indomitable spirit.

You may think you know someone's name and story, but you don't know their purpose and passion. As Jack Canfield wrote, *"Most of life is on-the-job training. Some of the most important things can only be learned in the process of doing them. You do something and you get feedback — about what works and about what doesn't. If you don't do anything for fear of doing it wrong, poorly or badly, you never get any feedback, and therefore you never get to improve."*

The only fighters who've never lost never competed. Because they never receive the feedback of loss, they remain bitter and small, deprecating others. As long as you continue to view other people's losses as defeats, your growth stays stunted — impotent to access your true perseverance.

My opponents may defeat my body without my consent, but they can defeat my spirit only with my consent. That is how you face loss and remain undefeatable.

True champions of the heart face life's inevitable losses, and persevere to fight again and again, despite repeated loss. They refuse to submit to smallness of spirit, to falling and staying down. That is a real undefeatable champion.

Life humbles us not to paralyze us but to empower us. Take a chance to reframe what you once considered failures and flaws, and instead see only life's lessons and gifts ... and transform both your attitude toward others and your perspective on your own life.

# FIGHTING FOR PEACE OF MIND

I can appreciate how some would misunderstand why I fight. Mixed martial arts can appear like a chest-thumping cacophony of punk-jitsu. But after enduring the violent fallout of post-traumatic stress in our family, which eventually consumed my father after his return from the Korean War, I gravitated to the martial arts as a cathartic release from rage and shame.

My father sacrificed more than a physical existence. His illness forfeited his entire family life. Ill-equipped to reacclimatize to domestic living, his alcoholism and abuse spiraled into our disintegration.

I externalized this drama repeatedly throughout my life, unwittingly seeking a solution to excessive stress. And violence became my bedfellow, as my peers smelled the victimization like chummed waters, bloodied by my obesity, learning disabilities and impoverishment.

Martial art, like yoga and athletics, became a proving ground for me to remain calm under stress. If I could face the strain of combative arousal, and keep mentally focused and emotionally controlled, I could perhaps find the solution to my family's, to my father's, post-traumatic stress.

I did not know this was my journey. I was only an actor in the storyline. Not until after I found my "perfect fight" — where I could remain calm in the storm — did the lifetime of struggle unriddle itself. …

Risking my business reputation and my body, facing opponents half my age and even 100 pounds heavier, jeopardizing my own family's livelihood, to emancipate myself from the cycle of rage of PTSD, winning the World Martial Arts Games was not a conquest for gold. I am honored to have gold placed over my neck for the US Team, but it was the gold placed in my heart that compelled me to compete.

I found my perfect fight and healed. The tools and techniques my teachers taught me allowed me to achieve that calm in the storm that was critical to my healing.

I have made a lot of mistakes over the years, and hurt a lot of people in my process of blindly seeking a solution to my drama.

But I hope to somehow compensate for any pain I caused by sharing these tools, and perhaps prevent the next generation from the burden of carrying excessive stress as their inheritance.

This was the motivation behind my book "Primal Stress: Revive — Survive — Thrive."

# YOUR TRUE PURPOSE MAY BE HIDDEN

As I was running down to the grocery for water and food, an elderly Orthodox Jewish man, visibly panting, asked me, "You're Jewish, no?"

I replied that I wasn't and slowed to walk with him.

He said, "Don't worry. Nobody's perfect." He continued by telling me that he had been praying to God for help. When he had finished his prayer and opened his eyes, he saw the pin of the Israeli Sheyetet 13 (their navy SEALs) on my shirt.

(It was actually the TACFIT logo, but that's another, longer story.)

He asked if I was in the military or security protecting temples. Shaking my head, I asked him if he was okay.

"For now, yes — Thank God. But three men are following me. I am too old to run, or even yell for help," he replied, pointing back toward three men striding toward him with determined eyes leveled.

As he pointed fearfully over his shoulder, he stepped into oncoming traffic. Horns raged and tires screeched. There wasn't any time to grab him, so I instinctively (foolishly?) jumped between the old man and the oncoming garbage truck. As it slid to a rubber-burnt stop, I leaned into the grille for the leverage to help me scoop the man in my other arm and jump forward …

… Straight into another oncoming lane of traffic. *Sheesh!*

Holding the man close, we spun together between the lanes of traffic and behind the passing car before the next arrived.

We were almost graceful if it weren't for the flying appendages of two unlikely gentlemen pirouetting together down a busy NYC street.

The next car was able to stop, thankfully, for although I had gotten the old man across I would not have made it in time.

Accepting the onslaught of curses from the driver with a bumpkin shoulder shrugging, I yelled, "Sorry!"

I escorted the man into the restaurant of a hotel, found him a seat and went to talk to security. However, they had seen the entire event and had already called for medical assistance.

The men he had thought were following him were gone and he was safe. Needing to return to my family, I checked in on him one last time. He said "I prayed for help but I thought it was from men following me, not from traffic. Thank you!" He smiled a great smile.

Overwhelmed by the event, I needed some time to take it all in. The universe acts in such complex ways and yet so elegantly; a tapestry of our actions interwoven with others in a constellation of unpredictable threads.

Our prayers are always answered, just not how we initially may think and always in our better interest.

Lawrence Block defined serendipity by suggesting, *"If you look for something, you'll find something else, but realize that what you've found is more suited to your needs than what you had thought you were looking for."*

On many days, I had been in this man's place and in many more, he had been in mine.

I pray for the courage to embrace the challenges I am sent, and for wisdom to understand them for the gifts they are.

As Nancy Long writes, *"Whether we name divine presence as synchronicity, serendipity, or grace matters little. What matters is the reality that our hearts have been understood. Nothing is as real as a healthy dose of magic to restore our spirits."*

# PUT ASIDE YOUR AGENDA, CHANGE A LIFE

We arrived at the gym at 0630 for our final TACFIT Rings session before we departed on our respective flights home for a quick break until we were to regroup in Argentina in a week.

About 20 young athletes were leaving, but they recognized Alberto. They all stopped to shake his hand. I pulled down my hat and quietly stepped around behind the group to jump on the mat for a workout unnoticed, because time was short and I wanted to TACFIT before wheels up.

As I was about to start the clock, I heard one of the kids explaining to the group that the creator of TACFIT fought across the planet, collecting animal movements, gymnastics skills, and old combat weapons to put together the best way to train fighters. Another pointed at me across the room, "You mean Scott Sonnon? That's him over there."

They ran over and asked for photos and autographs while Alberto laughed at my failed ninja routine.

Selfishly I wanted that time for just myself without interruption. However, I had not anticipated the impact that even a brief meeting could have on these young men and women. Like my mentors, idols and heroes had upon me, we often forget the impact that meeting them can have … in my case, changing the course of my life forever.

One young man shook my hand and said, "You don't know how much you changed my life, Coach. You just don't know." While taking a photo with him, I realized his entire body was trembling about the opportunity to take a photo with someone he had looked up to so highly. I said to him that he did it all himself, that even the best system won't work if he hadn't. And that I was honored he was part of the family.

Precisely those moments of selfishness, gaps in conscience, and lapses in awareness, have been my most squandered opportunities for significant impact upon the lives of those I've met. Reflecting upon meeting my idolized coaches and teachers, those moments that they took away from their lives for me, recharted the course I took in my life. They could have chosen to sneak unnoticed off to their own desires and expectations, but thankfully they gave me their attention for a brief moment. And that made a world of difference to me.

Respect to my teachers. Oss[1].

---

1   A term of Japanese origin used in the martial arts that conveys elements of respect, friendship and determination.

# BECOME BOTH STRONGER AND GENTLER

I have been a fighter, whether I've wanted it or not, all my life. I take no joy in it; in fact, I dread both facing violence, and the degree to which I must counter it with my own.

I'm not guiltless. I've hurt people — a lot of them. What I could do to another person causes me to lament the prospect. Being in more and more altercations over the years, I haven't grown desensitized to it. If anything, I've grown MORE sensitive to the tragic consequences of physical violence. Someone always gets hurt, and usually everyone involved does; many with long-term consequences; a tragic few… with finality.

Considering the above, most people don't understand why I have competed in so many styles of martial art. I have competed because the martial arts have allowed me to develop physical governors for my actions. They've given me greater granularity of control, more precise proportionality to counter violence, the ability to think, see and breathe calmly in the face of crisis.

This degree of control allows me to minimize the amount of damage I must do to others, even when they aim to do the maximum to me. That practice has become a directive: I train now, not to increase my capacity for dealing violence, but to decrease the damage I must do in order to neutralize it.

I recently told someone that my teacher taught me this, but that's not entirely accurate. My LIFE has taught me this, but my teacher has brought it to a conscious level of daily practice.

Amma is my Guru: a term I usually hide from others, because being a disciple of a guru isn't easily digested in the West. So when people ask me about her, I say that she's my "compassion coach." This makes some of the men with whom I have the honor of working flinch a bit, and I fully understand that reaction … as I too was suspicious of compassion in the face of violence … until its truth became incontrovertible.

Compassion isn't weak. It's gentle. Gentleness isn't impotent; quite the opposite. The compassion to increase one's skill to the point where you can CHOOSE to be gentle, especially in the face of violence, is perhaps true strength.

"Love all. Serve all. Trust none but God," my teacher said during a recent visit to Seattle. Appointed as lead for her security detail (with a team of incredible people), I captured what moments I could off-duty to let my external awareness ebb, and reflect upon her teachings.

My team was on the floor, my teacher had begun speaking, and everyone was captivated by her gentle words and compassionate energy. Suddenly, a distraught woman charged the stage. Before I rounded the corner, she had already ascended the stairs.

My team rushed forward, but she was already screaming violently and thrashing about, hitting people on stage. In a few steps, I was behind her.

Smiling and unfazed, my teacher told the woman to sit down next to her. The audience of over 2,000 held their collective breath at the sight. The woman acquiesced, but then angrily shoved aside one of the translators, and threw her body across my teacher and began kicking anyone within reach. I put my body in position as a shield, letting her kicks glance off me instead.

Any of us may find ourselves emotionally drowning at any point in the day - whether from missing a meal, misunderstanding each other in an argument, or from more serious lapses in lucid comprehension. I could see this woman drowning. I've been there, and knew that sinking feeling.

My teacher told me to let the woman stay, but I carefully scooped the woman and lifted her like a parent would carry a baby. She flailed and kicked as I carried her off the stage, punching me in the face, and kicking at anyone in range. I kept whispering to her, "You're okay. You're okay." And when others came over to stop her from hitting me, I told them, "She's okay! She's fine!"

I've been hit many times by some of the most skilled fighters in the world. I knew that the psychologically open water in which she was scrambling to breathe was frightening enough without me trying to forcibly restrain her, and I could easily accept the limited damage she was causing. I was strong enough to carry her; familiar enough with fighting to know she was not going to harm me; and skilled enough to keep her from harming others.

The crowd collectively sighed as they saw how gently she was being helped out of the hall, and I knew that we had avoided casting a shadow over the event. In fact, we had actually accomplished something positive, demonstrating how we could elevate our ability to face violence in the world: assertively, conclusively, but gently and compassionately.

It was her gift to me that I could realize such a blessing. And I mean that. I am grateful to her for this realization, though not from her conscious doing, obviously.

I hadn't known the extent to which I could remain 100 percent calm in such a situation until the gift of this event.

I have a duty in my daily practice to be better than the day before, so that as my skill increases, so does my ability to protect first myself, then others, and, finally, even the would-be drowning soul from whence the violence comes.

Some harm will come, to those who have slipped under the water so deeply that they will claw over anyone and anything for one more gasp of air, and, far more tragically – to those who have resigned themselves to sinking but in their overwhelming sorrow, seek to drag others with them. Harm will come to them, unfortunately, and from our hands. I dread those moments, but I will face them. And I will be better prepared each day to make lesser harm a trained option.

My teacher has helped me to realize what my life has been trying to teach me: There are no opponents; there are no enemies; there is only ignorance and the desperation it creates. Realizing that the capacity for that ignorance lies within each of us, allows us to expand our sphere of compassion. It also compels us to train harder and smarter every day, so that as we protect ourselves and others from harm, we can minimize the harm we must visit upon those ignorant of the consequences of their actions.

I don't fear violence any less than when it was visited upon me as a child. Perhaps, I fear it even more. I am just done reacting to it with the same mindlessness that created it, and perpetuates it from one generation to the next.

Thomas Edison said, *"Five percent of the world thinks; 10 percent of the world think they think; and the other 85 percent would rather die than think."* I practice every day so that I can enter and remain in the 5 percent, so that I can open my heart as well as my eyes. Just because most don't, doesn't mean we can't.

My brothers-in-arms call this the "sheepdog attitude" — closer to the predatory wolf-mind than that of the unguarded sheep-mind (into which we all must relax and deserve to take sanctuary throughout our lives). At any point in time, we may be given the chance to act as a sheepdog for ourselves and the innocents of the world, to protect against the frenetic panic that causes sheep to mutate with wolf-minded choices and in that desperation, bring violence to others surrounding them.

I believe there's another hopeful step: that through the righteousness of our gentle hand, we minimize the damage we must do to the wolf-minded, so that even if they do not transform themselves, through our example, into sheepdogs, then those watching, touched by our striving for self-betterment in the face of violence, could perhaps choose to become sheepdogs themselves, rather than wolves. ... And perhaps — though a crazy, impossible dream — in generations hence, the number of wolf-minded choices may decrease.

Love all. Serve all. Trust none but God.

A victory for love ... Amma

*Kailash*

# CONSENSUS COULD HOLD YOU BACK

When I coined the term "mobility training" in the early 1990s teaching at my university, other professors scoffed at the notion.

When I published my book on the flow of natural movement impacting emotional state, the industry laughed at the idea of a primal mind-body connection to exercise.

When I patented Clubbell swinging for three-dimensional movement strength over a decade ago, they became angry at the idea that we adapt to systemic movement, not segmental muscles.

When I launched the discipline of "tactical fitness" as a focus on accelerated recovery from excessive stress, they argued it was unnecessary and that only more powerful output was needed.

When I published the phrase "compensatory movement," suggesting that we must always specifically unload our actions, they claimed over-training is impossible.

Now, each of those ideas has become an established sub-industry in itself.

My career has been built upon standing alone against the incumbent opposition to my ideas. Had I folded to their resistance, none of these ideas would have had a chance to come to life. And that will not stop. I will continue to ruffle feathers, and encourage the new generation in our community to do the same.

Even now, they will be upset, claiming that only ego would attempt to take credit for accomplishments. Only our teachers deserve acknowledgement for creating the possibility of our achievements. But it takes your courageous temerity and obstinate stamina to resist the ridicule of others and remain true to yourself and your convictions.

As a result, I cannot endorse consensus as the highest form of social development. Rather, I hold authenticity as your most important contribution to others. YOU are the contribution! Compromise is a critical strategy for conflict resolution, but never let them pressure you to comprise your integrity or values… Or you will rob us all of the unique genius only you specifically could teach us.

# RELATIONSHIPS ARE A MARTIAL ART

My ex-girlfriend had had a viciously hot temper, which strangely attracted me in my early years as she seemed to be full of audacity. In reality, she was just dangerous; and my attraction to it, a product of my familiarity of being reared in an environment of violence. A toxic relationship, I had sought to extricate myself, resulting with a blowout where most of my apartment began flying toward me.

When I ended the relationship, I found myself entering a new one too quickly. Not violent but highly argumentative, words flew and often I became angry at what had been said. I wasn't innocently a victim, and had participated. I own my contributions. I ended it but not before awful things had been uttered by us both.

In the next relationship, few words had been spoken; never an argument. I had thought it must be perfect; and even said so to a trusted friend. When I flew quite literally around the world to visit her where she had studied abroad, she disclosed she had had sex with another man. Not fists, not words, but rather values had been thrown. They had skulked by invisibly and hurt the most. We ended painfully.

When I got married to my wonderful wife, I began studying with a teacher. He never seemed to get ruffled during controversial topics, and stated when he comments on an issue, he firstly asks himself if he speaks from his truth. He then asks himself if his comment will be necessary. Lastly, he asks himself if his comment will be kind rather than nice.

He explained that niceties are lies we tell socially to avoid our truth because we believe it to be more important to be polite than kind. Kindness on the other hand speaks your authentic truth even if the other considers it to be not nice. Speak your truth when necessary, and do so with kindness in your heart and you'll remain unaroused with no anger regardless of what is said or done.

When people debated with him they often found themselves frustrated and losing their temper but as soon as they did, my teacher never escalated emotionally or psychologically, so they would defuse or even apologize.

My wife and I don't agree on everything. Being different genders doesn't help us understand each other; though our same sex couple friends don't seem to have it any easier. But we love each other and are best friends, so we continually practice improving our communication, opening our empathy and lengthening our patience.

We both practice asking ourselves if it is our authentic truth which we speak, if it is necessary to say it, and if we are truly kind in our heart when we utter it.

We have difficult spots, but by practicing deepening our relationship we've learned a great deal about each other and increased our fulfillment as a couple.

Relationships are like martial art. Practice getting better every day if you intend to remain calm and centered when misunderstanding happens. Speak authentically your truth. Say what is necessary to resolve the misunderstanding. And like the reflective surface of a calm lake, keep kindness in your heart so you can mirror the compassion with which you wish to be treated.

# WHAT'S THE PUNCH-LINE IN YOUR LIFE?

On July 1st, 2009, I was given the honor of speaking as keynote for the Mensa National Conference. Considering the course of my life, institutionalized in a psychiatric hospital as a child for my learning difficulties, presenting my story to the "High IQ Society" had seemed like an ironic punch-line in the riddle that has been my life.

It's one thing for me to somehow get "lucky" enough to pass the intelligence examinations to be inducted into Mensa, but quite another within one year to be featured in their national journal, and then keynote at their national conference!

With not an empty seat in the William Penn Conference Center in Pittsburgh, and mostly a more seasoned crowd, I shared with my fellow Mensans the story of when I co-presented with the immortal Francois Henri "Jack" LaLanne — the Godfather of Fitness — at the Arnold Schwarzenegger Active Aging Festival.

Obviously, I felt intimidated following one of my childhood heroes. This is a man who pulled 70 boats while swimming shackled and handcuffed… at 70 years old. How could I follow Jack LaLanne?

Jack saw that I was nervous and put his arm around my shoulder to lend me a bit of wisdom.

He said, "Scott, I realize that you've traveled the world and mastered martial arts and exercise, but you haven't yet learned my secret."

Now… Jack was 92 years young at the time. You can imagine my boyish delight that I was about to peek into this ancient tome of fitness magic.

He said to me, uttering each word distinctly, "I… can't… die."

Confused but shaking it off with a chuckle I replied, "Granted you're the 'immortal' Jack LaLanne, but I hope you weren't bitten by lycanthropy as a child." (Jack had overcome childhood physical disabilities just as I had.)

He pulled me tighter and repeated, "I can't die. It'd be bad for my image."

Chagrined that I just let myself by snookered, I deflated. But Jack resumed in reconciliation, "Son, the secret's passion. Your PASSION," as he picked up my arm and waved it overhead like I had won the Olympics. "Ya either got guts or ya don't. And you have it in spades. It's not about intelligence or privilege or genetics. How can you not live forever when you feel so grateful to be healthy and strong and share that with other people? Listen kid, you're going to do exactly what you're destined to do and people will love you because of your passion!"

Those words will always echo around every episode through my life. Whenever I feel incompetent or ill-prepared. Which is often.

I don't really get excited unless the challenge is something bigger than I've done before. Why do what you've already done; you already know that you can do that thing, so do something that scares the hell out of you!

So, when I face a challenge, I remember Jack's secret… that it doesn't matter if I feel prepared. That's the paradox of bravery: Courage comes after the time that you need it. You only become brave by doing the thing you fear anyway.

Standing in front of an audience of some of the brightest minds in my country, I had found myself again facing a new challenge… but Jack's words reverberated through my preparatory meditation. Sharing my story, I received my first standing ovation in my speaking career…

The punch-line in my life has been that despite being the obese, learning disabled kid in the back of the class, the incredible teachers and mentors I've had helped me become the man who now gets to speak with the brightest minds in the world: YOU! Sharing that miracle with others is, as Jack said, "a passion which can overcome any obstacle."

What's been the punch-line in your life? What has been the source of inspiration, your passion, in your life? And what approaches have you used, or are you looking to implement to transcend the challenges you face?

# FOCUS YOUR FITNESS ON BEING HEALTHY

I watched as Jimmy slowly died inside; but back then, I had no tools to help him. I could only stay as close as he'd let me while he mentally circled the drain.

When he decided to compete in bodybuilding, the massive truckloads of powders and pills, the painfully ceaseless hours at the gym and tanning bed, and eventually, the "enhancing" needles came and siphoned his life.

Though we had once talked about futures and goals, first our church functions evaporated, then the erosion of our family events, and finally we stopped hanging out altogether. He had been skipping work to get extra time at the gym, and got into heated arguments with his boss about it, inevitably losing his job.

Even our discussions had stopped, with him telling me to get lost since I didn't know what being a real warrior was.

With Jimmy and his physique, there was no room left for our friendship. Everything devolved to his reflection in the mirror. I had lost him.

I watched from a distance, as his pains increased, with the pain killers to match. Then, his bicep had torn; followed by his quad. Lastly, he had blown out his knee, requiring reconstructive surgery. He had called me, crying, and divulged, "I'm never going to be good enough, bro."

I replied, "I can hear how much you're suffering. My family is going over to this taichi and yoga thing that the church is putting on at the park. Even if you can't do everything, come get some fresh air with me, and bring your little brother." He did.

Over time, through taichi and yoga and changes in his diet, he began to improve his health, detox off of his dangerous supplements, get off the needles, and start addressing the laundry list of injuries and pains throughout his body. He spent a lot more time hanging out with his younger brother. He started teaching free gatherings at the park for at-risk kids, and launched it into a personal training business which has now boomed, appropriately named, "Real Healthy."

One day he sent me a message, "Bro, I just wanted to thank you for saving my life. You gave me back my family, helped me see my purpose, and patched my body back together. I just won my first Jiujitsu tournament, and my kid brother won his division, too. We did it together and he told me that better than his gold around his neck was his brother's arm on top of it. Thank God for everything you do, bro. You've always been a REAL... Healthy... friend." I got the meaning of his business name.

When we tip hyper-focus onto our appearance, size and strength, out of alignment with our health and ability to move pain and injury free. It consumes all of our attention, and hemorrhages not just our psychological and spiritual outlook, but our involvement with family, friends and community. When people start to reclaim their health and mobility, they often reinvest their personal and spiritual orientation onto their family involvement and their community participation.

It's all about lifestyle balance.

I remember, before his death, standing on stage, teaching next to my mentor, the "Godfather of Fitness" Jack LaLanne.

He put his arm around me and said to everyone, "Do you know how I stay alive and fit for so long? Do you know why I am so passionate about exercise and nutrition? Do you know why I can keep jumping up and down like this year after year? Because it SAVED my life, and it is GOING to save YOURS. How can you not be passionate about something that'll change and save lives? NOW GET UP!!!"

And when Jack told an audience to jump up, they always did. He infected them with his vital enthusiasm.

Change and save your life, and those around you. You may not feel like you have tools, but if you make a choice, they'll appear in front of you. Get out there and focus on being healthy and moving well again. Get together with your family and do it, and you may just discover that even though you feel, do and look great, you've changed and maybe saved their lives as well.

# PRUNE AWAY UNPRODUCTIVE DENIAL

Recently a fitness professional stated that I am too hard on people, that I should just let them be happy and have fun; that if I really cared about people, I'd just let them enjoy their lives.

People have a right to live their lives, however they wish, without any judgment from others. However, if they ask for my professional help because they're NOT happy with their state, then I'm not going to enable people's current patterns if they're not contributing to their targeted growth and development. I don't see that as preventing people from enjoying their lives, but helping them.

I have had very good reasons for not being successful at reclaiming my health and fitness; very rational explanations for why I have not been able to get where I wanted and needed to go. And not one of those excuses mattered.

Just because you have a good excuse, doesn't mean you're exempt from overcoming it.

One of our team's leaders in Europe lost a hand during a horrible accident in his youth. Despite having a totally legitimate reason to exempt himself from succeeding, he succeeded anyway. When he first went for his physical test, we failed him.

The same fitness professional I mentioned above said I was a "horrible coach" for not allowing special exception to our testing standards. However, our European leader, despite that first failure, found a way, came back and destroyed the exam. He exemplifies everything I believe is honorable and pure about physical culture as a "way" of personal development.

Not ironically, he's one of the happiest, and most enjoyable people I have found to spend time with outside of training. Why? No excuses. No lamenting a circumstance or complaining about a situation, rather only looking for solution, enjoying the puzzle, appreciating the mystery, and reveling in the process. I enjoy listening to his ideas, and being in his company; something I cannot say of everyone.

It is not negativity to confront a problem. First, you must be willing to fight to change what you feel is unacceptable. Then, you can begin to see the benefits that challenge will bring you as a result of your courage to turn and face it. Finally, the opportunities from that situation and your willingness to address it appear.

If it is truly important to you, you will find a way. If not, you'll find an excuse. A good coach, like a good friend, won't sugarcoat it with false smiles and pretend hugs, but will tell you straight. I'm not telling you it's going to be easier, because frankly, it's probably going to get a lot harder before it gets any easier. I am, however, telling you that it's going to be worth it and I believe you can, if you set your mind to doing it.

All dreams ARE unrealistic by definition, because they're not real YET.

The people closest to you often resist your continual change the most strongly. Not because your dreams are unrealistic, but because the reality of their own dreams feels too heavy to believe that anyone could carry the burden. They don't believe in themselves YET, though your example of going alone when you must may give them reluctant courage to do the same.

Everyone looks down the road of their dreams, and consciously or intuitively acknowledges the massive resistance they'll encounter. The ONLY foolish dreamers are those who wish or disbelieve any resistance will be met. Sometimes you'll have to go it all the way alone. But those who have realized their dreams will nod in sympathy, as everyone who has made their dreams REAL, has walked in solitude and faced the trials of transformation. … And everyone in their sphere of influence has benefited from their persistence and determination.

# DISCIPLINE IS CONTAGIOUS – USE IT

How you do one thing is how you do anything. This applies to food and movement. Master one thing, apply those lessons to all disciplines, and you will most assuredly be correct.

As I continue to deepen my study of other disciplines, the reflections of my own core mastery appear.

As one of my critical means of sharing information and insights is through writing, I invest at least two hours per week in expanding and refining my writing skills. Verlyn Klinkenborg, non-fiction author, New York Times Editor, and self-farming advocate, in his course, The Genre of the Sentence, mandates, "Anything you think you need in order to write — or to be inspired to write or to get in the mood — becomes a prohibition when it's lacking. Learn to write anywhere, at any time, in any condition, with anything, starting from nowhere. All you need is your head: the one indispensable requirement."

I have found this to be true in my own discipline of martial art, in both competition and in surviving confrontations, and I also discover this true in both exercise and nutrition.

In exercise, you cannot rely upon a gym, a training partner, a personal trainer, a piece of equipment, a workout program, or a particular movement. Wherever you are, whatever you have, no matter your circumstances, decide upon the time that you must (within an hour after waking, and before your first meal), start your exercise.

If you're too tight, sore and tired, do your mobility, but get up and do it for 20 minutes. The appetite comes with the meal: you may find yourself able to do more once you switch on your nervous system through movement.

In nutrition, you cannot depend upon a meal plan, diet, restaurant, grocery store, recipe, nutritionist, cook or particular food. Whatever money you have, wherever you happen to be and have access to, schedule your meals at least a day in advance, and if you cannot, then have a glass of water, sit down, and think of your best option. Shop before you're starving, but if you wait until it's too late, then shop the perimeter of the store to avoid the processed packaged "quick" crap.

Once you eat a little of good food, you'll be able think more clearly, have better energy and be able to create an effective plan for getting more quality food.

All you need is yourself. That doesn't meant that you cannot reach out to those you trust in times of need. But if they're not available to inspire, motivate or support you, STILL do it. You are all you need. Trust yourself, and do it, no matter how convincing your excuse, reason or circumstance. Do it anyway, even if only a little. You'll find yourself able to do more and more, little by little.

# LET FAILURE BE YOUR FUEL

Another startup company of mine had failed; this time losing several thousand dollars of investment collected by family to support our initiative. We had started a gym, invested in the equipment, and launched our classes. Knowing too little about marketing and business management at the time, within a year, we had to close doors.

I was devastated, broke and disheartened, until a family member told me of his own failed business venture, and how it taught him to focus on the real questions being asked by the end-user. He suggested I continue to bring high quality to my clientele, but organize my service so that they would be self-willed to share the news about the quality.

I doubled down on my efforts, at redesigning the system I had been teaching so that it pre-incorporated the marketing punch needed to make entry into local markets and compete with big box health clubs. I began with the question, "What would give this quality system wheels and traction outside of the classes? What would cause people to want to virally spread it by word of mouth?"

Implementing it in a new gym, and then another, and another, it rapidly spread across the globe. TACFIT has now been named by one of its own competitors "the fastest spreading fitness system in the world."

An arrow can only be shot forward by pulling it to the rear, and a bolt can only be tightened by first turning the socket wrench backward. Had I not had my decisive failure at my initial start up business, I would not have been compelled to redesign my system in such a way that would give it the legs to travel to success. Perhaps I would have continued with mediocre success at that one facility. Perhaps it would have failed anyway from the toil of teaching everything myself for long hours with little compensation for my family. But that gift of failure gave me the perspective to revisit my strategy.

Aikido training taught me that when I encounter great opposition, to absorb the resistance I faced, confluently blend with it, and bring about a great resolution through joining with it. I continue to apply this in my vocation as a writer, speaker and entrepreneur. As George Leonard wrote in his 1992 book on Aikido Mastery, *"We fail to realize that mastery is not about perfection. It's about a process, a journey. The master is the one who stays on the path day after day, year after year. The master is the one who is willing to try, and fail and try again, for as long as he or she lives."*

Failure is so paramount to success that you should find something you're willing to die for and live for it, because you'll need the faith and courage to recover from your falls, reorient on a more effective strategy and redouble your efforts. Try and fail, but don't fail to try. You must fall backward, like the arrow or the socket wrench, for advancement to occur.

# FOLLOW THE HIGH ROAD

My attorney contacted me, so we had to end our family vacation early to return home. When we crossed the border into the States, my phone lit up like a Christmas tree. Flabbergasted by the thousands of remarks and comments on my Facebook page, I saw 1.25 MILLION readers in the past week alone!

This is my REAL work. Yes, I write health and fitness books and produce video workout series; and thanks to my teachers, true friends and loving family, I've become one of the leading spokespersons in the industry. But my real work, I do happily for FREE!

The books I write, the seminars I teach and the videos I produce subsidize my ability to reach out online to those who face truly difficult challenges every day, but I get to do this in a non-transactional way. There is no "fee" my audience must pay. Certainly, a portion of you, when able, sponsor my ability to be online, by reading my books and following my workouts. But that patronage allows me the latitude to invest my time for free.

On the phone, I advised a colleague not to worry about recent attempts to repackage my work by others who were claiming it as their own. Why? Because those books and videos are merely things I've done. They are neither what I do, nor who I am.

Yes, I'm proud of the programs I've created, as well as my ambassadors in 32 countries. But my REAL work is for free. It cannot be stolen, because it doesn't require a transaction. It cannot be repackaged, because it isn't contained within a package to purchase. It's given away for free.

A colleague, friend and fellow writer, Dan Millman, once said to me back in the early 1990s, "Scott, you have to be willing to sacrifice what you are, for who you can become." His truth still holds today. Who I can become is not defined by what I've done in the past, but what I can offer to the world TODAY.

I will not scurry about desperately squabbling with those who squeeze pittance by repurposing work I once did. I won't be policing my intellectual property for fear of "loss." There's nothing I can lose. I HAVE nothing to lose, because God has given me a way to make a living offering my time to those who need it. I am finally free, because there is no price tag to who I am. Imagine, 1.25 million readers to a single post in one week.

Despite all of the trolling immaturity some visitors may muddily tramp through our discussions, a difference is being made.

Keep going. Millions are joining us. Don't allow yourself to be pulled down by those who truthfully need us to remain on the High road. We are doing it. Like Mooji said, *"Don't remind the world that it is sick and troubled. Remind it that it is beautiful and FREE!"*

# BE PATIENT, DAWN APPROACHES

A friend going through a hard time asked me when I first saw light at the end of the tunnel. Honestly, I never did. For me, it wasn't traveling toward a tunneled light, but rather a pinhole of hope poking through my obscurity, like light sneaking in behind the fabric of a blindfold. Fortunately, the worst is not as dangerous as we imagine.

For example, a disgruntled former student threatened to recruit others to abuse my trademarks until they became "household terms" — as a result, causing us to lose our ability to protect our work from loss of value. I was prepared for the challenges of failure, when nothing I had was worth anything. But, I had not prepared for the challenges of success.

I felt very worried for the families who survive from my work, so I consulted with a trusted coach. After listening to my concerns, she helped remind me of five critical points:

1. Write down the following four salient points as they may again slip into unclarity. This reinforces my vigilant awareness through the kinesthetic anchor of handwriting.

2. Remember that I'm always objectively protected, despite the temporary illusion of disconnectedness from the disorientation of threats from broken trust. This restores my faith in the indirect process of giving support without any expectation of reward, and allows people to come to me because they believe in my value as a professional and as a person.

3. Remove judgment from events: neither castigate them as bad, nor struggle to perceive their good. They just "are." Remain non-judgmental and assume the purpose will reveal itself over time with courage.

4. Remain true, or perhaps even truer, to my authenticity. Transparency allows others to identify with my message, and aspire to trust in their own process. Courage is a contagion that infects others. If I withhold my courage, it diminishes the opportunities others may have to stay strong.

5. Stop attempting to avoid being hit. If you try to prevent being hit in a fight, you're always reactionary and never blending with the opponent's energy to find a mutual resolution to the conflict. Instead, recover rapidly WHEN my attitude takes a hit by focusing on what I value most.

Once in Russia, my coach told me of a Cossack rite of passage. The young cadet's father would take him into the forest, blindfold him and tell the boy to sit on a stump the whole night. He is told not to remove the blindfold until the rays of the morning sun shine through it. He cannot cry out for help, and must face his ordeal alone.

For once he survives the night, he is told he will become a MAN.

The boys are naturally terrified. They hear all manner of noises. Wild beasts must surely be all around them — maybe even a human to do them harm.

Though the wind may blow the grass and earth, and shake the stump, the cadets are required to sit stoically, never remove the blindfold. Even in the mind of a child, they know their courage to sit quietly unmoving would be the only way they could become Men!

Finally, after a horrific night, the sun would appear and they would remove their blindfold. Each cadet would discover his father sitting on the stump next to him, at watch the entire night, protecting the son from harm.

We, too, are never alone, even when we don't know it. However you define God, I believe, should be your own right. Just find Him when you're sitting on your stump of hardships, terrified under your blindfold.

You may lose your faith in your dark nights. But still sit there, because we are given these opportunities not to punish our lack of faith, but to develop greater courage in spite of our fears.

If we tear off our blindfold early, or we await until the sun basks us with warm pinholes of hope, either way, we will discover we were never alone. But if we wait, if we exhale and calm ourselves, steel our will, when we remove the blindfold at the beckoning dawn, we will be so proud of ourselves, and the greater maturity we have developed through our courage.

Stay strong. It won't be much longer. Dawn comes, and you are not alone.

# ESCHEW QUICK PAYOFFS FOR TRUE VALUE

Sitting in front of one of, if not the, largest infomercial companies in the world, I was being courted regarding my system, which I had invested over a decade building, teaching and refining. It was anticipated to become the "Next, Big Thing!"

Question after question came, "Could this be changed to be more like our current program? Could that be changed too? What about this? Do we need this? Can't we use what we've already found to sell?"

Eventually, I laughed and replied, "Two things cannot both be the same, and be different. I've spent years isolating and amplifying what makes what I teach a success to all levels of people, not just a niche. I cannot guarantee injury-free, superior results we've validated by making my program into what you've already done. I can't change what I've found to safely and consistently yield high results in order to promise high-volume, rapid sales."

I couldn't lie. I couldn't compromise my values for the allure of millions. Many have called me crazy for allowing my Puritan principles to "lose" the opportunity I had been given at that time. Crazy I can accept. But the mighty oak was once a little nut who kept its ground. Now, my system has been adopted by more special units and federal agencies than any other approach in history. Sometimes, being a little nutty pays off in the long run.

I may have lost that "golden" payoff, but I won a clear conscience by not perverting my integrity. And I won a community of excellence, of ambassadors who honorably strive to represent the principles and integrity which made us our best.

As Miyagi said to his student Daniel in Karate Kid II, *"Never put passion in front of principle, for if you do, even if you win, you lose."* Though I never became the huge flash trend of popular television infomercial programs, even though it has taken me years longer than it would have otherwise required by selling out to the lowest quality denominators for the highest bid, I've been able to slowly build a legacy into a legion.

Delicately probing for the file which had been closed on my life as a minor with learning disabilities, a doctor once asked me if any of our family suffered any mental conditions. I replied with a smile, "No, we all seem to enjoy them just fine, thanks."

You have to be a little crazy sometimes to stick to your values, especially when offered a seductive opportunity to cave in and sell out. But remember, no matter how attractive the payoff may seem, what awaits you for keeping your integrity and staying true to your honor FAR, FAR outweighs any fool's gold bedazzling our dim-sighted greed.

# FOLLOW YOUR DREAMS ... LITERALLY

One mental technique I use to solve encountered problems involves a process often alluded to as "lucid dreaming."

Immediately before falling asleep I reflect upon the challenge I am facing and begin imagining a solution which actually transforms the challenge into an opportunity.

In my research, I had discovered that when the brain hemispheres are severed, the left, speech-centered half will "confabulate" — make up — explanations as to the actions the right half is doing.

Dyslexia predominantly involves "mixed dominance" (including ambidexterity) where the sidedness of the brain is connected across both hemispheres like a lightning storm. Certain skills will be left handed and others right handed; some both.

I noticed early on, and then later confirmed in my research, that this same neural network which storms throughout the neocortex creating mixed dominance also allows dyslexics to step outside otherwise orthodox boundaries of the currently possible through this process of confabulation.

This same phenomenon allowed famous dyslexics like Albert Einstein to think outside the conventional parameters of his field. As Einstein once said, *"I very rarely think in words at all. A thought comes, and I may try to express it in words afterwards."*

Einstein's solutions weren't particularly complicated; in fact they were very simple in process and product, but how many thousands of other thinkers were completely incapable of thinking through Einstein's simple mental exercises and create solutions which have changed our world?

My technique, used by many other thinkers, lets the dreaming thought process sidestep learned rigidity and consider flexible, rule-bending solutions. Rarely are these solutions complicated.

For example, I was born with a joint disease called osteochondrosis, where conventional weight lifting created great pain to my underdeveloped connective tissue due to the dramatic compression the exercise causes.

Programming my mind one night before sleeping, I had sought to create an alternative to this problem. "How could my disease be an advantage here," I asked. My dreams allowed me to use "non-directed thinking." I dreamed of being in a large battle wielding a club where the stronger my opponents the stronger I became. When I awoke I recorded my dream in my journal to encode it into my waking "directed" thinking.

During my morning run up the mountain where I had lived at the time, I had recalled the Tajikistan Team at World Championships practicing another sport called Zurkhaneh (including swinging heavy wooden clubs) as an activity before their grappling matches.

The hypothesis dawned on me at the top of the mountain in 2001:

1.  If compressive forces caused me joint pain,

2.  and tissue grows just as effectively from traction as it does compression,

3.  and traction was one of the recommended curative solutions to my connective tissue challenges,

4.  wouldn't exercising in a way that creates traction, make me just as strong but without pain?

Two years later, I brought my patented line of "Clubbells" to the world using the sports biomechanics I had studied in Russia to make the system of progressive resistance known as the "Circular Strength Training" system now found in 68 countries. Some know me exclusively from that line of equipment and training system.

It wasn't a particularly complicated solution. But no one else had brought it to the world because exercise had been considered a compression-only activity. I merely had thought, "Instead of lifting, why not swinging weight?" That one lucid dream confabulated an idea which eventually (after many years of hard work and teaching) transformed the fitness industry.

Once practiced, you can use this "back-burner" technique to simmer solutions even while awake and performing other automatic tasks, such as driving, showering, walking, and gardening.

Your brain is so much more powerful than you can imagine. Give lucid dreaming a try for a few weeks, direct your problems before sleeping (but don't try and directly solve it to avoid becoming an insomniac). Think about the current problem; ask for a solution that can transform into new potential. Record your lucid dream as soon as you awake, and then allow the idea to sublimate to your conscious mind throughout your day.

# FIND THAT INNER BADASS

I was struggling financially, a new father, husband, and fledgling businessman with only several years of my own company under my belt. At a family holiday, a distant relative snickered at me after I answered his questions regarding my goals.

He scoffed, "Well, I guess you'll be able to make it by teaching martial arts." Out of respect to the family function, I smiled, kept silent and didn't exacerbate a drama already tense from his bombastic behavior.

I was named one of the six "most influential martial artists of the century" by Black Belt Magazine, have had my courses officially adopted by federal law enforcement agencies, special operations units, firefighting academies and mixed martial arts gyms in 21 nations, and become the first ever federally POST approved program in history.

I often wonder if I ran into that relative what I would say, and then I realize that I have changed.

I'd shake his hand and ask him how his family was doing.

Ignorance and fear are the only real enemies. Ignorance of our own true potential, and fear of our incompetence. When we illuminate those shadows, they evaporate … if we're brave enough to turn on the lights. And our basements are EACH cluttered and dirty.

Never let anyone tell you what you ought to do when it's contrary to your character and core beliefs. My best coaches never told me what to see, but showed me where to look, and then awaited my discovery so I owned it … no matter how long it took me.

No matter how long it takes you to realize it, look inside. There's a badass within. Defy status quo. Speak from your own authentic power. Support others with the courage to do the same, and protect them when they have not. And don't you dare give up on yourself and your dreams. Ever.

# AUTHENTICITY WILL ALWAYS TRIUMPH

Give a pernicious attitude sufficient rope and it will hang itself.

An individual started a doppelgänger company of TACFIT, and began spreading slanderous rumors about my background to discredit my reputation and further his standing in the marketplace.

I was asked to contact the organizers of an event where he would be presenting, in order to apprise them of his deceptions.

Observing behavioral patterns from an objective "coaching" perspective, when a behavior proves unsuccessful and destructive, evolve your world view or expect repeated failure and destruction. Though I've had a different perspective in the past, my viewpoint has changed over the years, using this litmus test for success.

I will provide proof of every single claim I've made and will diligently continue to do my own work at my own prolific pace, but I won't police others' behavior even if it infringes on me.

People who prey upon your success in order to duplicate it as their own, and who defame your name to elevate their own, will destroy themselves, because they do not have a sufficiently developed attitude, necessary for abundance and growth.

We cannot succeed by reducing our behavior down to their antagonistic level. If you're following your passion, then others will attempt to reproduce your success. They are following you, because they cannot yet comprehend your true nature of empowering positive development and fostering community support through the expression of your personal power. An attitude of drama will fixate on reproducing success perceived in the marketplace, rather than truly innovating and stimulating growth.

Ultimately, people want progress, not purchases, authenticity not drama, transparency not rhetoric, so they WILL discover the difference between an innovator and a duplicator.

In my experience as a martial artist, you ultimately lose when reducing yourself to the level of an opponent who attempts to cheat to win, who attempts to harm others unjustly to further their position.

Instead, the more honorably we fight with higher consciousness in mind, the greater triumph we bring to both ourselves AND our opponents. We both win, when we continue to take the "high road," and resist delving into competitive drama.

We succeed for us AND FOR THEM in leading by powerful example of how we ought to behave for abundance and growth, ESPECIALLY when faced with the choice of joining in the injustice, or choosing the harder path of remaining above it.

Stay the course, brothers and sisters. Fight with honor by doing your best work, following your true calling, and listening to your inner compass.

Win the real fight within … for all of our sakes.

# WIN-WIN IS A WINNING BUSINESS STRATEGY

Seeing me walk out of the house with determination, my wife asked me where I was going. I replied, "To pick a fight."

I had made an appointment with the local fire department's fitness director. I told him the police department believed they could beat them in a fitness competition. We would collect pledges for each repetition — say $1 per rep. The biggest total pledge collection would win, and proceeds would be donated to rebuild the local Boys and Girls Club house, which had burned down.

He replied that firefighters are always ready for any fitness challenge, especially against the police; and since they're constantly doing charity fundraisers, it sounded like a great fit for them.

I then traveled to the police department and told them that the firefighters believed they could beat their department in a fitness competition. ... They asked if it could include boxing, and laughing, I said no, only fitness.

The police training officer said that even though the firefighters don't work real shifts and have the luxury of exercising all day long, they would still beat them.

It was on.

Earlier in the month, I had been driving in the city past an auto accident, and observed a police officer and firefighter in a heated argument. I thought to myself, "How could I turn this into a positive? What good could I convert this into?" A crazy idea bubbled to awareness.

One year earlier, I had brought my new invention — the Clubbell — to a local health club, proposing to train people from their facility. They had responded with a, "No."

Not to be derailed with a rejection, I continued to attempt many ideas, though none resulted in providing me with a location to train others with my equipment.

Banging my head against a wall, I kept at it knowing eventually a successful idea would appear.

Returning to that same club, I told them that the police and the fire departments wanted to hold a competitive fitness charity drive on neutral ground — a commercial gym. The radio, newspaper and television media outlets would attend and give exposure to whomever hosted the event, and I would personally give the winning department free training for one year.

The health club loved the idea and jumped at the opportunity to have so much good community work, interacting with the police and fire departments, while getting huge local exposure as a result.

It had all come together: the police and fire departments, the health club and all of the local media, even the representatives of the charity. Because of their incredible effort, and one big crazy idea, the community came together, did some good, and got "caught" by the public doing it. Everyone benefited BY benefiting everyone.

It benefited me too. The fire department won the event, and the health club converted part of their facility into the first TACFIT gym in history. The health club opened up my classes to their members, and I started a revenue stream to subsidize my gratis work to the competition winners.

Establishing my coaching, my equipment and my system as a result, TACFIT and its energetic avalanche began to spread, and gained gyms across 32 countries in the eight years that followed.

Marianne Williamson wrote, "You must learn a new way of thinking before you can master a new way to be." When you encounter resistance, sometimes you have to push, but most often you have to reconsider WHERE you're pushing. When you encounter a wall, think laterally, and scan around you. You still have to push, but find the right spot.

Ask, "How can I get everyone involved to benefit from my idea?" Make your desire to help others wider than your fear of personal failure, and deeper than

your desperation for individual success. You will be amazed how short a time it can take for wonderful things to happen, when you have the courage to pursue your crazy ideas for everyone's benefit.

# USE POSITIVE STRESS TO YOUR ADVANTAGE

Early abuse, shame, violence and fear compelled me to think critically about decisions of the heart. My concept of self-mastery evolved from that early bias toward thought over feeling: The mind must control the passions of the heart.

However, my idea was born from a wounded heart and the raw emotional tempest it stormed.

Through years of support from my family and friends, and daily effort to heal and embrace the gifts of my circumstances, my wounds healed and my bias shifted to the push of my heart over the pull of my mind. When you come from a centered place of peace within, then the mind no longer needs to paralyze your passion.

The Mind can only ask, "WHY?" before it decides. As it should.

But the Heart when healed asks, "FOR WHOM?" before it commits.

Commitment binds much deeper than decision, for when confidence fails — when evidence compels you to quit and run away — the decision your mind made wavers and falters. However, despite the weight of evidence to give up and stop pursuing your dreams, when your confidence fails, if your heart has committed, your courage will remain to fight on.

Therefore, *"When at a conflict between the Mind and the Heart, follow the Heart."* ~ Vivekanand

Where I once, from a place of wounding, necessarily favored the scrutiny of the mind, healed of the burden I no longer carry, I now favor the guidance of my heart in committing to helping and loving others.

*"Mastering others is strength. Mastering yourself is power."* ~ Lao Tzu

But …

Though self-love is necessary, it is insufficient for a fulfilling life. Only love fills the soul.

The ultimate measure of our health, fitness and even character is not our response in times of convenience, but rather in the moments of great challenge. We NEED stress to grow, and to step into our true potential, but why do we feel "stressed out?"

As you read in my earlier notifications, there are two types of stress:

1. Eustress: Productive, positive, adaptable stress.

2. Distress: Destructive, negative, non-adaptable stress.

The more eustress in your life, the greater you grow, the richer your quality of life, and the more potential you can unlock within. You need stress for your health, fitness and longevity. However, as I wrote earlier, researchers have identified a very specific moment when eustress begins the avalanche into distress. The aches, pains, injuries, illnesses and diseases, the mental gremlins that corrode your attitude, the emotional sinkholes that cannibalize your confidence, all appear at this one singular point in time. I am sure you agree that since stress-related disease is our number one killer, it'll be important to know exactly where that point is located.

Even if you're only interested in a pain-free physique, then it'd be important to know how you can adapt and grow, without aches and injuries, because it happens at this same point in time. Yet, conventional health and fitness approaches tell you to "get tough" without any guidance on how to do so. They don't understand the stress physiology that defeats our attempts to modify our movement and nutritional behaviors. Either these professionals have never needed to climb from the bottom of the well, or they climbed out and warn you not to fall down there.

Before you can be tough, you must be resilient:

Resilience: your ability to recover from excessive stress when it happens.

Toughness: your ability to resist excessive stress before it happens.

You can't resist that defining line between eustress and distress unless you have the ability to step over it and recover underneath it rapidly. How could you resist excess if you don't know where it is? People telling you to just "be tough" is like being told to not fall in a pit while walking in a completely dark room. Is it any wonder why we become frustrated over our pitfalls in unlocking our vitality, refining our pain-free physique and improving our quality of life?

Resilience is your climbing gear. Once you are resiliently anchored, then you can belay if you begin to slip. Once you gain resilience, you by definition know the defining line, and gain toughness.

Because I started so far down at the bottom of the well, born into the violence of post-traumatic stress, amplified by my learning disabilities, obesity and joint disease, I have had to invest my life in studying the impact of excessive stress upon our health, fitness, performance and longevity. Gaining resilience saved my life, and has given me the opportunity to help others change their lives.

There are measurable, trackable patterns to excessive stress, and if we know them, we can turn the lights on, and continue to improve our health and fitness without diminishing returns, without plateau, and without backslide into pains, injuries, illness and disease.

# EMPOWERED CHILDREN ARE LABELED 'ABLED'

Gifted programs often contain those of us who have earlier been labeled learning disabled. In light of research in neuroscience, we are better described as "otherwise wired" for our special skills and talents. If the right teachers use the right methods in the right way for our unique learning ABILITIES, we will excel even beyond our mainstream counterparts.

Asked to be the keynote speaker for the Mensa annual conference, at first I felt intimidated. My wife gave me poignant feedback, propelling me to fly 3,000 miles to stand in front of an audience of some of the world's brightest minds.

She said, "I didn't fall in love with you for who you were. I didn't fall in love with you because of your accomplishments. I fell in love with you because when you find something that needs to be done, and is the right thing to do, even if everyone says you can't do it, you think about, plan it out, prepare every day, and find a way to make it happen."

She loved the "righteous rebel" in me, who, when witnessing an injustice, will devise any means possible, even if I have to invent entirely new ways of thinking about the problem.

To my Mensan listeners, I explained that I didn't understand why I was so frustrated with how slowly and inadequately I comprehended scholastic academics. You assume you are the problem; that it's not the delivery method at fault. But like people trying to communicate in a country where they don't know the language, my frustrated teachers would yell slowly, as if I were deaf or didn't understand their words.

I had to invent a translator for myself. Therefore, I began with studying my own language — how I uniquely think and process data and experiences. Through this study, I was able to create translation methods for my learning disabilities. I didn't teach myself what to think, but how to think about inbound information.

Teachers have come a long way in the thirty years since. Now, many no longer teach children what to think, but HOW to think. When you empower children this way, expect them to challenge you. Challenge them to exceed you, and empower them with the insight that they have latent talents, which when cultivated and refined will give them the power to exceed you as their mentor much more quickly, because of your belief in them.

# HAPPINESS ISN'T THE GOAL – IT'S MORE

During a meeting to discuss details of an upcoming book release, someone remarked that he's seen me become so much more relaxed over the years, and, well, happier. Absolutely true, but only as a result of confidence gained in a particular discovery.

Nothing can make me happy. As a child, I dreamed of becoming a world martial arts champion so vividly, I could hear the music being played, see the lights shining in my eyes, sense the smell of the mats, the cheers from my team and audience. And when I had won, it wasn't happiness, but closure that I felt, for I would no longer be plagued by the persistent specter of realizing that dream. The medals hung round my neck, yet the spontaneous happiness never manifested.

Coming from a trailer park, food stamp, blue-collar upbringing, I felt compelled to become financially independent and never suffer the oppressive weight that my mother experienced providing for four children in an economy much worse than the current one, with no skills or opportunities but her hands and her courage. And yet with each new financial milestone achieved, not one thing made me happy. Financial success removed the childhood dread of impoverishment, but only like a removal of weight, not a presence of lightness. What now could make me happy?

Repeating my story of overcoming hardship, abuse, obesity, learning disability, joint disease, poverty, I fought for higher and higher levels of validation. Yet the more recognition I received from greater authorities, federal agencies, special units, educational institutions, halls of fame, magazines, the more plaques I received, the more I recognized that these accolades did not bring me any happiness, but merely extinguished the oppressive weight of feeling invalid and unworthy.

When I discovered that no one can determine my worth as a person, the compulsion for acknowledgement disappeared and left me unfettered, but still driven to help others do the same. Just no "happier."

Nowhere (no place) could make me happy. When I was young, I thought I'd never "get out." Yet, with each expanding circle of my adventures, to more exotic wonders around the world, no happiness could be found. Farther and more often I traveled, with my new family, to stunning landscapes surrounding the globe, and yet, as picturesque they might be, no sudden bliss erupted within. I got out, but I only wanted to "get back" to a place of trust.

A life of violence, abuse and abandonment can engender great fears and mistrust. Finding myself dissatisfied with the veneer of most relationships, I searched for teachers, for friends, and for my own future family.

And after decades and thousands of acquaintances, I found truly honorable and loyal family, around the world, and the most loving wife and children I could have imagined. And yet, even they could not MAKE me happy. Relieved. Confident that integrity isn't an obsolete dinosaur, and relieved that substance and depth of love can be found, but not any happier.

In Hawaii, teaching for the government, something happened, though: my mind stopped. If you can imagine living with a deafening roar for a lifetime, and suddenly all went quiet, what shock this would hold. Others have remarked that I'm prolific in my work, but I experience it as being afflicted with an incessant muse: until I finalize each obsessive idea, it haunts me like an incomplete puzzle; I can't sleep, focus or function unless I heed solving it. I don't try to think about ideas. They just bubble to consciousness and assault me until I realize them.

My life has been so infused with this perpetual productivity, that when my muse went silent, initially I felt afraid, "What if it's stopped forever! What if I have no more ideas? How will I contribute?" But in the gentle respite of that silence, I reflected that not one of my ideas has ever brought me happiness, only relief from their cessation, and then another would immediately barge in queue for attention like a hungry, demanding child.

It seems silly to timestamp happiness, but during that reprieve, I eased into the experience of allowing ambition and desire to dissolve away, and looked with clarity for the first time. What a wondrous journey of weight being unburdened from my awareness. Achieving my desires for recognition, success, independence, community, family did not MAKE me happy. When the weight of those attachments lifted, I saw lucidly for a moment, and recalled a lesson from one of my great teachers:

When you say, "I want to be happy," remove the "I" who is desiring. Then, remove the "want" of your desires. Only happiness remains.

I, my personhood, became the circumstances that compelled predictable desires to which values strongly attached.

When those lifted, when they went quiet, happiness was lying there as a mode of being, as a birdsong or an ocean wave. It just was. I couldn't achieve it any more than I could capture music in my hands.

Words fail, and attachment to their success ensures their failure. But I never found a way to be happy… for happiness is the way.

Deepest love for all of you, the journeys and trials you face, and the "falls" when we have not yet realized, and when we forget that we live in the way… Happiness is.

# RECOGNIZE WHEN DRAMA LEADS YOU ASTRAY

We often feel offended because there's an element of truth to an insult. If we truly know that something said has no basis in reality, we can laugh and let it roll off us like water off a goose. My Pappy used to say, just because it's true, doesn't mean it's unkind. But then again, anything he said could sound mean. He was the toughest, but most actually loving man, I had ever known. And he lived such an honest life that nothing ever perturbed him.

My grandfather once said to me that if you want things to improve for everyone, then make everything you do excellent.

He taught to avoid speaking negatively about others, but encouraged unreservedly sharing positive experiences when asked. He would not associate with a toxic individual even if it might have led to personal gain; refused to abandon friends by concealing his relationships with them; and refused to withhold good opinion of trusted colleagues when asked pointedly.

Accept demands that you abandon friends or conceal your good opinions for fear of retribution, and you import their scarcity into your heart. Should you be so commanded by someone, avoid the entanglement of drama altogether. Take great care with those who offer you financial, physical or emotional rewards for turning your back on your own good conscience, in exchange for your silence. Stay true to yourself and what you truly believe in.

My grandfather once said, "Be careful what you do, because whatever it is, you'll want to get better at it. The more you improve, the more there is to improve. So choose wisely your efforts."

This idea infected my martial arts training, my business development, my coaching pedagogy, even how I approach relationships.

It was a seed my grandfather planted so early, that I didn't realize, nor could predict, how deeply I would be influenced.

# 'LEGION' IS OUR GLOBAL FAMILY

When others hear us use the word "legion" to refer to our community, we are often misunderstood to be an army of chiseled 300 style warriors. But as you can see, older people and children are part of our family. So what does legion mean?

Originally, it began as a salutation between Alberto Gallazzi and I by email, as a result of our commitment to working toward our collective goal, though thousands of kilometers separated our individual efforts. We believed we were brothers in a cause stronger than blood: helping to protect those who protect us, helping those who want to help others, and helping those who, from sacrifice or tragedy, cannot help themselves alone.

No matter who we help, we believe them to be part of our family, rising above any national or cultural differences.

Both of us students of ancient military history, we also refer to the Roman legion. The word legion derives from the Latin root, legere, which means to choose. Those who choose to lead not by preaching rhetoric on their own interests, but from the front by example for the sake of others' welfare, for the men, women and children to their right and to their left, are "Legion" to us.

We are a family. When we train together, our sweat becomes our blood. We learn to trust each other, watching to make sure we are honest with our technique. This supports us and motivates us to work harder when our technique can hold more effort, and takes care of us by reminding us that our preparation and our compensation are the most important parts of our workouts.

When we train and eat together, we use our positive pressure to help each other realize our individual goals, and as a result we grow stronger together. With each new member of our family, every member of the family grows stronger. As Legion, we choose to be a deliberate, conscious family.

# PRACTICE STRENGTHENS RELATIONSHIPS

My ex-girlfriend had a hot temper, a vicious one. It strangely attracted me in my early years, because she seemed to be full of audacity, but in reality she was just dangerous. Finally recognizing it as a toxic relationship, I tried to extricate myself, leading to a big blowout where most of my apartment began flying toward me.

After I ended the relationship, I found myself in a new one too quickly. Not violent, but highly argumentative. Words flew, and often I became angry at what had been said. I ended it, too, but not before awful things had been uttered.

In the next relationship, few words were spoken and there was never an argument. It must be perfect, right? After years together, she disclosed she had cheated on me. Not fists, not words, but rather values had been thrown. They appear invisible and as a result hurt the most. We ended painfully.

When I got married to my wonderful wife, whom I've known for 17 years, I began studying with one of my teachers.

When I remarked that he never seemed to get ruffled during debates on controversial topics, he replied that when he comments on an issue, he firstly asks himself if he speaks from his truth. He then asks himself if his comment will be necessary.

Lastly, he asks himself if his comment will be kind rather than nice, and explained that niceties are lies we tell socially to avoid our truth, because we believe it's more important to be polite than kind. Kindness on the other hand is speaking your authentic truth even if the other considers it not nice. Speak your truth when it's necessary, and do so with kindness in your heart and you'll remain unaroused with no anger, regardless of what is said or done.

When people debated with him, they often found themselves frustrated and losing their temper, but as soon as they did, and my teacher never escalated emotionally or psychologically, they would defuse and even apologize.

My wife and I don't agree on everything, and being different genders doesn't help us understand each other. But we love each other and are best friends, so we are continually practicing improving our communication, opening our empathy and lengthening our patience. We both practice asking ourselves if it is our authentic truth we speak, if it is necessary to say it and if we are truly kind in our heart when we utter it.

We've had difficult spots early on but approaching our 10-year anniversary I can say that by practicing deepening our relationship, we've learned a great deal about each other and increased our fulfillment as a couple.

Relationships are like martial art. Practice getting better every day if you intend to remain calm and centered when misunderstanding happens. Speak authentically your truth. Say what is necessary to resolve the misunderstanding. And like the reflective surface of a calm lake, keep kindness in your heart so you can mirror the compassion with which you wish you were treated.

# DON'T DROWN IN THE PAST

My mother's drunken boyfriend held me under the water. Struggling, flailing, scratching, I clawed at his forearm, but at only 8 years old, I could only peer up through the shimmering water at his distorted image. Finally, I gave up and just waited, unmoving, praying that drowning would not be very painful. But he suddenly pulled me back out.

Many years later, after he was no longer with my mother, I ran into him at a restaurant. He came over to me and my girlfriend. Shocked, I stood and shook his extended hand, and answered his questions about my life. "I heard you won some kind of world championship in fighting," he said, "See? I guess all those years I was tough on you paid off."

A fuse blew inside me. I was no longer under the water, and I could easily choke out this old man and make him feel the water I had gulped into my 8-year-old lungs. But my girlfriend touched my forearm gently, and as I turned to look at her, my eyes cleared, and my awareness reopened.

I came back into myself.

"It is not what you wrongly did to me, but what I correctly grew within myself. It is not what you put me through that defined who I am. It is how I got through it that has made me the person I am today." Having said these words, I put money for our bill on the table and we walked out.

Today, my children have both lived beyond the beginning of my trauma at their age. I don't have an experience of how to be a healthy father at their age, so I must consciously fabricate what I ought to do in each situation. My daughter — the compassionate, serious, driven one... Always looking out into the world; my son — the affably oblivious and charming one... Always entertaining others (and himself)... Parenting them is yet another coping skill I must develop on a day to day basis. Recognizing that I'm 'making it all up' to parent them as and where they are, allows me to enjoy my confusion.

Your coping skills you develop to combat traumatic circumstances, and the lifetime of healthy experience you must "make up" are a credit to you and those who have loved and supported you through them. It can be hard to own them, when you have suffered having had your power victimized. However, you now deserve full credit for being a survivor and a victor. Circumstances, or the people who cause them, do not deserve any gratitude for what they did to you.

Be grateful for the opportunity you have created within yourself to grow. Certainly, you can feel gratitude that events and people happened in your life, because when they happened, you discovered and cultivated within yourself that your resources are far greater than you had imagined them to be.

As Wayne Dyer writes, *"With everything that has happened to you, you can either feel sorry for yourself, or treat what has happened as a gift. Everything is either an opportunity to grow, or an obstacle to keep you from growing. You get to choose."*

When you face a crisis, don't ask, "Why did this happen to me? Can I even get out of this?" Ask yourself, "What would I have to access to resolve this challenge, and how will I grow from the coping skills which will result from facing it?" You can. You will. You choose.

# BUILDING TRUST TAKES TIME, EFFORT

The night I met my future wife, a gun had been held to my head. Friends of hers had invited her to a party at my college apartment, hosted by my roommates. From my training, I unconsciously snatched the weapon from the gunman's hand, yelling for him and his henchmen to leave. As they cautiously backed out the door hands held high, I threw the handgun out after them, and slammed the door, yelling, "And don't come back!"

Turning around, my friends screamed, "Why did you throw the gun back to them???" I hadn't even recognized that I had taken it from him, much less thrown it back at him. My body started to uncontrollably shake, and my friends pulled me into the back room to hide my near-catatonic body and call the police.

Fortunately, my future wife had already left my apartment, and I didn't officially meet her for another two years, in 1994, when she had signed up for my martial art school. She quickly excelled and became a national champion Sambo fighter within a year. Her technique was magical. It was hard for me to not be distracted by the messenger of that movement.

We had an unstated magnetism between us. But as a policy I avoided romantic relationships as they're unfair between "coach" and "athlete." So two years after she had begun, she walked into my office departing for university on the opposite side of the country. Slamming her fist on my desk she asked, "So that's IT? You have nothing to say to me?" I replied that I couldn't as it would be dishonorable to even utter; I had already felt conflicted about my feelings. She turned and stormed out of the school.

For the six years that followed, she didn't speak to me: angry and hurt that I had withheld my feelings toward her. I regretted my decision month after month. But departing for Russia, I became consumed with my studies there, as she similarly immersed herself at her university.

One distant Christmas evening mass, I saw her walking through the pews. She floated by me, not recognizing my long hair and beard, as I had recently returned from the cold, Russian winter. Instantly standing, I had dashed after her, but she had been nowhere to be found. In the days that followed, I tried to find her, but her rightfully-protective mother had refused to disclose her phone number or email; though I finally convinced her to at least convey mine to her.

An email appeared in my inbox, succinctly asking what I had wanted. So, I explained that I had hoped to buy her a ticket to fly back and go out on a date with me. She didn't answer for a week, but later reluctantly agreed. Sending her the ticket, I received a check in the mail from her parents for the price of the flight which read: "...so our daughter does not feel obligated."

Our date felt awkward and fumbling, confusing and uncomfortable, and had totally confirmed my suspicion that I had been in love with her for the many years since I had met her.

She disclosed that I had hurt her greatly, yet her life was finally where she had wanted it, and that she hadn't wanted major upheaval again.

She flew home, and I hadn't known if she had ever wanted to see me again. She had given me a letter and had made me promise to not open it until she departed.

As the tires lifted off the tarmac, I opened it. In it she told me everything, from the beginning of our story together... And had disclosed her true feelings. She had loved me as well, but feared my tendency to abruptly change when I had felt so inclined. She did not want to be hurt again.

The next week, I packed my car, closed all of my accounts, and found an apartment on her side of the country. (Perhaps validating her concern about my abruptness!) In two and a half days of crazy 15 hour sprints, I had arrived on the West Coast.

Rather than drive to my new apartment, I drove straight to her at work. She was shocked: of course if I could do something so rash as to move across the country to date her, couldn't I then make a reckless decision and abruptly end our blossoming relationship?

Although it appears from the radical nature of my life's choices that I make decisions in haste, my mother had taught me:

1. When you believe in something, you must be willing to sacrifice everything to pursue it.

2. If it doesn't work out, trying to force it will bring you great suffering and failure.

3. Knowing the difference between 1 and 2 is the hardest thing in life.

"I always wondered why birds stay in the same place when they could choose to fly anywhere on the Earth, but then I ask myself the same question," wrote an unknown author. The hardships of my early life opened the cage to travel anywhere passion had compelled me. Fortunately, those childhood challenges drove me directly into the arms of my best friend and love of my life.

Building trust in a relationship takes time, especially when you're facing the chaotic events of adolescence and in the unsteady beginning of your career. We both believed in our relationship, and were passionate enough to commit to a life together.

Very difficult trials would lie ahead for us individually and as a couple. But like a gemstone is not polished without rubbing, a relationship is not grown without commitment to the other's individual growth and fulfillment... especially when you could, rather, focus all your efforts to shining.. alone. A life without her would lack luster, no matter the efforts I had made to polish it. So, I left the cage of my prior security, and adventured out to find her, to earn her trust, and to spend the last of my days together loving her.

Birds don't choose to stay in one place because they're afraid to fly away. They stay, because they're home.

Wherever my beautiful bride, and the exuberant little cherubs we've created together, live... There, I am home.

Often, the most difficult choices are between the sane arguments of our mind and the crazed intuitions of our heart. As a man of reason, formally schooled in logic and rationality, I've come to learn... No matter how much it may seem stressful, choose heart. Your mind will create every convincing excuse for you to not follow your heart, under the illusions of some stress free fantasy, but sometimes, only those crazed foolish dreams are sane.

Fortunately for me, she said, "Yes."

# OWN YOUR TRUTH, THEN SHARE IT

I told the truth to my wife, fully expecting her to leave me. In past relationships, I had learned to not share all of the painful experiences of my childhood as those dark trials frequently frightened my prior relationships into abandoning our connection.

Friends or girlfriends, I had kept a shamefully undisclosed hold on my institutionalization in a children's psychiatric hospital for my learning difficulties. Simply a moment in ancient history before multiple learning styles were understood, prior relationships had reacted with horror.

Committing to invest myself in a permanent relationship with my then future wife, we could only begin our relationship with honesty. Better to have her leave then with truth, than remain with a lie. To love each other deeply, we need the courage to honestly disclose.

Instead of the repulsion, she looked at me with empathy, "That must have been impossibly hard, and yet you still grew into who you've become. You are an incredible man, and I love you for it." Years of bottled shame released, and like the river bank we sat upon, flowed clean with my choked embrace.

To this day, approaching twenty years knowing my wife, I still encounter others who recommend that I shouldn't disclose my past, that I should tuck it away and hide the truth of my history. But only truth can begin connection with another, whether a new friendship, or a student I shall only ever meet through writing.

It may seem silly to have guidelines for honesty for some, but when you fear judgment, hold shame, and know pain, disclosure comes cautiously. So, when sharing with each other, these 10 guidelines for honesty which I learned from being married to my wife have helped me communicate... and grow.

1. Ask questions for which you're prepared to accept an honest answer, even if it causes you discomfort.

2. Don't judge someone for being honest about a past experience you weren't part of. Feel grateful they shared it with you. Remember who they are now. Love them for both enduring, and further opening up to you.

3. Expect as much disclosure as you give. We are hard-wired to tell the truth, and when we hold back, our body screams out what our lips shut tight. Loved ones intuit your degree of disclosure.

4. When someone's shares private experiences, listen instead of providing solutions, opinions or feedback (until asked). The hardest part of healing is relearning to trust in disclosure. Talking it out may be enough for now, and they'll restructure over time purely through sharing.

5. When asked for your thoughts, be authentic. Acknowledge the difficulty of sharing private issues, and express your gratitude for their trust. Ask them how they would prefer to hear your thoughts, and be ready to learn the "rules of engagement" for communicating with them.

6. Be kind rather than nice. A nice remark is fluffy, trite untruth. A kind remark is an uncomfortable, compassionate truth.

7. Speak your own truth in kind, rather than saying what you think the other may want to hear.

8. If you trust disclosing to someone, trust in their response. Should they react rather than respond, remember that they too are growing as an individual. If they're hurtful, admit that the way their remark was received felt hurtful and then create distance until they process their own communication growth.

9. Don't hold back your truth, or you'll grow resentful. Sounds simple. Ain't easy.

10. Decide in advance that what you're about to say is necessary: motivated by my personal growth or for our growth together (and not some careless, flippant, or irrelevant remark). Clearly communicate your motives for sharing your thoughts, even if you only admit that you do not know, but feel it to be important to you.

If I forget any of the above, I ask myself: Is it NECESSARY? Is it my TRUTH? Is it KIND?

You can be your own living proof in the power of your necessary, kind truth. As I read the daily messages in my inbox, I remember the love I felt from my wife when I had dared lay bare my soul. Because of her, my courage has turned into confidence that those who belong in my life, will stay in it, not in spite of my past, but because of it. And as I grow, we grow.

Finding one relationship in which you can be totally honest about yourself infuses you with the confidence to remain boldly "you" to all people at all times. Do not fear your truth. OWN it. As Mary Shelley wrote, *"Beware; I am fearless, and therefore powerful."* Be fearlessly honest. And we will grow together.

# CONFIDENCE FLED BUT PRAYER WORKED

My neck had snapped again. My cervical spine remains like popcorn after having been shattered during the 1994 Grand National Championships.

Sudden tension against my neck now causes instant spasm to defensively brace against the perceived threat. This protective mechanism ironically can — through the strength of these spasms — pull on my spine so strongly as to actually renew the injury.

Two months ago, while teaching a choke in Jiujitsu, a student slipped and placed too much weight upon me, changing the choke to a crank.

The loud "POP" wasn't followed by pain, but numbness. I immediately knew the severity of the issue. Pain would have been preferable. Pins and needles were a bad sign.

At the time, I had been the strongest I had ever been in my life, able to move weight in a way few people could; and glowingly confident having had just vindicated myself and honored so many thousands of others through my TEDx Talk on overcoming the labels of learning disabilities to discover my own unique array of learning styles.

Three major trips loomed imminent on the horizon: Vegas, NYC and Australia ... and I had lost about 80 percent of the strength of my right arm. How I was going to do my job? Wasn't my job about being strong? Wasn't I then lying to my students?

Maybe I had just become too old to be able to do my job as I once had done, having accumulated too many severe injuries in my quest fighting in different martial art styles around the world to find alternative forms of movement education. Perhaps the cost of my discoveries had finally outweighed the benefit. Had I now faced a self-selected obsolescence?

When you overcome weakness to become strong — in any aspect of your life — and then return to weakness, you can have the most corrosive thoughts. What if I had been a fraud all this time, and now, through my own arrogance, created a job for which I am no longer competent. The old negative childhood thoughts flooded in, so long held back by a levee of physical strength, overwhelmed by the nerve damage.

I hid the injury, as I had through the many years of skilled camouflage, from my students; demonstrating exercises on my strong side, scuttling off to the shadows to ice the ubiquitous pain in my neck and shoulder.

Calling upon all of the movement therapy I had learned over the decades and developed into programs of my own, I worked diligently to heal myself. The improvement was so imperceptible that it remained invisible to my awareness.

Ashamed of my weakness, and frightened that I had ruined my family's livelihood, I confided in my wife, the fraud I worried I might be. Hadn't I overcome this imposter syndrome with the public disclosure during my TEDx Talk? Evidently not.

My wife said to me, "This is all happening for something better. Your strength isn't only a physical thing. That'll come and go; you know that. Your real strength is in your heart; not in how you have fought with others, but in how you now fight FOR others. Maybe if you can zoom out and see this situation for the benefit it is, no matter how physically painful and emotionally overwhelming, you'll find out how this is helping you grow into something bigger than muscle."

Through tears of gratitude, I recalled Ashley Willis noting, "A strong marriage rarely has two people strong at the same time. It is two people who take turns being strong for each other when the other feels weak."

My wife, like no other person could, helped me realign my internal gaze upon a higher purpose. She told me to pray on it.

Yet as it did, I prayed... not for what I would have imagined I would have prayed for. I prayed that before my strength fully returned, before the pain subsided, before the numbness stopped, that I would rather experience an even harder physical challenge, than lack a complete understanding of the growth it offered.

I prayed that instead of restoring my body, I'd rather face another hardship so that I could fully grasp its benefit.

I couldn't afford to miss this again.

That prayer surprised me. I had lost my confidence, but not my courage.

Confidence is belief in evidence, but courage is faith despite a lack of evidence. When I had lost my strength, I had compared my prior weakness to my temporary period of strength. But regardless of my weakness, past and present, my wife had reminded me of my true purpose, and my courage took over.

I had never given up on my daily consistent therapy. Despite no evidence of progress, I continued to face the weakness of the day as bravely as I could.

Dribs and drabs of progress, taking months to observe, turned into sudden lurches of advance. Ten percent of my strength came back, then twenty, then forty percent more. I continued with the daily therapy, and my physical strength in my arm has nearly fully returned.

Confidence is a fickle fair weather fan, who visits us only when the game is going in our favor, but flees to cheer the other side when the scoreboard shifts.

Yet even when our lack of confidence taunts our losses, a deeper faith erupts: a courage, blind to how far behind we may appear to be, and the bulk of evidence to the contrary of our unlikely success.

This courage had always been within me. I had found it as a child. But it had taken many years back then. With one person, who knows you better than anyone on the planet, whose judgment you trust more than your own, who reminds you of your higher purpose and the ultimate benefit ALL challenges hold, then the attitude to find your courage can change not over years, but over days, or even in a single moment.

# DO YOUR BEST, DON'T FEAR THE WORST

"Now if YOU had one of these special cards, we could be driving over in the fast lane, but nooooooo, you have to use passports," I joked with my wife. She harrumphed and ignored my ("lack of") humor.

As we pulled up to the customs gate at the U.S.-Canada border, the agent asked, "Your Nexus card isn't activated. How long have you had it?" My wife snickered to herself.

"Well over a year, and I've been using it internationally now that it has been accepted in the Global Entry program," I replied.

The agent kept my family's stack of passports and told me to park and go inside. My wife curled her mouth, remarking, "That is SOME special card you have right there, Babe," as our kids untangled themselves from their gear and we all went inside to a full waiting room.

Instantly my mind flooded with concerns: how did I deactivate the card; was there an activation step I neglected, will this incur a fine, did using it in an unintended wrong way internationally flag my account, should I show alternate ID from my government work, who am I going to have to call to get this cleared, will my family be detained?

The concerns cascaded through my mind as I was taken back to my years in Russia, where administration changes could suddenly find me in a country with an expired visa, incorrect stamps, invalid ID, followed by arrest, fines and jailing.

"This was my own country. Calm down. You didn't do anything wrong. It must be some kind of error," I told myself.

The agent returned and said, "Sorry Mr. Sonnon. Somehow your card deactivated on its own. We reactivated it. On a side note, we appreciate what you've done for our agency. Our apologies for your family's inconvenience."

Resuming my drive home with relief, I wondered to myself why it happened. Life is a metaphor for itself: Nothing happens by accident, and everything happens to teach us something. So I tried to learn what this needed to teach me.

"You need to learn that the government is incompetent," my good friend's voice chided in my head, and I laughed to myself at the irony of his high federal position. No, in my life, I've found as Eckhart Tolle wrote, *"Life will give you whatever experience is the most helpful for the evolution of your consciousness."* My life runs very smoothly when I presume that everything happens to teach me a new or deeper lesson.

And then the insight dawned on me. … For the past few weeks, I had been facing a surreptitious set of lies from an individual. My default setting is to search for what I could have been doing that may have precipitated this behavior: How had I caused this situation, what did I do to contribute, where was I the wrongdoer in the issue?

After weeks of soul-searching, I frustratedly could not find anything that I could do or improve.

I had felt out of control. Finding that I was doing something "wrong" almost would have been easier than this situation, because at least when you're wrong, you can fix it. But there was nothing I could change, so I had to just … remain calm, unattached to the lies and rumors being spread about me, and wait it out.

Finally, the truth began to be discovered, and this person indicted himself with his own lies. People who I had worried might be manipulated by these untruths were coming to tell me they'd caught this person in his deceptions. Huge sigh of relief!

My mind raced back to the customs agent and my Nexus card. When things appear to go badly, you can catastrophize the worst, and scramble in anticipation to prepare for a hardship. A life full of trauma can certainly contribute to this tendency, but I have been working for many years to consciously elevate my default mental patterns, and rise above my reflexive panic at crises. But it evidently still has had a bit of a hold in my life, where I worry sometimes, and immediately move into damage control planning mode to expedite the solution to a perceived problem.

However, not everything is a problem. Sometimes, there are just accidents that need to work themselves out. There is nothing you can control or do. Just patiently wait it out, and stop worrying. You haven't done anything wrong, and the truth will eventually be uncovered if you relax and hold your ground gracefully.

This insight has huge implications for my life, and I'm excited to see how it reticulates throughout all of my responses to events.

As Pema Chödrön spoke, *"Nothing goes away until it teaches us what we need to know."* When you find a type of event repeatedly returning to your life, it could be that you haven't yet reaped the full benefit of what it has to teach. Just because something "bad" appears to be happening to you doesn't mean that you're necessarily doing anything "wrong."

It could merely mean that you can stand your ground gracefully, live your truth patiently and allow your continued personal evolution to unfold as a metaphor in front of you.

# TO THE ONE WHO DESERVES YOU

Two contrasting messages regarding spouses appeared:

1. A person living in a domestic abuse situation asked how one could deal with physical violence, since they felt obligated to make the relationship work. This person believes that to truly love someone you must work, and can't throw away relationships just because they're damaged.

2. Another person has a caring spouse and large family, but felt they'd "fallen in love" with a coworker from afar. This individual believed one should follow one's heart, but they don't want to hurt their spouse's feelings and lose their children.

I find it both ironic and teachable to myself to observe the stark contrast of these two messages. It has helped me appreciate the impact of growing up in household of serial violence, and how challenging it has been to refuse to accept abuse of any type in my life, and to find someone I truly love and invest the effort to make it work.

I watched my mother beaten, first by my father and then later by drunken boyfriends. My violent childhood didn't teach me to commit violence, as can happen, but it did condition me to believe that sometimes you must accept violence. It took many years to realize that never, not under any circumstance, even when I did something "wrong," did I deserve abuse.

My early default setting had become close to that of the first individual: When something breaks, don't throw it away; fix it. But ...

What's broken in the cases of domestic abuse isn't the relationship; because if you are suffering violence, you are not in a relationship. A victim and a victimizer do not have a relationship. What's broken is our perspective. Under no circumstances is violence acceptable or possible in a relationship. If we are suffering violence, we are not in a relationship. Get out now.

Similarly, because I had developed a high tolerance to abuse, I got involved in many relationships where I tried to do everything possible to "fix" all problems; to be present, available and giving. But to many of those women, that became unexciting. My ubiquity and constant care eventually became unattractive. They wanted someone who would challenge them, who kept his mystery and did not overwhelm them with the permanency of a long-term relationship.

I had to learn that to be truly of value to someone, I needed to highly value myself and my own needs. So instead of focusing on what my future, potential partner would need, and try to make myself into that imagined person, I refocused and concentrated on becoming my best at my passions, pursuits and purpose. The person who deserved to be with me would want to be with me because I was living true to my individual growth and development as a person. (And I with them.)

When I found that person, my wife, I discovered that she too has her own individual path. We don't have all the same interests, and sometimes even have opposite ones. We both believe, however, in working our asses off, in learning how to communicate with each other: to hear and listen, and to think and express, back and forth, to respect and improve our understanding of the other's path.

There have been many arguments. There probably will be still more in the future. With anyone, it is going to take effort, because they're a completely different and unique person. You know how hard it is to get to know yourself. Is it any surprise that an entirely different person whose thoughts and feelings you can't immediately (or ultimately) know, like your own, is MUCH harder?

But when things are hard in your current relationship, and you meet someone else, attractive, flirtatious, and mysterious, you aren't falling in love with them. Love is that what remains after it's no longer convenient to you; it's what powers your commitment to being in a relationship. You're not following your heart when you cheat on a commitment; you're following your groin.

Lust is only nature's temporary help to get to know each other enough to survive the long haul of a true relationship. Once lust dissolves, then love appears. To follow your heart, be true to your values and your commitments.

Marriage is like fitness and diet. You can't cheat on it and expect it to work. To make it work, you both need to.

Everything you truly want, wants you. You just need to be willing to take action to earn and to deserve it. There is someone out there who truly deserves you, who is busting their ass to value themselves and be true to their contributions to society by being true to their gifts. To earn their presence in your life, you must be true to yourself and your needs ... and then re-honor your commitment.

If someone is violently robbing you of your energy, you're not in a relationship. You're being victimized. It's not that it's broken; it doesn't exist. No matter how much you think you're working to fix it, you're only prolonging your suffering. You're never going to find the person who deserves you by devaluing yourself. The person who truly deserves you cannot FIND you because if you devalue yourself, that makes you invisible to them. Respect yourself and expect what you deserve in a safe, loving relationship, and you pop up on their radar. They'll find YOU.

There will be very hard times in any worthwhile relationship, so collect resources when they are abundant. Droughts will come, but they will pass. Catch and store energy of the easy times, so that you will have the emotional sustenance during the hard ones. When you're facing hard times, get "all in" or get out.

But know, that when you do find someone you love, you WILL face hard times with them too. And then what?

You won't ever get out of hard times by cheating; just like you cannot ever get your scorched soil to yield new abundance by throwing your seeds in a different field and watering that one instead of your own.

Value yourself enough to be "in" a relationship. Love isn't a fleeting feeling of falling in and out. Love is the strength to be in a true relationship, no matter how challenging it becomes to grow together, as long as you both remain committed to growing together. You deserve it.

# SELF-WORTH IS ESSENTIAL TO A RELATIONSHIP

Several men have written me about how to deal with concerns of "losing a woman."

Noel Coward reminds us that, *"It's discouraging how many people are shocked by honesty but so few by deceit."*

You can't lose your woman, because you don't have her; you never have and no matter how hard you try, you never will.

My first real girlfriend cheated on me after three years. I drove four hours on a suspicion that she was with another man. She was.

The woman I nearly married after four years, I had flown from the USA to Russia to Australia (48 hours of flying) to discover she had cheated on me there. Devastation.

It took me years until I could date again, as the betrayals triggered longtime anxieties of abandonment and revived my lack of self-worth.

When you've been cheated on, you can empathize. But no matter how many shoulders you're given to cry on, it won't change the fact that only we, as individuals, can change our attitudes regarding our own self-worth. When we truly value ourselves, we won't be in a place where betrayal can affect us. We get exactly the lessons we're supposed to learn ... until we finally learn them.

You can either let her go and be happy that she stays or suffer indefinitely worrying she'll leave ... and probably make the small (or large) choices in actions which will cause her to do so. We repeat the circumstances with different people and events until we have addressed our unlearned lessons.

It's not easy and took me years of a loving wife to overcome my lack of self-worth. Ultimately, there was nothing she could or can do for me. I had and have to do it alone and be a man.

I don't know if I could have been successful without being graced with her ongoing evidence that self-validation enables growth together in a relationship. But I still must work on myself rather the illusion of working on us; which is merely a rationalization for trying to keep from "losing her."

As men, our biggest challenge is often not a lack of effort but too much. I've been guilty of trying to fix arguments rather than HEAR her concerns, of trying to solve problems for her rather than support her process in the way she has expressed that she wants it.

The most successful relationships I've observed have been between those people who've felt loss and found their way out of the depths of feeling individually unworthy. These couples have a sensitivity that fills them with compassion and patience for each other's process.

Let us work at not trying to make it work; but rather work at letting it work by unapologetically being ourselves, by realizing our inalienable worth and living confidently next to her.

# TREASURE EACH MOMENT WITH FAMILY

I did not grow up as my children do. I did not trust in life. I did not feel safe to take great risks. My limits felt like prisons, not the playgrounds my children make of their challenges. Only through force of will, alone within myself, and rebellious against all resistance, did I lift out of my dire circumstances. They just float, no sandbags upon their balloons.

Where I feared risks in my youth, needing to excavate courage from a dry well, they run right at their challenges, with humor, excitement and curiosity. They are more my teachers, than I am theirs.

My son said, "Dad, if I get up and pee every night, does that mean I am a 'Mock-Turtle.'" After processing what he was trying to say for a moment, I replied, "No, you're not a pretend turtle because you pee at night. You just need to stop drinking water before you go to sleep. And the word is 'nocturnal.'"

My daughter chimed in to my wife that she was very sad because "Daddy's travel season was beginning." Now, I'm migratory?

Too many NatGeo documentaries, LOL.

It's these precious stories that I miss when I depart. I'll never get them back. If I miss one, it is forever gone. My effort and expertise are nothing, compared to the time that I lose with them.

I love my job. I wouldn't want to do ANYTHING else in the world than helping people. But I hate leaving my family at home.

Love you so much!

# LOVE THE JOURNEY THAT AWAITS

My daughter described a teacher's aptitude evaluation that suggested she should consider becoming a veterinarian or animal trainer. I felt so happy seeing her joy in the outdoor education programs my wife found for her, and the support she receives from her teachers, family and community to pursue her love of helping animals.

Asking about my childhood, and what my teachers advised me, I told her the story of my guidance counselor who recommended I should not set my hopes "unrealistically high," and should consider an "honest job with good pay" working at the chicken processing plant. I began working third shift at the chicken plant for the summer, snapping the necks of hanging carcasses on an assembly line.

Each horrible night, I'd stand on the stainless steel deck, smock smeared with guts and refuse, feeling like I was wasting my brain. So, at the end of the summer, I returned to school and told the guidance counselor that even if she was right, even if I set unrealistically high hopes, I would rather go out into the world and fail to achieve my dreams than rot away in a lifetime of mind-numbing regret. So, off into the world I trod.

My daughter stared off after my story with both disgust and incomprehensibility, so my wife and I alleviated her discomfort.

We told her that we felt so happy with her teachers and community for supporting her in her interests and guiding her to fulfill her goals of helping animals. But even if she had no support from them, or even from us, she could still achieve her dreams. Having the support allows her to do it with less suffering in doubt of whether she could accomplish her objectives.

I changed my unacceptably traumatic circumstances: traumatized and terrified, sickly and obese, legally blind and learning disabled, impoverished and unsupported.

But without support, being told by elders and authorities to accept my lot in life felt like an immovable mountain of inadequacy. I doubted myself with each step I took.

Looking into my daughter's daring eyes, I can see that she holds little, if any, doubts. And it baffles me, frightens me and thrills me simultaneously. How far could a child go, and how happy she would be, if she believed whatever she was doing was what she loved, and never doubted a step she took?

But even if she should doubt herself in the future, I know that at least I can provide her with the certainty that doubts do not destine you to fail. Doubts can be ignored for the convincing illusions they are.

I feel immense gratitude for my innately courageous daughter showing me by her example what life could be like for a child free of doubts; and grateful that having survived my own hesitations and fears, should she face them in the future, that by being next to me, she will know to step toward love regardless of any doubts she may feel.

The first step to getting anywhere comes when you decide you no longer will to remain where you are. Not for hate of where you are or have been, but for love of where you could go, step forward. Never doubt yourself, ever, but when you do, step anyway.

# NURTURE THE GENIUS WITHIN EACH CHILD

I was named a "sped," an acronym for special education. "Retard" didn't have the powerful derogation it once had. Sped hurt enough. Yet, now we understand that 1 in 7 people is dyslexic, albeit most do not know it.

Teachers called me "Dazer" because they would begin teaching according to their dominant learning style and cause my brain to switch off. Yet, well over 5,000,000 kids currently line the pockets of Big Pharma. The USA consumes 90 percent of the world's Ritalin supply, though no one has proved the geographical density of its need.

My membership card for Mensa — the High IQ Society, arrived in the mail. My daughter, seeing it on my desk, asked what it was. When I told her, she remarked, "Was it a contest? Did you have to win it?" I told her about the entry exams and she beamed that I must be one of the smartest people in the world. I laughed and hugged her.

"No babe, but I do get to hang out with truly smart people. Your Dad is just good at blending in."

One day I dream that this little girl will become a woman who realizes that true intelligence cannot be found in a test, a membership or approval. True intelligence, as Stephen Hawking said, is the ability to adapt to change.

She's gorgeous, bright and beaming. But most of all, she lives for new experiences. She adapts. She's genius.

She works very hard on her grades and has become an exemplary student, but her real beauty lies beyond memorization of books. It is the application of knowledge — wisdom — that marks true intelligence. How is it that someone so young can seem so wise?

Fortunately for me, sometimes people with the worst past can manage to create the greatest futures. I looked into her eyes today and dared to consider something I don't often allow myself to ponder: she has her parents' unconditional support, an incredible community of loving, supportive teachers, friends and families, healthy, generative food, a safe, cozy home and a spiritual life free from abuse and ridicule. Where could I have gone, how much would I have been able to learn, absorb and apply, how many people could I have reached coming from where she blissfully stands with confidence and courage? Compared to her, I was forged in fear and shame.

Let not one child go to sleep at night worrying that s/he is inferior, incapable and incompetent. We are not speds, retards or dazers. We are geniuses within. Erupt, and incite the dormancy within others to awaken.

# THAT INTUITION MIGHT JUST BE GOD'S TOUCH

The woman next to me glanced over at my wife and children, remarking, "You have such a beautiful family."

After I thanked her, she asked an interesting question, "My son came to me and asked me how you know when you're in the relationship you're supposed to be in. He's going to do his duty to his newborn son, but he feels overwhelmed by being a new Dad, and disconnected from his rightly preoccupied mother of his child. What was the first time you knew for sure that you were in the relationship you were meant to be in?"

I told her the story of how my wife and I finally started dating.

She had invited me to visit with her family on Chincoteague Island in Virginia, which was an interesting coincidence, as my family had vacationed there every summer since I was very young. Her family had vacationed there as well ... across the street from us. We wouldn't have known each other in those early years, as my wife is much younger than me, but the irony of most likely encountering each other on this small island impacted us.

We got married and had children, living far off in Bellingham, Washington, 3,000 miles away from both of our Pennsylvanian families. But every year, we all reunite in Chincoteague, and spend our time kayaking, swimming, playing beach volleyball, having oceanside bonfires, cooking seafood and enjoying the pony penning festivals.

One year, my brother-in-law and I sat on chairs at the beach. Our wives had offered to take the kids back to the house to shower, so we could have one day to just sit on the beach together and chat in the evening hours. We sat with newspapers, reading unrelated articles, enjoying the white noise of crashing tide. Despite the chance to talk, we merely went quiet, enjoying the view together as two Dads, both appreciating the break.

I thought to myself, how coincidental that after all my travels around the world, and despite all my painful memories of childhood, my favorite place to return was this tiny, relatively unknown island where my family had vacationed. For one moment, it popped into consideration, "Did I never escape my childhood traumas; did I make my way back here by unconscious accident? Maybe I steered my way into this relationship so that I would reconcile the bad memories by overwriting them with good, in a common place?"

Shaking off the intense thought at such a light time, I looked back down at the newspaper to an article on the National Headquarters for Chincoteague Ponies. Chincoteague Ponies are a breed only appearing on the island, and population controlled, to prevent their extinction. Young ones are sold at the island auction every year, with the proceeds funding their protection.

And the largest number of Chincoteague Ponies outside the island lived at this ranch at the headquarters ... in Bellingham, Washington.

The location almost didn't register, because I had seen it so many times as a resident. I had "randomly" moved with my family many thousands of miles away, to the very town that served as the national headquarters to our mutual childhood ponies.

Einstein said that coincidence is God's way of remaining anonymous, but I think I was given a sudden shocking glimpse of the undeniably divine presence orchestrating my life, my wife's, our families' lives. The probability of a vast set of unconnected people and events coming together in such a meaningful and elegant way is so incredibly low and unlikely that it simply cannot be considered anything other than a destiny intended.

We so often doubt. We hesitate. We feel lost, disconnected, alone and confused as to our course of action and direction.

We often lose faith, but we always have intuition. If your gut tells you so strongly that this is right for you, trust yourself.

You may not know the underlying story. You may never be given the chance to glimpse behind Oz' curtain. But everything is so carefully organized for you, if you have the courage and conviction to follow your intuition.

# FOR MEMORIES, GOOD AND BAD, THANK YOU

The universe provides instantaneous feedback, devoid of randomness, and holding immediate relevance. Put words to feelings, and it provides an augured mirror of insight. The ubiquity of teachers and meaningful lessons awes by its sophisticated elegance of purpose and growth.

My wife and I were discussing this very issue. Since the birth of our first child a decade ago, I buckled down, kept my chin tucked and ran with it. Though I followed my passions before then by exploring the world, after bringing children into the world, I could no longer follow, but rather had to lead my bliss.

Before children, I was purely trying to figure things out. After children, I was too busy trying to make things work to understand them. But now, I feel a clarity appearing, revealing a rich canopy of lessons I've been given, though had not the time to truly appreciate, embrace and consciously apply with consistency throughout all facets of my life.

Upon reflection, the past seems feverishly rushed. I've been shaking my head to free the flashes of memories from the coffers where they've been cached. And these reflected moments each feel like treasures I've not had the opportunity to honor with due attention.

Though I regret the moments I did not cherish as they were happening, they weren't lost. They were tucked away until later, when they could be loved with fond reverie.

I take this moment to express my gratitude for you. We are here for a reason, and our purpose: to know and grow from our connection. Soon this will be all gone, but for now, we are better from or touching each other's lives. Thank you for the positive impact you've had upon my life, and for the (misperceived) negative impact, because I am growing in my personal development as a result.

# GIVING IS IN OUR NATURE

I cried for my mom to give me the final piece of milk toast at dinner, because I was still so hungry. She smiled and handed me that last piece. I didn't know that she had not eaten at all yet.

Looking at my two sleeping children now, I understand her sacrifices. Compared with the confusing and narcissistic sensations of childhood hunger, it is not as difficult as an adult to work without food when you get to feed your children because of it.

When my wife and I moved into our first house, a wood burning one-room shack in the mountains, she was very frugal and managed to stretch our budget of $700 per month to pay all of our bills, and feed our newborn. We lived on beans and rice in bulk, and anything else we could squeeze from the coins we found in the couch pillows.

I don't know how we managed, and there were some desperate nights, but my wife always managed to awake smiling at the sunshine, flowers and our baby's face. God loves that woman.

We try to volunteer our time as much as we can. She's constantly involved in the community. One of my investments involves my best use: writing my articles to help inspire and motivate others through their hardships and challenges, to which a friend remarked, "You spend an hour every morning writing for your audience. Shouldn't you better use that time in your projects; or at least try to monetize that writing, so you can get a return?"

Not everything should be transactional. Sometimes, you just need to give without any expectation of receiving. When you recognize how much you actually have, and how many problems others face, like my mother and my wife, it is not so difficult to give.

When you are at your job, unapologetically insist on getting paid the true value of your skillful labor, and nothing less. But outside of your living means, if you give, you will have all that you need.

# HOW TO THWART THE CRIMINAL 'INTERVIEW'

A man attempted to rob my son and I. He screamed obscenities while I retrieved money at the ATM. I leaned in, to whisper.

My son said, "Whoa, Dad! How'd you make him run away with your words?" I replied, it takes practice to not need to hit someone. Sometimes you must, but only because that's the thing to make him run. This time: It was the right words said in the right way.

What I said was unimportant. It's how it's said. Like I hoped to have introduced to my son, it takes practice to work a gesticular, postural, proximal and emotional level. How you move, stand, enter and engage hold more influence over the conflict than the techniques employed, should escalation happen. In this case, it defused and disarmed prior to escalation.

He saw a man and a little boy walk up to an ATM. I observed him see us. He walked up behind us and leaned against the wall. I covered my PIN and angled so I could watch him in the reflection of the screen.

The "interview" technique he used to try and "excuse" himself while I was typing my PIN, received a very certain "NO!"

He stammered, "Hey, asshole, I just wanna know where the best place to watch the Seahawks game is," as he walked toward us.

I said, "We can't help you. Please step back out of our space until we are finished, Sir."

He said he "didn't need no damn machine to get money," escalated with obscenities and entered my space. I turned, nudged my son behind me (who was already doing so), and placed my heel against the wall. When the subject advanced to chest-bump me with arms wide, I knew he was only posturing and not really ready to throw down.

I considered putting him down right away to just get it over with. But his face was flush red, so he wasn't in "fight" mode yet biochemically (though I kept watching to see if he blanched as his blood rerouted to large muscles).

So, smiling, I leaned in and whispered, "I know you don't want me to call down to the department. Why don't you just save yourself the trouble and leave now," as I reached in my pocket and pulled out my phone.

He held up his hands saying, "No man, sorry, sorry, sorry, God bless!" And took off running.

It's not what I said that was important, as those specific words may not have worked on someone else. Rather it was that I "failed" the criminal interview four times:

1. On his first approach with the "excuse me" while at the ATM, where he collided with a sharp "NO!" interrupting his attempt to sidetrack me.

2. On his second attempt with the "Seahawks" comment, when I made him aware that I knew he was invading our privacy.

3. On the posturing attempt at a chest-bump when I bridged my son and loaded against the wall.

4. And when without any fear in my body I leaned in, smiling to advise him of a much easier course of action than the one he was about to face.

Criminals are looking for easy goods, easy prey and easy escape. He wasn't getting any of that from my son and I, so he went on to greener pastures. (I called it in anyway, since this was obviously a rehearsed routine, and someone else may "pass" the criminal interview.)

I shared this to celebrate my son's bravery. Afterward, I asked him if he had been scared. He replied, "No, Dad, I don't get scared and I'm never ticklish." Chuckling at the last bit, I said it's okay to be scared; dad gets scared too. He nodded his head and said, "Yeah, I know, dad."

It was interesting for me to watch his reactions while I was addressing the hostile subject. My son just observed, unattached, stepped behind me when the subject began to circle his way, but just continued watching. (I saw this in the reflection behind the subject.) Never growing up with my father next to me, because of the Army first and then divorce, I was constantly in a state of panic; that's not surprising considering the violence I lived in. But I was both proud and shocked to see this confident boy calmly bridging the suspect so I was in between, watching him and waiting for my signal. So proud of my little man.

We are all going to encounter disrespectful people; some, outright pernicious, others, innocuous but energetically vampiric.

Don't let them hurt you. Don't let them pierce your skin with vile embitterment. Keep your dignity. Remain true to your values. And don't permit yourself to be sucked down into lower versions of yourself in reaction to their words and deeds.

They need help. But it is not up to you to fix them, nor to put up with it. Just smile, realize that this has nothing to do with you, and walk away. When and if they ever become ready to evolve their behavior, they'll find help instantly. But until then, the absolute best service you could give them involves giving your highest self a chance to set an example for them to experience.

# LESSONS FROM THE DOLPHIN DADDY

I had taken my son in the kayak out into the ocean for the first time of the season. He loves to paddle the boat, despite being only 8 years old, and not able to propel us far. It can be frightening to look down into transparent seas, and become aware of tremendous depths ... perhaps only for me.

The family was waving frantically from the beach. As I watched their antics, I caught a glimpse of movement to my far right. Looking, a pod of dolphins breached the water only 50 yards from us. Asking my son for the paddle, the "Dad engine" started charging off toward the pod.

Within 20 yards, one of the babies, not three feet long, veered off from his family, jumping and tail-slapping straight toward us. When it came within arm's reach of our starboard side, I moved the paddle into our kayak to avoid accidentally hitting the infant, who threw himself into the air, and whacked his tail playfully. My son was enthralled, "Dad, he's SO amazing! He acts just like me." Too true, I thought.

While the two adolescents connected across their marine playground, my intuition caused me to lift my gaze and scan the water. As I did, something white, something massive, headed on a collision course under the water toward our kayak. Crazily, it first appeared like a beluga whale. But the seemingly predatory energy of its intercepting trajectory brought a harrowing realization: I was helpless to defend my son against a threat.

Within a few feet, the white mass spun under our kayak, and popped out of the waves: the largest of the dolphin pod. With scars lining his fins and torso, he patrolled around us in two slow circles.

Mesmerized, I watched until he paused in front of the bow. My son, who'd never stopped watching the baby, announced sadly, "Dad, awww, he's leaving," as the baby darted back to the rest of the pod. But my eyes had remained transfixed on the big male dolphin. He scanned me with what I can only describe as a familiar parental expression: simultaneously assessing my intentions, while warning me to pursue them no farther.

When the baby had safely returned to the pod, the big male glanced one final time, eye to eye with me, then submerged, passing under us, and flashed back to his family. My son threw his hands in the air, and cheered, like a soccer goal had just been made at the world championships.

In contrast, I exhaled with relief.

Brian Piergrossi points out, "Excitement and anxiety are the exact same energy channeled in a different way." The disparity between my energy and my son's perfectly illustrated this.

My early traumatic experiences of violence and abuse had led to my highly suspicious and protective approach to parenting. I trust in the universe, but still prepare daily to defend my family with nearly OCD precision. I realize the root cause of my distrust of others derives from my childhood experience of a violent, absent father who suffered the ravages of PTSD. So I've frequently felt ... over-mobilized for potential threats.

With the big male and his baby, I felt like I had experienced an ordinary reaction to extraordinary circumstances. A father's totally normal response to a potential threat involves internal suspicion and external warning, if not physical protection of one's young. Certainly, I must remain aware of the potential for my childhood distortions to impact my current perspectives, but for once, I finally felt like a normal parent, with ordinary anxiety.

As the character Tyrion Lannister advised in Game of Thrones, *"Never forget what you are, for the rest of the world will not. Wear it like armor and it can ever be used to hurt you."* Rusty armor, you should dismantle; but some pieces, some experiences, are given to you as a gift, not a burden, to be of aid to others, and protect them from harm.

Everything you can imagine is real ... to you. Use that reality to choose and chart your course, unconsciously as a slave to your prior experiences, or consciously as a master to your own destiny of attitudes and choices. Let your imagination create the most positive future possible, even if that includes the normal, ordinary anxieties of protecting yourself and others from harm.

# HOLDING HANDS, HOLDING HEARTS

My daughter and I were in Italy for my work. On one of my days off, we and the rest of my family were touring through the tight cobblestone labyrinth of Milano, and were about to step onto the major Corso Buenos Aires, a tangled monster roadway of speeding machines.

To be honest, I was a little scared of my daughter being distracted, so I asked my little girl, "Sweetie, hold my hand so that you don't get hit by this traffic."

She looked up and me quite calmly and replied, "No, Daddy. You hold MY hand."

Chuckling, thinking her being goofy, I asked her, "Oh? Okay, what's the difference?"

"There's a BIG difference, Daddy," she replied. Continuing, she said, "If I hold your hand and something happens to me, I may not be strong enough and my hand may slip. But if you hold MY hand, for sure, no matter what, you'll never let me go."

She then grabbed my right hand with her right hand and placed it over her left wrist instead of her hand. "See? Like this. That way I won't ever slip away."

Gulp.

When my parents divorced, I felt like I had slipped out of my father's hand, and had gotten lost, for a very long time. Even though, after his passing, my father and I had resolved our past misunderstandings and healed our separation in peace, I now still clutch my children's hands a little too often and a little too long, never wanting them to feel alone or lost.

Harriet Beecher Stowe wrote, *"The bitterest tears are shed over graves are for words left unsaid and deeds left undone."*

To my daughter and son:

I don't want you to feel those bitter tears, so I write this now, for you to read one day. If I am taken before you grow strong and sure, until you are holding your own children's hands, and know the sobering confidence that gives you, I pray that you know how immensely proud I am of your incredible uniqueness, of how much I adore every second with both of you, even when you act like mischievous little imps, and of how excited I am for the world that they have the chance to experience the greatness within you.

One day, I may let your little hands go, but I will never, ever let your heart go without me. Always holding you.

Love you so much.
Dad

# PUSHING HARDER HAS ITS PRICE

My 10-year-old daughter lost it yesterday. I wasn't present, but my wife was. She's been pouring it on lately, with impeccable grades, disciplined nightly ballet and choir practice, as well as voice and instrument lessons.

The vinegar to her water sometimes is her 8-year-old brother, who in his affable daze behaves like an impish Loki in his endless quest for levity. Life to him is a big romp, and he still remains oblivious of the impact he has upon others with his infectious silliness; such as he does upon his very intense sister.

She has discipline twice her age, but still she's a little girl who's trying to figure it all out, and she unloaded on her brother after school because he once again guerrilla'ed her with his incessant pranks. At home, she was in tears. It was really the first time I sat and saw the adult who was trying to come out of that little body.

She said she felt awful that she was so mean to her brother, and embarrassed for losing her temper. Hugging her, I noted that she seemed like she had been working extra hard lately with a lot of pressure to improve her grades, performance in dance and music, and on her relationships with some of her "friends" at school who too often mistreat her, while she practices forgiving them. She burst out crying again and lay her head on my shoulder only managing a "Yeah" between her sobs.

Oh, do I understand that self-pressure to improve. She had that infection too. Nature or nurture, I wondered to myself; did I cause this, or was she this driven as well? So, I reflected to her that I lose control like she did and I neglect to pay attention like her brother does; often making both mistakes.

She paused to look up at me, and said, "But you always seem so in control and focus on everything at once." Laughing, I replied, "Ha! You have no idea. I practice every day to exhale and not lose it. I'm only peaceful on the outside (some of the time) because I'm fighting to let go on the inside (all of the time).

"We see you working extra hard lately. Realize that pushing harder ALWAYS comes at a cost. Anything you work harder for is going to require that you release the pressure, and recover your energy. It's good to work hard, especially for others. But all that energy gets caught up, and when you're first learning how to let out the pressure, you make mistakes and unload too quickly at the wrong time for the wrong reason."

Glassy-eyed with tears, she remarked, "I just don't know how to let it out, Dad. I feel like such a bad person for hurting him."

Smiling, I replied that's how she should know she's not a bad person; only people with good hearts regret carelessly hurting others. What would be worse is not caring! I said, "When you have a good heart, you can still hurt people at two times: when you lose control, or when you're not paying attention. You lost control, like we all do; and your brother wasn't paying attention, like we all don't.

"It happens a lot when you're a kid and too often when you're a grown up. It's totally fine. When you do, then apologize for your mistake and make up for it, not by trying to be extra-nice but just being a little more forgiving when the other person makes the same mistake. Forgive your brother for being a pain in the butt, and forgive yourself for pushing too hard without releasing and recovering the price of that pressure."

She hugged me tightly, took a deep breath, and it all seemed to evaporate instantly. Amazing. I wish I could be that resilient, facing the daily troubles, challenges and tragedies I encounter. But then I realized that I needed to better apply this lesson in my own life.

# EVERYTHING MATTERS TO SOMEONE

My daughter slipped out of my hand, running down the sidewalk toward a man in a tattered trench coat and grimy wool beanie.

Body in motion, I ran, but she approached the man from behind faster than I could catch her. Bending over, she picked up a crumpled wrapper, tugged on the man's sleeve. Looking down at my little girl, she said to him, "I'm sorry but you accidentally dropped this, and I know that you'd never want to hurt the Earth."

Overhearing everything, I prepared to deal with any gruff or potentially antagonistic reaction from the man. And then he said, "Ahhhh, you're right kid. Thanks." Grabbing the garbage, shoving into his pocket, he turned the corner and off he went.

Originally intending to advise my daughter of the dangers of running up to strangers, I looked into her unwaveringly confident gaze and lost my words.

From the mouth of babes come the clearest truths. At that point, I realized, my wife and I had given birth to one of my new teachers. … And that my goal was to protect and support her, until we could all understand her clarity.

Edward Everett Hale proclaimed, *"I am only one, but I am one. I cannot do everything, but I can do something. And because I cannot do everything, I will not refuse to do the something that I can do. What I can do, I should do. And what I should do, by the grace of God, I will."*

You may feel like nothing you do will ultimately matter, but it will matter to one. One is a world of enough. If you are aware, mature and compassionate enough to do something, do it, for you could change that world through your courage.

# BE YOUR LITTLE ONE'S LION

Leaving for camp, my daughter wrote this note to me as a present.

"Everyone thinks the lion is ferocious and dangerous, but they are only right about how ferocious he is. The lion loves his family and fights to keep his little ones safe from mischief and danger. He is big and warm and gentle and safe. When he's ferocious, it's because he has to, not because he wants to. He's gentle because he gets to be, not because he has to be. You are the bold lion, Daddy."

OMG. Eyesight. Already. Bad. Must. Resist. Crying and Driving...

# FACE LIFE AS IT IS, NOT AS FANTASY

After posting a photo of my son's first day hunting, I received belligerent messages from "peace activists" who wrote, "why don't you teach your son to just go get his food from the supermarket like normal people, instead of teaching him to murder beautiful creatures?!"

Food doesn't spontaneously appear in a Star Trek Replicator behind the stockroom doors.

Whenever possible, we prefer wild, free-range, local and care-taken animals and plants. When optimal, we harvest those ourselves, as we know that we will invest honoring the food that we take into ourselves for the sacred experience it is.

We have become so distant from the natural world that we have forgotten the industrialized process that intervenes in it: a process within which you cannot control moral growth manipulation, acquisition, processing, distribution, preparation and recycling.

My children learned DIRECTLY to honor the life cycle: Other creatures die so that we may live. Whether vegan or paleo, you DO take life every day so you can continue to live. How you honor taking that life determines everything from vibrance and health, to your perspective on living in the world.

Marcus Aurelius remarked that, *"Everything we hear is an opinion, not a fact; and everything we see is a perspective, not the truth."* These are my opinions on living healthy and honorably. This is my perspective on the cycle of life. It may not resonate with you. I respect your right to your way of life, so long as you reciprocate.

Remain struck by the wonder life brings us, and continually seek to challenge your beliefs against the universe of wonder each day brings. But do not allow unchallenged beliefs to distort your opinions and perspectives into quiet lies, fed to you by a marketing machine to pit us against each other and distract us from our direct experience of the cycle of life.

I deleted photos of my son's first day learning to shoot and going deer hunting with his uncles, because of the insensitive, derogative remarks made about my boy and my family.

I am a simple man. If you want to have a discussion, I will be happy to help you with the research and experiences I've had over my life. But you do not have any right to express self-righteous judgments about my children and family. You do not have a right to free speech; you only have a "right" (protected by warriors) to not have your speech censored by government.

Threaten to not buy my books, videos, or attend my seminars if I support my son's education in the safe use of firearms and the necessary skills of hunting and fishing. My community is composed of people who have a diversity of lifestyles, from vegan to paleo, from soldiers to pastors, from athletes to artists. They all have in common, respect and honor.

Act without those: Then, you have not yet earned the privilege to learn what my teachers have shared with me.

So, exhale, and think very carefully before you make a derogative comment about my children or family. Banning you cannot be undone. For those of you reading who have already been banned, I strongly encourage you to take a long hard look in the mirror ... What has you so seething with hateful remarks could be a slow painful suicide.

Life doesn't come in a box or a can. We hold a simple reverence for the plants and animals we hunt and gather. We eat them together as a family. You are very welcome to your lifestyle, and I support what helps you improve your health and fulfillment as a family.

# BALANCING PARENTING AND COACHING

My son recently lost a basketball game in his first season learning.

At 8, losing a game doesn't feel like that big of a deal, especially when you're just learning how to dribble, run and pass/shoot: a skill set that should truly amaze us if we look at how complex the timing.

As the group of great kids gathered around the coach after the game, the coach proceeded to tell them that they did badly on both offense and defense. Disheartened, my son walked over to me, head hanging while muttering, "Sorry Dad. We did badly at everything."

As the group of kids and parents began turning to walk, I said to my son, "Being told you did badly isn't helpful. You already feel badly about the score." I said a bit more loudly for the other kids to overhear, "Coaching is about helping you know where you specifically had improved and where you can specifically continue to improve for next time.

"You did a great job at improving your dribbling and shooting skills. Let's work together on our running passes and shots at home since those are totally different new skills than the free throwing and standing passes you've been successfully practicing. But you did a rock star job improving since the last practice in working together to run the court and set up the shots as a team."

My son replied, "But Dad, we LOST! That means we DID do badly!"

I laughed thinking about how many times I've lost over the decades I've competed. "Son, losing a game doesn't mean you did poorly like winning a game doesn't mean you did well. If you played the Seattle Sounders and your team lost, would that mean that you did poorly?"

He chuckled, "Dad, no. They're pros. We're just kids."

"And if you played against a team of three-year-olds, when your team won does that mean that they did poorly," I asked.

"They're just little kids, no," he said.

I continued, "So that also means that you didn't necessarily do 'well' if you beat those three-year-olds?"

"Well, we COULD have done a good job but it'd be a lot easier because they're little kids," he thought aloud, "just like the Sounders beating us only would beat us because we are kids..."

"Exactly," I said as we walked to the car, "how well or poorly you do has nothing to do with whether you win or lose the game. It has to do with how much you work on improving your skills yourself and as a team, over the last time you played."

He looked up at me almost as if what I had been saying was clicking; a rare and precious moment for any parent who means well but knows that they often appear to be tuning you out, and only click when they hear the same lesson from an external source.

But this time, the "coach" wasn't actually coaching; and wasn't reinforcing good sports attitude for these kids.

"So, we didn't do badly, Dad? We lost but we got better and we know what we have to work on for next time. Right?"

Holy Smokes, he got it! "That's exactly right, bud. I've lost more fights than I've won, but great coaches taught me how to learn from each loss and each win, so I started to lose less, but eventually the result on the scoreboard wasn't as exciting to me as the results of my betterment," I reflected.

I continued, "Son, you really impress me with how you understand how to get better. I feel excited to see what you do with this understanding!"

Not all youth coaches have been taught how to coach or even the difference between teaching and coaching. That can be frustrating for parents. It's hard not to undermine the authority of a coach when he does something that is unproductive for youth development. But you do want to give coaches an opportunity to improve; which also involves mistakes.

It feels great when your kids encounter a truly great coach, but how can you expect a child to have that opportunity; when firstly, coaching isn't taught until university, and university coaches aren't frequenting the pivotal age groups that desperately need great coaching to develop healthy attitudes for lifetime growth?

I've been a national team head coach for several sports, each with a staff of amazing coaches. I've also had great coaches myself, who have changed my life and have given me hope when no one else could.

The best that I can do as a parent is to steer my kids to coaches who have the most awareness of their far-reaching impact on the kids' attitudinal development, and when they make mistakes, model for them effective coaching strategies.

The one I used above is PCP: Praise — Correct — Praise.

1.  Congratulate the kids on where they specifically had improved.

2.  Ask them or help point out where they want to improve for next time.

3.  And reinforce that they HAVE improved and will continue to do so because they have already shown the ability to improve; so though losing is sometimes a reality, improvement is a guarantee ... and winning an inevitability.

Parenting athletes isn't easy. We are going to make a lot of mistakes. And sometimes we have to tell our kids that despite our opinion they need to put their faith in their coach (who we have selected as a parent), even if we disagree; so our kids can see that they can choose which "coaching" to internalize.

But sometimes we must advocate for quality coaching by modeling how we feel coaching should best happen.

# FAIL? THAT'S IMPOSSIBLE!

"Daddy, the only thing I'm worried about on my first day of middle school is making a mistake and failing. I want to make you and Mom proud, and want to learn as much as I can to become a veterinarian," my daughter said to me.

I replied, "Babe, let me tell you a secret ... you are ALREADY the person we'd dreamed you'd become. You know how we know that?"

"No," she admitted. I asked her what she would do if she came home with a failing grade. She conceded saying she'd "probably cry all night and get up the next day and try harder."

Sitting her down, I said to her, "That's what I mean, Sweetheart. You ALREADY have all of the qualities we'd hoped for you. You were born with those virtues, and you're not afraid to let them out. You're not afraid of crying when you make a mistake. And you're not afraid of getting up the next day and trying harder. That's why it is ... IMPOSSIBLE ... for you to fail."

She sat quietly considering what I had said and then rebutted, "But, Dad, I make mistakes all the time!"

Looking her in the eyes and grabbing her face, I said, "Babe, so do I. But mistakes aren't failure. Mistakes are how you learn and improve. If you don't make mistakes, you probably haven't learned anything new. To do new things, expect to make mistakes. The only way to FAIL is to stop from trying something new because you're afraid of making a mistake, or to quit trying after you make one. So, since you're already the kind of person who won't do those things ... no matter what you do ... no matter what you face ... no matter how many times you make mistakes ... it's IMPOSSIBLE for you to fail. Just go out there and do everything you dare to dream, Sweetheart."

Staring at me with a strange mischievous grin, she said, "Hmmmm ... So, Daddy, I've really been dreaming about having my own laptop computer? Does that mean I can have one now?"

"No," I replied wryly.

She smiled, bubbly, saying, "Don't worry, Daddy. I can't fail, so I won't quit asking."

I pretended to frown saying, "That's okay, Kid. I won't fail either ... so I won't stop refusing."

Then, I opened the door to the car to take her to the Apple store in Seattle.

# ADVICE ON MY DAUGHTER'S FIRST CRUSH

I met the boy my daughter has her first crush on at eleven years young.

He seems healthy, athletic and happy, but I don't know anything about what it was like to be like that as a boy. I wasn't any of those things at his age.

So, out of pure curiosity, while driving my daughter home from a dance, I asked her about him.

She confided in me: "Dad, it's no big deal. He's not even interested in me anyway and I wouldn't know how to be interesting to him."

I replied, "You don't have to try to interest anyone, sweetheart. You're brilliant, courageous, graceful and gorgeous. I find you to be fascinating, and continually surprise me with the things you do and say and think, just being yourself. Boys don't know what they want because their brain won't stop being cooked until they're 25, but after then, they have a chance to become adult men. Then, the right man will realize how awesome you already and always are."

The conversation felt like it went well, but last night, I thought longer about her comment. Remembering an article from a writer named Kelly Flanagan to his own daughter, I adapted what I had remembered and wrote out what I'd wanted to say to mine:

Sweetheart,

You never need to try to be interesting to anyone, boy or girl. That's not your job in life. Your only job is to know in your heart without any cloud of confusion or fog of hesitation that you are worthy of anyone's interest without trying. You are perfectly worthy just as you are; just like everyone else is, even if you or others (or your Mom and I) get confused about our individual worth, or about the worth of each other.

If you continue to believe in yourself, you'll radiate. Boys, and eventually when you're grown up — men, will be attracted to you because of who you really are in your heart of hearts. You won't need to try to be interesting because the second most important man in your life will be interested in everything you are (the most important man in your life — me — already is and always will be).

I don't know much about what it is to be a healthy, happy boy. Your Dad hadn't been those things. But I can tell you what it's like to be a healthy, happy person: You don't need to keep the interest of healthy, happy people. They're interested in you purely because you are confident in your fascinatingly unique, wonderfully weird (in other words — AWESOME) self.

One day you'll meet a boy and he will be overwhelmed by you, and you by him. When you're young and someone likes you, it feels like the entire world is in the moments you are near each other. But your worth isn't dependent upon him feeling this way toward you (or you toward him). A good boy will feel this way about you because you are perfectly worthy of it... Already and Always.

When he comes to our house to meet us, you'll be scared of what we think of him because of how you feel when he's so smitten by you. Even if he sets his sights on audacious goals, as long as he places his eyes on you when you tilt your head and lift your shoulders when you giggle at your own silly jokes — and then can't look away — then we will love him too.

Even if he doesn't want to wrestle with me, come training with me, or go hunting with the other men in your family during holiday get-togethers, if he can romp with the beautiful children you create together, and fawn in all of the wonderfully frustrating ways that your children are exactly like you, then we will love him too.

Even if he doesn't dedicate his life to his finances, if — like you — he follows his passion to help others, while standing right next to you as you do, then we will love him too.

He doesn't need to be strong like your Dad. As long as he exercises the most important muscle — his heart — by loving and honoring you as much as your Mom and I do you (and each other), then we will love him too.

We don't care about his politics or viewpoints, if he makes you the most important person in his life and considers how every action impacts you, as you do him.

We don't care about the culture he comes from, or the place he was born, as long as he calls standing next to you wherever you are — home.

It doesn't matter to us what religion he practices, if he understands that you and your relationship together are inherently sacred, and every day that he gets to spend with you — a blessed gift.

I don't care if he has nothing in common with your Dad, for if he's completely different in every detail, he and I will have the most important common interest worthy of our complete dedication: you.

In the end, the only thing you'll ever need to do to keep our interest is just be you, already and always as you are each and every moment.

Love you,
Dad

I thought to share this with you because the world may be changing at a very rapid rate, but the confusion of being a Dad — and total absence of a fatherhood instruction manual — causes me to reach out to those of you who are facing similar conversations with their growing children. Consider writing a similar letter to your own son or daughter.

Perhaps, together, in our individual heartfelt love of our little ones, we can help create a generation to understand that they don't need to try to be a certain way to be worthy... to be happy. They only need to be perfectly themselves, as they already and always are.

# AN OPEN LETTER TO MY SON

Honestly, every day feels like it could be my last. I look at my wife and my children, and I feel as if it could all end at any moment.

In reality, this may indeed be very true. But psychologically, I know this feeling of imminent finality originates from having my parents violently divorce when I was only four years old.

Having had no father in my life, I feel that as a father now myself, I could quite suddenly just ... disappear. If I did, will I have said everything that I wanted to say, everything that I could, to my children?

I shared a letter to my daughter which brought the two of us together in a way I hadn't imagined. We're a very strong team.

But my son is still quite young, unable to avoid the "SQUIRREL!" distractions in life, so I wrote to him a letter that we will read and discuss in a lucid moment, but it is more of a roadmap for the future, left to him in case these were indeed my final words to him as his Dad.

My "Rules of Engagement for Becoming a Man"

Little man,

You're only turning nine years old, but you asked me to write you a letter like I had written your sister. Here it is.

Some people say eight is too young to worry about manhood, but I believe if you don't know where you're headed, you'll have trouble getting there. You won't be able to spend all your years as a boy, and then suddenly know how to be a man. On your 18th birthday, you may be told be in your identification that you're an adult, but it won't magically be in your identity that you're a man.

You're already trying to put on a man's shoes in certain circumstances, so if you know which direction to walk, perhaps you'll have an easier time figuring out how to walk in them... and be okay when you trip.

I did not. I'm not afraid to be honest with you. My father was gone when I was only four, which means it's been years since I've been your Dad that I've had an example of exactly what to do as a father. I don't have a specific plan to tell you what you'll need to become a man. I have had to figure it out by myself, and through the father figures in my life as my coaches.

So, I can begin by telling you what I've learned a man is not.

It's not an age. No matter how others make it seem, there isn't a magical age: not 18, 21, not even 45. As you grow older, you don't automatically become more of a man. When you grow taller in your shoes, deeper in your voice, or hairy on your face, you won't be any closer to becoming a man. I wish, Son, it was that simple.

A boy thinks and behaves as if he's the center of the universe. This isn't about age, but about behavior, action and thought.

Even at my age, we can behave and think like boys; as your Dad does when I make mistakes and behave childishly. I am still practicing the difference between a boy and being a man. I can still choose to act like a boy, even though I'm five times older than you. Behaving like a boy means putting your own interests first (your hunger, thirst, sleepiness, pleasure, happiness, cravings, sadness, anger and so on) and getting those desires met before considering the needs of others.

A boy takes (because he's learning) but a man gives (because he's learning more). To become a man, you have to place others' interests before your own. It's not easy, because you have to think about how your behavior impacts others, and then imagine what the world looks like from their perspective, and how what you do, think and say makes them feel. Just because you feel you're right, doesn't mean you should do it, say it or even think it. That's a hard one. To do this, you can't be at the center of your own little world.

You can't even only think about what a man would do, you have to act upon it. When big challenges come, you don't even have time to think. You only have time to act; often when you don't know what you should do. How you act then, tells you if you're a boy or a man.

I think about these challenges a lot, even as a "grown-up." When they come, I think, will I have the courage to be a man, or will I allow fear to overcome me, and act only as a boy, concerned only about my own needs? Even your Dad won't know until it happens, what he'll do. You can only practice becoming a man in the small, daily, simple, normal things, so that when the big, scary, difficult things come, you have had enough practice to act as a man. This is what people mean when they talk about your "character."

Throughout your life, you're going to have these opportunities, and just like your Dad, you won't be great at them all right away. You'll make mistakes. You'll fail to live up to your own expectations. You'll be too afraid to remember your courage, and you'll act like a boy, rather than remember to practice becoming a man. That happens to us for the rest of our lives, Son.

I am still practicing even — and maybe especially — as I write these words to you. You have to find a balance between being firm with yourself, and pulling yourself off the ground, turning toward your fears, and the mistakes you've made, owning them and pushing through even when it hurts; with being forgiving and gentle with yourself when you repeatedly get knocked down, get overwhelmed, make huge blunders, and shrink away from them because you've hurt yourself from pushing too hard for too long.

I haven't mastered it myself, but I keep practicing.

I didn't have my Dad around when I was your age, so I looked to my coaches to act as my father figures. And they did. I grew from their lessons. You will find teachers everywhere when you need them, and even when you don't, because you need to practice and learn from a teacher before the big challenges come, and after they knock you down, and when you get back up again and again.

Be ready for disappointment. Don't think it is you. Sometimes you win and sometimes you learn. When you feel disappointed, remember this letter, and read it again, please. Because when you're disappointed, and hard on yourself, that's when you're growing, and being given the chance to become more of a man. At the same time, you're going to have plenty of happy times, and lots of laughs, victories and achievements. Don't get too attached to these once they're over. Celebrate them, and let 'em go. A boy collects them, but a man moves on.

You're going to experience weakness, failure, vulnerability, worry, surprise and even terror. I can't protect you from these feelings, but I can help you get prepared for when you feel them. It's wonderful to feel strong, invulnerable, confident, certain and brave. But sometimes, those feelings seem to disappear for awhile. They'll come back, but only when you do one thing: get up anyway. Get up when you know you've failed a hundred times, when you know it'll hurt and you feel completely exposed and unprotected, when you know that people will be upset when you own up to a mistake you've made, when you don't know at all what to do. You get up, and do the right thing anyway... even if you fail again. That is the difference between behaving like a boy and like a man.

Sometimes I just want to curl up with your Mom and have her hold me, because even at my age, I get overwhelmed; I feel out-gunned and under-prepared, hurt and angry, alone and tired. It's okay to do that, Son. It's okay to take a breath, to feel comforted. And then, you'll know that it's not yet time, that you could stay within that warm embrace longer and feel safe, but you get up anyway to face it. That Son, is becoming more of a man.

The things you're going to go through will be different than what I did, Thank God. What you'll face will be unique to you. I won't know all the answers, even if you feel like your Dad could face any challenge. I know I don't know. But I know that I have to do something even when I don't know what to do. So, I can't tell you what's going to happen. But I can tell you for absolute certain, that you will be given exactly what you need to become a man: you'll either do a great job at it, or you'll learn how to do it better the next time. I've learned a lot, which means I've made a lot of mistakes. And I still am. A man never stops learning and practicing.

You'll have your own challenges, but you should always know that your Mom and I are behind you, until you're man enough to go it alone. And then, we'll still be with you, in one way or another. You get to choose how to live your life. You get to choose how you want to face a challenge, how many times you must repeat that challenge until you overcome it. Or if you choose to do nothing about it at all and hope to escape it. That's your choice. I want the best for you, so I'm going to do my best to always provide you with support and love, but you can choose to not heed my advice. That is your choice, as you become a man.

Being a man sounds like a lot of work, like it's very hard, and there aren't many benefits. But let me tell you, Son, being a man is "good." We get to feel tough and choose to be gentle. We get to feel strong, and choose to be compassionate. We get to feel freedom, but choose to be responsible. Remember what I wrote about "character." It's what you decide to do when the pressure is on. There's no better feeling than that, really: to feel like everything is pushing and pulling you in so many directions, and yet you stand your ground and speak the truth, and act righteously.

When we behave like boys, we can lie, cheat, steal, even hurt others. When we act like men, we keep our word, even when it's easy not to. We remain reliable, when someone needs us, yet spontaneous and unpredictable. You can be hard on yourself, fair with others, and compassionate with everyone. When you feel pressure from others to do what might seem "fun" but could be hurtful, deceitful or in any way "wrong," even though it makes you "unpopular" you'll find the courage to do the "right" thing anyway.

You may think you'll be able to get away with it, because no one is looking, but there's always someone watching: the boy inside you who's becoming a man. He's always watching. Help him grow; don't hurt him and keep him small. You'll hear that voice cautioning you, and sometimes, you'll ignore it, and make a mistake. It's okay, your Dad screws up, too. But becoming a man means owning up to those mistakes, facing an even harder crowd of peer pressure afterward, and doing the right thing eventually. The more you run from it, the harder it will be when you do, but you can ALWAYS clean the slate and start over. Just remember that the longer you wait to own up and come clean, the more people will be hurt by your choices, and the harder it will be to face. But you CAN face it. A man should.

Be proud of who you are, and where you came from. Your name means something. It is a bank account, and you've inherited a huge savings. Put more into that account for your sons and daughters. Protect it, honor it, and then pass it to them. Put more into it throughout your life than you take out. Take care of it, because you don't own your name. You carry it to the next generation.

Your family is the most important; this one with me, your Mom and your Sister, and then one you will create when you become a man. Protect them before yourself. Provide for them above your own desires. Put them first and foremost in your thoughts, actions and behaviors. LOVE THEM AS BIG AS YOU CAN! All of our lessons as a boy prepare us for that privilege as a man. Live as an example to your children. And pass on these lessons I'm sharing with you, with them.

Stay humble, for your gifts are God given. Be grateful for your fruits are delicate blessings which come and go. Work hard but be smart about it. Don't waste a second; invest it in your growth. You're told to "be happy," but remember that you won't always feel happy and that's okay. Being a man means doing hard things that won't make you immediately happy, but they'll make you eventually happy. Often instant pleasure is the worst thing you could feel, because of what it will cost you to stay a boy, and not become more of a man.

Breathe. Take it all in. Let it all go quiet sometimes. Sit. Smile. This is your domain where you get to help as many people as you can. That is an honor. The worries will come; and when an army of them swarm around you, sometimes you start with the biggest guy and knock him down first; other times, you start with the closest and easiest just to get rolling. A lot of times, you'll feel like you can't breathe, and you're never resting. That, too, is what it means to be a man; so when you knock out a few of your responsibilities, remember: sit, breathe, let it go, relax and smile. You're doing it.

Believe in the nobility in becoming a man. You are learning how to become a King. Even when we act like precocious, pampered, spoiled little Princes, we are all still learning. Sometimes we need to shake off the boyish behavior, stop accepting mediocrity and charge toward our dreams. ... My mother once told me that she wanted a better life for me than she had; and I do want that for you. But to have a better life, you'll need to make different decisions than I made. I promise you that I will continue to practice becoming more of a man, when you come to me as a man, and tell me that you're choosing to not heed my advice and go a new direction. Together, as two men, we will support each other, as you head off in that uncharted path. (But try your best to consider the counsel of your elders before you make that choice, please. Sometimes, men do know what we're talking about.)

Most of the time, just like your Dad, you'll be making it all up as you go along. Be ready to improvise, adapt and overcome. Expect that you will not know how to do something, that no one else can or is willing to do it, and that you'll have to just figure it out on your own while doing it. There are a lot of different ways to solve a problem. Even if you don't figure out the fastest or most efficient way, keep going, because you will figure out a way eventually, even if no one else has done that way before. Just don't stop going. Fail and fail and fail and fail and one day, you'll be doing something completely unrelated and the solution will come to you (so remember to step away from a task for a moment if you can, to take a chance for it to come to you). You're so much smarter than you can imagine, because that brain of yours comes from God. Those ideas are divine gifts. Treat them as sacred as a church and bring them to life as piously as a prayer.

You'll feel tempted to try and figure everything out, and fix all problems you see. Remember that it's a mystery to be appreciated, so stay curious. Watch how others create solutions. Listen to how they came to their conclusions. Look to understand rather than only to "fix." Ask as many questions as appropriate when time permits, because you can always at least learn a different perspective on the same problem.

What you say and what you feel aren't always perceived the same way by others, so you're going to need to practice being better at communicating all of your life. That's one of the reasons that you never finish becoming a man. Sometimes you have to say something in order to realize how you really feel, sometimes you have to correct what you've said because it came out the wrong way, and most times, you're going to need to remember that it's that way for everyone else too; so be patient, ask questions to confirm what they meant in words you understand. Ask them to do the same when they don't understand you.

Here's the hard one. No matter how much it will feel like you're exposing yourself, share how you really feel with those you love. This is the most important type of sharing as a man. You can share things, and tasks, and tools, and thoughts, but sharing feelings is a very hard one because we are told to just "man up" and get over it. Listen, Son, when it comes to those you love, "manning up" IS sharing how you really feel. So, remember that you also need to really listen and hear when loved ones share with you. It's how you will really connect with them and understand the WHY in their life; and how they can understand the WHY in your life; why we do, behave and think in the peculiar ways we do...

No matter how firm and disciplined you must become in your challenges, remember to love yourself, accept who you are, and always remain true to that man you're becoming. Others will try to control you, and dictate what you should do in life. Remember to love and honor yourself. Try to be compassionate with them, and acknowledge that sometimes the most compassionate thing you can say to people trying to control your life is, "No." I will stand behind those, "No," responses with you, even if you feel totally alone, even if my body isn't right next to you when you do it.

Truly mean it when saying you're sorry; because you'll be saying it a LOT. Expect to do a lot for others without recognition; in fact, although it's hard for us to realize when we think like boys, but that's the best kind of thing to do. So, pick your friends carefully, as many people will try to exploit your generosity. Don't prejudice them but consider their values; will they help you become a better man, and will you help them become better men and women? Do they make others feel bad, and do they honor that you're becoming a man of character, and hope for them to practice the same? Commit to your word, and you'll find that your friends are able to do the same more often. It takes time, sometimes years, but how you behave, think and act is like a rock dropped into a lake: the ripples move outward, affecting everyone around you.

Honor this body you've been given like you would protect and help your own son grow. Be honest with your growth so you can keep healthy. And when your strength wanes, and your health diminishes, remember to respect your Spirit which cannot die ever, and will always be strong no matter how big, scary and difficult the challenge.

Like I said, Son, sometimes you're going to win; and other times you're going to learn. It won't seem fair when we think like a boy, but as you become a man, you'll see that you create fairness: you equal things out for others, when what they've experienced has been unfair to them, you will be the one to extend an anonymous helping hand. It'll keep you humble, and keep you busy.

So, remember to laugh... and cry. These are two of your best tools as a man. Laugh at yourself, and cry for others' hardships. Being more human means you're becoming more of a man.

Things in life may come and go, but your character is yours for life. Appreciate things while they're here, and help others when they're not. Because that "character" of yours is the only real thing that makes you a man.

You have everything you need to "make up" this life for yourself. You can do it.

Whatever you need will be there for you when you need it, once you commit to improvising and taking action even when you don't know what to do.... especially so.

Whatever happens, no matter today or 70 years from now when I'm gone, know that I am always proud of you, and the man you are becoming.

I love you so much, Son.
Dad

# I AM FREE

What could a man with such a dark, traumatic past truly dream of? It would be a dream beyond comprehension; a wish so foreign to my experience that I would dare not dream it for fear it would be unattainable, inaccessible, unavailable to one such as me.

Most of my life I have lived in shame so silently secret, I compensated through over achievement, building myself into a formidable fighter, a champion athlete and a successful entrepreneur. Surely, I thought, no one would recognize my shame if I trapped it in the camouflage of socially validated recognition, like induction into Halls of Fame and photos on magazine covers.

One person saw through my emperor's cloak. She didn't care about my trophies, medals and belts. Each time around her, I felt naked. My rusty armor weighed awkwardly in her presence. And piece by piece, her clear gaze pierced me to take off that ill-fitting suit.

I broke down, and thought that raw, exposed emotional flesh would endanger me. Unearthing my shame from early life, I'd try to pick up the pieces and hold them against me for fear of unknown, ubiquitous threats. What if I was discovered for the defect, the flaw, the fraud I felt. But the pieces would fall clattering back to the earth noisily.

Then she'd smile. A smile so delicate and courageous that I felt her to be the strongest person I'd ever met. I still haven't met anyone who compares.

She restored innocence to my life, by allowing me to be vulnerable. ... And to be totally free of shame for who I am. She represents divine sweetness; a name given to her by our teacher. Sweetness. Innocence. Wholesome. Unfettered, Unadorned and Pure.

The dream a man like me had fearfully, reluctantly dared to wish was to live in the peace of that sweetness, unencumbered by the trappings of shame's overcompensation.

I am free because of observing her fierce freedom. I am courageous enough to be unabashedly real only because I have studied her vulnerability.

She is my best friend. My savior. My love. My heroine. My most adored role model. My reawakening to the divine in each of us, and a mirror so clearly reflecting sweetness that even a man like me can be reminded and become restored.

My sweet. Saying I love you speaks to a lifetime you have given back to me through your example.

— *Kailash*

# ABOUT THE AUTHOR

Scott Sonnon overcame dyslexia so severe that he was hospitalized in a children's psychiatric institution for his "disruptive classroom behavior." Despite being advised that he should not set his expectations very high, he went on to become a five-time world martial arts champion, award-winning producer, prolific author, patent-holding inventor and fitness industry magnate with his books, DVDs and equipment now available in 68 countries worldwide.

Ironically, Scott became a keynote speaker for the genius organization Mensa, and his acclaimed TEDx talk challenges the notion of "learning disabilities" through the creative genius of alternative learning styles.

Using his "unique neurological wiring" to create innovative health programs, he was named one of the Top 25 Trainers in the world by Men's Fitness Magazine, "World's Smartest Workout" creator by Men's Health Magazine, and one of the seven most influential martial art teachers of the 21st century by Black Belt Magazine.

Scott was named an adjunct instructor for the U.S. Federal Law Enforcement Training Center, and lecturer for the State and Local Law Enforcement Training Symposium. His training systems have been used by more than 50,000 federal agents through the US Customs and Border Protection Advanced Training Center and the US Marshals Service Academy.

Scott has been a featured speaker at the Arnold Schwarzenegger Sports Festival, the National Strength Conditioning Association and many more.

Scott has now taken his success in martial art, fitness and yoga off the mats and into the classrooms, as an international speaker. He advocates for children and adults battling the labels of learning difficulties, the ravages of obesity, the trials of post-traumatic stress, the dangers of bullyism and the challenges of accelerated aging in joint and soft tissue.

He lives in the Bellingham, Washington, area with his wife, Jodie, and their two children.